ENGLISH POLITICAL PORTRAITS
OF THE NINETEENTH CENTURY

THE DUKE OF WELLINGTON AND SIR ROBERT PEEL

From a painting by Winterhalter in the Collection of His Majesty King George V

ENGLISH POLITICAL PORTRAITS
OF THE NINETEENTH CENTURY

BY G. R. STIRLING TAYLOR

WITH
ILLUSTRATIONS

Essay Index Reprint Series

BOOKS FOR LIBRARIES PRESS, INC.
FREEPORT, NEW YORK

First published 1929
Reprinted 1967

PRINTED IN THE UNITED STATES OF AMERICA

PREFACE

THE seven statesmen chosen for the miniature character portraits of the present book are interesting in two quite different ways. There is, first, the personal, individual and psychological interest. Each of them was a treasure house of subtle shades of mind which would make the reputation of any novelist who could re-create them in fiction. But, strange to say, the reader of fiction is content to be supplied with the portraits and stories of the smaller people, who play with life on a small scale. The romance-loving public is content to read of rather insignificant matters of domestic life, whereas the figures of the present book threw dice and played for the fate of kingdoms and parliaments. One does not suggest that a kingdom or a parliament is a more important matter than the welfare of the private soul. But the scale of the picture is greater and more exciting.

However, quite apart from the scale of the *mise en scène*, the personal souls of all these seven were of the most alluring kind. Wellington had a heavily veiled background of intellectual and romantic imagination which was perhaps the chief quality of his character; and his wonderfully complex mind is one of the most absorbing problems in psychological study. Peel rouses the important question how such a small mind ever gained so powerful a place in the world. The portrait of these two men standing together — the famous soldier who was perhaps first a poet, and the great statesman who had the intellectual scope of a small tradesman — raises most of the problems of psychology and history. Then there is the abysmal contrast between Disraeli and Gladstone, who are hard enough to comprehend in their public affairs, while their private souls have the unsolved mysteries of the most perplexing mazes. There are moments when Gladstone's "complex" mind was as near a saint's as a politician's; and Disraeli tried the bold adventure of balancing philosophy and political charlatanry on the high pole of buffoonery. Yet, when we survey the performance from the distance of years, it seems possible that Benjamin Disraeli got as near saintship as Mr. Gladstone reached with all his theology.

The second interest of these political characters is that although, on closer inspection, it will be found that they somewhat helplessly floated on the top of the social current, rather than directed its course, yet for this very reason they are most valuable evidence of historical progress. Peel, for example, did not make the history of his age; but he was the most complete illustration of the social, economic and political drift of England in the first half of the nineteenth century. He was, down to the smallest detail, the type specimen of his day. Disraeli, on the other hand, was the representative of an older age which Peel was wiping out of English history. Canning was the prince (in a somewhat tawdry theatrical dress) of the political adventurers who were the final and natural result of a hundred years' rule by oligarchs, to whom places were more important than principles. Queen Victoria, finally, was in many ways more interesting than all her Prime Ministers; for, paradoxical though it may seem, this hereditary monarch was a more complete representative of her people than the parliamentary representative system seems capable of producing.

So it is not suggested that these seven statesmen were the controlling minds of their nation's progress. They are offered, rather, as concise summaries of the national spirit which swept them along in its irresistible way. They are not leaders but symbols. One does not say of a signpost that it leads; it merely points in silent passiveness — though one would have to apologise for applying such words as *silence* and *passivity* to some of the persons of this book!

For those who do not care for the technical, and sometimes sordid, details of political biography, it is suggested that each one of these political personages had also most of the qualities necessary for the heroes and heroines of romance. It is no disadvantage to a romance that it is true. It is only the timid and more trivial readers who are satisfied by the milder and less convincing tales of fiction. It is a very remarkable thing that there are people who find the average novel more interesting reading than the Greville diary, or the Croker or Creevy papers, or a score of other sources for the period covered in this book. It is an ill-furnished and dull mind that can be satisfied with fictitious adventures when there are within reach Sir Herbert Maxwell's two big volumes on the Duke of Wellington, or Messrs. Monypenny and Buckle's six volumes of Disraeli's life, in all of which there is not a dull page. Sir John Fortescue's "British Statesmen of the Great War" (of the Napoleonic times) is one of the most brilliant judgments in historical literature, and is an ideal introduction to the succeeding period discussed in the present volume. Any first-class students' general history of the period will supply a bibliography of the main sources of evidence, and it is unnecessary to repeat it in a volume which merely reduces those endless sources into miniature portraits. It has been the serious endeavour of the author never to tamper with the exact truth for the sake of some trivial effect — a treason to historical science unfortunately not unknown in an age which is endeavouring to make knowledge a popular commodity. The writer would even venture to hope that the historical student will sometimes find in these pages a more accurate clue to the truth than the text books disclose in their bare summary of so-called facts, which are, too often, only partisan fancies that have grown plausible by much repetition.

CONTENTS

Preface
· v ·

The First Duke of Wellington
· 1 ·

George Canning
· 51 ·

The Second Viscount Melbourne
· 101 ·

Sir Robert Peel
· 153 ·

Benjamin Disraeli, Earl of Beaconsfield
· 203 ·

William Ewart Gladstone
· 239 ·

Queen Victoria
· 285 ·

Index
· 321 ·

ILLUSTRATIONS

The Duke of Wellington and Sir Robert Peel
· FRONTISPIECE ·

Duke of Wellington
· 24 ·

George Canning
· 66 ·

Lord Melbourne
· 132 ·

Benjamin Disraeli, Earl of Beaconsfield
· 206 ·

William Ewart Gladstone
· 252 ·

Queen Victoria, the Prince Consort and Family
· 300 ·

THE FIRST DUKE OF WELLINGTON
1769-1852

THE FIRST DUKE OF WELLINGTON
1769–1852

I

Arthur Wellesley, the first Duke of Wellington, has always been a much underrated man. He was certainly the most famous and the most honoured figure of his period — it was even notorious that kings were nervous in his presence — but not many people realised how much his worth exceeded the praise they offered. He was covered with laurels during his life; and historians have recorded him in ten thousand books since his death. Yet it is not untrue to say that he remains one of the most unknown and misunderstood men in history.

He made one fatal blunder if he desired the knowledge and highest praise of his neighbours and successors. He did too much in the world. He won too many battles; he scored too many civilian's triumphs. He aimed too high; and, for a punishment, he has been buried beneath the enormous mass of his accomplished deeds. There has been a further difficulty in the case of the Duke of Wellington; for he was a man who shrank, in a very sensitive way, from that public shout of applause, which in the modern world is the final proof of success; and often indeed (by careful advertising) its first cause. This great Duke carried his modesty too far; for he wrote thirty-six volumes of despatches; which were clearly sufficient to conceal the greatest of reputations. Whereas a skilful journalist could have made him famous in half a dozen columns.

The Battle of Waterloo destroyed our last hope of understanding the true character of the great man who won it. For it had such a stupendous effect in the world that ever afterwards the delicate outline of Wellington's mind was lost in the din and glare of a noisy fame that was on everybody's lips and in all eyes. It caused the further obscurity, in that, coming after the Peninsular War, it confirmed the erroneous opinion of all dull observers that Wellington should be finally judged as a great soldier. Whereas, in fact, he was a far greater statesman. After Waterloo, it was as impossible to read Wellington aright as it would be to enjoy the subtleties of Shakespeare's sonnets or Scarlatti's fugues amid the rattle of the traffic of New York or Birmingham. The fine shades have been lost in the noise and confusion.

It is an interesting problem to discover whether it be possible to rescue the real Arthur Wellesley out of the tremendous bustle of his tumultuous and lengthy life; whether anything of the true outline can be recovered from the endless details of his despatches, from the vast mass of contemporary evidence which surrounds the student of his history, or the lighter reader who is content to know something of his magnificent romance. The more one considers this evidence, the clearer it is that Wellington was a far greater man than merely the happy, victorious survivor of the physical chaos of the field of Waterloo; greater even than the brilliant soldier who made the Peninsular campaign a chief classic of military history; greater still than the Prime Minister of England, which he later became.

The peculiar biographical allurement of the Duke of Wellington is that on careful examination it will be found that behind all the public achievements, which the historians catalogue as great landmarks in the world's career, there is a strangely evasive figure of a man in the background, who seems to be far more momentous than his great deeds, which have been placed in the foreground of the picture. There are elements in this stately ducal portrait which denote qualities of character beyond the reach of most generals, and almost unknown in these places where ministers of State perform their ambiguous professional functions.

It would be no surprising thing if even the gigantic figure of Wellington had failed to emerge, in a distinctive way, from the European background of 1800 and its surrounding years. For it was a tumultuous scene of extraordinary confusion. The position has been repeatedly described by the best historians, who have usually followed the orthodox evidence supplied by the diplomatists and soldiers. But no prim official language can ever sufficiently relax to do justice to the complete anarchy of that time. It may be more exactly described by the simpler proverbial picture of the china shop during the visit of the impatient and unreasonable bull — which in this case was of the Corsican breed.

There were too many reasons for this deplorable condition; but one alone was almost sufficient to account for the dire peril of social affairs. For the last half-century or so Europe had been under the control of benevolent despots and literary persons whose hobbies and art had taken an earnestly reforming turn. There were those royal beings, Joseph II of Austria, Frederick the Great of Prussia, and Catherine the Great of Russia, on one side; and the bourgeois figures of Voltaire, Rousseau, and many other people of encyclopædic minds, on the other. There was even an occasional alliance between these two groups of benevolent kings and superintelligent philosophers; and when the two combined the strain on the normal social organism was too great and Europe was left in a condition of revolutionary insanity. The "reformers" — as they too hastily considered themselves — produced the French Revolution and all its noisy, ill-bred children.

To understand the Duke of Wellington in any complete way it would be necessary to analyse in full this European background, against which he is only one figure which stands out more clearly than most of the others. Yet the essential (if paradoxical) fact about Wellington is not that he was an abnormal, exceptional man — like the selfish and brutal Napoleon Bonaparte, the mentally deficient Robespierre, or the amazingly ignorant Younger Pitt, for example — but, rather, that he was more like the multitude of his fellows; and therefore a more organic part of the background than the freakish figures of comedy and tragedy that so often appear in the foreground of history.

The chief fact about Arthur Wellesley is that he was a very sane, very honest, very well-balanced — even commonplace — man; who did more than any one else to restore order and common sense in a Europe which had been turned upside down by the genius and insanity of men whose benevolent intentions were better than their deeds, and whose deeds were less lofty than their principles.

The philanthropic kings and the half-witted philosophers had experimented with social institutions as a chemist makes daring mixtures with his chemicals in his laboratory. The results had been disastrous. Joseph of Austria had made so many "improvements" in his empire that it was on the verge of explosion. Frederick of Prussia had "reformed" his kingdom into a barrack yard. Rousseau, not knowing how to manage his own life, was wandering round Western Europe telling other people how to manage theirs. Kant, having less physical energy — being content with the limited facts to be found within the borders of East Prussia, and the conversations of his housekeeper and a few college friends — with equal dogmatism was telling the whole world how to think.

Driven desperate by the reckless experiments of well-intentioned theorists and confused rulers, European civilisation burst its banks in the torrent of the French Revolution. From 1789, for almost three decades, the Continent was a whirling confusion; in which the genius that is near akin to insanity linked arms with every rogue and adventurer within reach; until, by the survival of the fittest, Napoleon Bonaparte, the rogue and adventurer who had most genius of them all — or, perhaps, only most callous selfishness — came to the top of the devil's cauldron, and Europe was within measurable reach of a complete anarchy, that was resolving itself into an absolute tyranny, which has always been the inevitable historical sequence of social chaos.

In large degree, it might seem, by the efforts of one man (but really only because that one man was so truly representative of the bulk of outraged humanity) European civilisation was saved from the threatened catastrophe. This representative leader of sanity and common sense was Arthur Wellesley; who was made a duke, not (as had been the more usual custom) because he conquered other people, but because he prevented some one else conquering Europe. It should be one of the closest bonds of friendship between the French and the English nations that it was a British general who saved France from being captured by a ruthless Corsican bandit, whose chief need for subjects was that he might turn them into corpses on his battlefields.

Arthur Wellesley was a mystery even in his earliest days; there was something uncanny about him from the beginning. It demands no large amount of superstition to suspect that his birth was not a purely natural phenomenon; for his mother said it happened on one day in one place; while his nurse said it occurred in another place on another day; and modern criticism has decided that they were both wrong! It will not need many more generations of myth-making to believe that Wellington had a supernatural origin. Then, again, his mother never cared much for this son; and the new school of psychoanalysis could doubtless prove that this was a subconscious instinct that the relationship was not quite natural. She said: "I vow to God, I don't know what I shall do with my awkward son, Arthur." One cannot be hard on her impatient annoyance; for his most serious biographer, Sir Herbert Maxwell, says that the boy had "a slow thick speech and dull manner which gave him an air of stupidity."

As a youth he was, if we can believe the best evidence, dull-witted and lazy; both strange facts, seeing that when he grew older he was to fascinate and dominate the world by the amazing accuracy of his judgments, and his stupendous energy in putting that wise judgment into practice. However, of all this there was at first no sign. He went to a military academy, and we are told that he could find nothing better to do than loll about with a pet dog — though this may have been a sign of intelligence in a youth who had probably realised that a military school had nothing to teach that was worth the consideration of an original mind. But years later in Paris, just after he had won the Battle of Waterloo, Lady Shelley tells (in her diary) how, at a great reception in the Tuileries, the Duke suddenly dropped her arm, in order "to greet and kiss with reverence the hand of the most charming old lady of the *vieille cour* that I ever met. The Duke introduced me to her as the Duchesse de Seran, in whose society he had passed the happiest parts of his life, and to whose matronly kindness he owed more gratitude than he could ever repay." The Duc de Seran was chief of the military college just mentioned, and Lady Shelley says that it was from these two fine aristocrats that Wellington had learnt fluent French and distinguished manners, the only useful lessons that Wellington brought out of his military academy. The Duchesse gave Lady Shelley a more revealing glimpse into the real man than the biographers (who worry excessively about the evidence of official documents) usually grant us; for she "spoke to me of the noble qualities of mind and heart which had, in those early days, endeared Wellington to the Duc de Seran and herself."

Wellesley had thus learned the most important lesson of

his career; he had made himself think and act as a gentleman — not in the trivial sense of the snob, but with the deepest meaning of that phrase. Wellington was to become famous because he always thought and acted as a gentleman in a Europe that was filled with selfish adventurers and egotistical diplomatists. At least, that was the greater part of the reason of his fame. It was the most important fact of his life.

One now begins to suspect that his apparent laziness was due to the other fundamental quality of his character — his persistent and unshakable common sense. He would never waste his time over the collecting of the sentiments and conventions which so often pass for knowledge — and not least in a military college. So it may be that it was not laziness or stupidity — but sound judgment — that made his youth so disappointing and regrettable at the first glance. He idled because he did not intend to learn to become stupid.

It was the blunder of his life that Arthur Wellesley ever went into the Army; and it is probable that he was always conscious that it was a profession which was beneath his ethical and intellectual dignity. He was by nature an artist. He had, for example, a real sense of good music, but threw away his beloved fiddle because he thought that it was entirely incompatible with the profession of killing one's fellow men. He had gone into the military service in the mere routine of his time and social class. The Army then shared with the Church a natural right to the services of the duller members of every well-born family of the period. It was agreed that Arthur Wellesley was the dunce of his house, so naturally he was destined for the trade of killing and being killed. The better paid and safer departments of State were filled with the more promising members of this ruling class, which controlled the government mainly in its own interests. The Wellesleys and Castlereagh, and here and there a few others, were the exceptions that saved their nation.

His first campaign, the one of 1794 in the Netherlands, convinced him that the leaders of the Army did not know their craft. They were also negligent of their duties; but that was all to the good; for Wellesley could, in their absence, apply his skill with less obstruction from their stupidity. He also recognised from the first that all the fine talk of "patriotism" was mainly twaddle, only useful for official speeches. He was to say clearly in later days, when he was still more capable of judging — and no one dared to contradict him — that the English Army was the "scum of the earth. The English soldiers are fellows who have enlisted for drink — that is the plain fact. . . ." There one finds early evidence of that other great quality which, after his honesty and common sense (perhaps it was their expression), made him the great man he was. That quality was his sense of reality. Wellington always saw things as they were; and not as the sentimentalists fancied them. In the world of action, whether on the battlefield or in the parliament house, the power of seeing the facts (instead of the fancies) gave this man a long start over almost every one else whom he met in public life — where they usually prefer some thing more picturesque and more convenient than facts.

Put beside the clear-headed realist who planned the lines of Torres Vedras and won the Battle of Waterloo, Napoleon Bonaparte, his great opponent, was almost a dreamer of dreams and the victim of schoolgirl romance. Wellington was not afflicted with fantastic visions that he could conquer Europe — or the world. His mind was steady with the most solid common sense; he could always distinguish the truth from the fictitious. When the dreamer Napoleon, with the finest veteran army the world has ever seen, came up against the realist Wellington at Waterloo, with a smaller army of raw recruits, the dreamer battered his empty head against the wall of reality, as a madman would try to brush away a wall of steel with a lady's fan. Napoleon's generals had met Wellington and his men before, and offered their anxious advice; but their chief, being unable to distinguish fact from fancy, rushed blindly to his fate.

This sense of reality revealed to Wellesley another important lesson in his first campaign. If the soldiers did not fight for patriotism, neither did it guide the diplomatists who did the civilian work safely behind the lines. One of his first duties in the field was to conduct (under a white flag) a diplomatic agent to a conference with the enemy leaders; and Wellesley came to the shrewd conclusion that this diplomatist was quite ready to betray his country. In the common-sense realism of this unusual soldier's mind, a great deal of the glamour of war had thus faded at the first sight.

Wellesley was one of the few soldiers since Julius Cæsar whose brain was of first-class quality. It is said that immediately he joined his first regiment he weighed the clothes and baggage a man had to carry on march; so that he might know how many miles per day he had any right to expect of his men. Such an intellectual effort was a red-letter day in the British Army, and had probably not occurred since the time of Marlborough. It is nearly the most significant act in Wellesley's career, for it gives the clue to that minute attention to detail which enabled him to beat all the reckless heroes who were raging over Europe. Wellesley was one of the few big soldiers who have treated war as a science. From the beginning of his career he made it a rigid habit to devote several hours each day to systematic study. In his Indian campaign, when his white companions were mainly drinking or sleeping, Wellesley was reading the Commentaries of Cæsar, and analysing the manœuvres of Hannibal.

Such being the mind of this unique British officer, it is not surprising to find that the first thing he did, on returning to

England after this first campaign, was to ask his influential friends to get him transferred from the military to a civil career! He had discovered that men with brains were not expected in the British Army; his fellow officers in the Netherlands had betrayed such an alarming amount of incapacity. To put it shortly in his own words: "I learnt what one ought not to do, and that is always something." But one does not care to go tiger-hunting with men who persistently do the wrong thing; and Wellesley instinctively distrusted his future in a profession where brains were of no importance and entirely unrecognised. As he told Croker in 1826, long after his military career was over: "I can't say I owe my successes to any favour or confidence from the Horse Guards; they never showed me any from the first day I had command to this hour. . . . I have a proof that they thought I could not be trusted alone with a division, and I suspect they still have their doubts."

But the civilian departments of State had no use either for this man of brains. So Wellesley was sent off with his regiment to India, at the age of twenty-six. He fell ill as he was waiting to embark, and his doctor recorded that his patient's "conversation is the most extraordinary I have ever listened to. . . . If this young man lives he must one day be Prime Minister"— surely the shrewdest prophecy ever made.

In India Wellesley soon showed his quality. The historians have devoted a large part of their books to proving that this soldier made endless blunders in strategy and tactics; and that many, if not most, of his successes were due to good luck more than anything else. But his blunders somehow persisted in ending as victories. In his first great battle, at Assaye, he broke most of the scientific laws of wars; but laws drawn up by simpletons can often be safely ignored by wise men. When a man is persistently "lucky" ninety-five times out of every hundred, "luck" seems scarcely the right word. When Wellington won almost every battle he fought, one may at least compromise and call his bad judgment the insanity of genius. Wellington at least could rely on "luck" with scientific certainty. To make luck a certainty is invaluable in any career.

From the first it was clear that he was a far greater civil administrator than a soldier. He only cared just enough about soldiering to beat everybody who crossed his path. From the beginning he had an intense dislike of war; and was reluctant to fight if he could in any way get his ends by intellect and personal charm of manner. He really believed that war was the last resource of fools. For example, he wrote to his superiors, begging them to give Tippoo every loophole of escape from the desperate remedy of fighting: he wanted the matter, almost at all costs, compromised off the battlefield. In his later years, when he was compelled to take steps to keep order during the Chartists' threats of a revolution, he concealed his troops so that the mob would not be incited by anger at the sight of them; and he made every arrangement by which the rioters should be able to escape, if it came to fighting.

Wellesley was far more interested in finer problems of the mind than he could meet in the crude struggle of war. That was one reason why, as far as possible, by careful organisation and precise attention to details, he won his battles before the fighting began. From the outset, in India, he himself attended to the household arrangements of his army; and the domestic orders, from beef to vinegar, can be seen written with his own hand. His whole brilliant career was built up not of theoretical heroics, but of an infinite number of atoms of the coldest, commonest common sense. For example, he wrote from the East: "I know of but one receipt for good health in this country and that is to live moderately, to drink little or no wine, to use exercise, to keep the mind employed, and if possible to keep in good humour with the world" — words that are more usual from an exceptionally intelligent family doctor, or a nurse from the latest training college, than from a brilliant soldier. But they were entirely typical of Wellington.

"If possible keep in good humour" — the words were of infinite significance in Wellington's career. For he was all his life surrounded by the irritating, inferior persons who have so often filled the ranks of the governing class. He insisted upon leaving the East for one of the haughtiest reasons ever given as an excuse for retiring: "I don't exactly see the necessity that I should stay several years in India in order to settle affairs which, if I had been permitted, I should have settled long ago." It was the severest trial of Wellington's career that he had to bear with duller men who would not let him do his work as quickly as his brilliant brain could have finished it. Wellington was always conscious of his own ability; but this occasion was one of the few times in his life when he allowed his personal conceit to burst out in a sentence of angry impatience: "I don't conceive that any man has a right to call upon me to remain in a subordinate position in this country."

So he came back to Europe in 1805, a major general and a Knight of the Bath; which were both quite inappropriate rewards for his services. He had certainly proved himself a great soldier, and had made Britain supreme on the battle-fields of India. But he had done much more fundamental deeds than driving horrified and inoffensive Indians into flight. He would have been more suitably rewarded by a very honourable degree in the higher ethics. For he (and his brother the Governor-general) had laid a foundation for the ruling of India by a scrupulous code of high honour and unselfish devotion to the good of the whole community. He had taught his countrymen that they must govern India as gentlemen who respected the interests of the people who lived there; not like bandits or commercial travellers, seeking spoils and profits. A subordinate officer once came to Arthur Wellesley with an offer of a present from a rajah who desired his protection; and Wellington answered with icy passion: "In respect to the bribe offered to you and myself, I am surprised that any man in the character of an English officer should not have given the rajah to understand that the offer would be considered an insult."

The rewards of this world are so clumsily inadequate; so — as we have seen — instead of returning with the halo of a saint, Wellesley came back from India in the uniform of a general. On arriving he continued his unselfish, saint-like career by marrying (in 1806) Catherine Packenham, to whom he had been informally engaged before he started for the East. He does not seem to have mentioned her once in his correspondence during his more than ten years' absence; and he married her now only on a point of rigid honour that his word should be kept at all cost. It was the weakest thing he did. This gentle, amiable, doll-like creature was as fitting a mate for Arthur Wellesley as a milkmaid married to a mathematician. There was this impossible wife — with an intellect as fragile as a Sèvres vase — in the background of the rest of his life. There was no open quarrel; indeed, every courtesy to her on his side, and adoration from her to him. But his marriage was a tragedy; and the psychologists must estimate if we have here the solution, in part, of his almost tragical personal loneliness in the midst of an adoring world. The big man must inevitably be much alone; it was impossible to mingle in perfect fellowship with companions who were worrying over molehills, while he was considering the ascent of mountains; and in the case of his wife, she would seem to have had only the gently flitting mind of a butterfly.

When Wellesley arrived in England, on his return from India, the war with Napoleon was raging. There was little chance of stopping his triumphant career, for the Younger Pitt was still Prime Minister; which meant that nothing was attempted except fantastic, useless schemes that wasted the strength of England in dribblets. Pitt was the precise opposite to Arthur Wellesley; who, himself, in later years explained to Lady de Ros why Pitt was so ineffective: "The fault of his character was being too sanguine, that he conceived a project and then imagined it was done, and did not enter enough into the details." England would have been almost as safe in the hands of a schoolgirl, as left to the lazy imagination of the Younger William Pitt. He once proposed to Wellesley some feather-brained scheme of a military advance through Prussia; but the soldier saw it was merely idle chatter and scornfully commented: "they fancied it could be done in a moment, but I knew better." However, in January, 1806, Pitt did his greatest service to his country — and died; and the national prospects soon began to brighten.

Wellesley became Chief Secretary for Ireland. But he soon determined that he could have no intimate relations with party politicians; for he was no more at home in the company of sharpers than in that of military dullheads. He had to spend a large part of his time answering applications for posts; which was obviously a repulsive occupation for a man who throughout his career refused to recommend any one on any grounds except merit. A relative in after years desired a government post, and wrote to his all-powerful kinsman, "One word from your Grace will be sufficient"; and the curt reply was: "Dear — Not one word. From yours affectionately, Wellington." So he went to war again as the commander of a division under Lord Cathcart, in the Copenhagen campaign of 1807. It confirmed him in his earlier opinion that war was a barbaric foolishness; and he begged his chief not to bombard Copenhagen, but try another method that would save bloodshed. But the politicians at home were clamouring for effective scenes that would be pleasing to journalists and mob orators; so he was unheeded, and Copenhagen was bombarded; though Wellesley did what he could for his enemies by sternly suppressing all pillaging. The Danish General Oxholm wrote thanking him for his kindness to the prisoners and adding: "it is a great pity that political views should counteract the private feelings of individuals, but, as soldiers, our lot is to obey."

Then Wellesley went back for a short time to his civil post in Ireland, and tried to smooth away the political injustices between Protestants and Catholics by granting them equal rights. Their theological hairsplittings were, of course, beneath the attention of Wellesley's realist, common-sense genius. But by this time the men in power had begun to realise that Wellesley had a brain worth better use than for the management of their rather ignominious political jobs. So they questioned him as to the possibility of arousing a revolution in South America, as a way of embarrassing their enemies in Europe. But Wellesley flatly refused to assist in any such work. As he told the story to Stanhope: "I always had a horror of revolutionising any country for a political object. I always said, if they rise of themselves, well and good, but do not stir them up; it is a fearful responsibility." Years after, when he was Prime Minister, he refused to allow any encouragement to be given to rebels — however good their cause and however abominable their tyrants. For he knew how horrible war was; and that it was almost always the political adventurers who started strife — hoping that they would be able to gather the spoils when the fighting was over. Wellesley never assisted rogues if he could help it.

At last his advice received attention. In 1808 he pointed out that Napoleon's armies were distributed over Europe: it was the moment to hit; for his far-scattered lines, "each portion of them having great objects and ample employments which cannot be given up without injury to his affairs, afford an opportunity which ought not to be passed by."

It was the germ idea of the Peninsular War; and conclusive evidence that a great mind had at last arrived. In June, 1808, he was made the commander of an expedition to drive the French out of Spain from a base in Portugal.

The whole conception of the Peninsular War, as Wellington created it, is one of the big triumphs of human art. Pitt had already wasted eighty thousand British soldiers on futile expeditions to the fever-infected West Indies. The beneficial results were not enough to cover a sheet of note paper. With the loss of far fewer men in Spain, Wellington bled Napoleon of three hundred thousand of his best French soldiers. The Spanish Peninsula was the open vein which sapped the life of the Napoleonic Empire. Wellesley (or Wellington as he became by his peerage granted in 1809) by a flash of genius soon saw that if he built himself the impregnable lines of Torres Vedras along the Portuguese Mountains, he could defy the French attack in front, while the untouchable British Navy fed him with supplies by the sea communications behind him.

It happened exactly as he had planned. He built these lines with perfect skill and in absolute secrecy — for he had infected the whole Portuguese peasantry with his own amazing spirit. Thousands of simple men toiled at the fortifications, yet not one of them played the traitor by revealing the truth to the French. Perhaps this was a greater triumph for Wellington than the military skill of the plan; for it proved that he was not only a great soldier who could fight more brilliantly than his enemy, but a still greater psychologist who could capture the mind of a whole nation.

When Massena, in pursuit of Wellington (as he thought — but really decoyed, as he was), ran his head against the lines of Torres Vedras, he was amazed. He turned savagely on his intelligence staff; why had they not told him of what was in front. They pleaded ignorance of the building of the

The First Duke of Wellington

lines; and Massena raged, "*Que Diable! Wellington n'a pas construit ces montagnes.*" It was the petulant cry of a man who had been outwitted by his intellectual superior.

From these lines Wellington was a perpetual menace to Napoleon's scheme of conquering Europe; behind these walls was the one spot in continental Europe which remained free from, and threatened, his power. The Peninsular campaign was the scheme by which Wellington, acting from the certain impregnable base of Torres Vedras, gradually drained the French army of its blood, until the day came when, in 1813, he was able at last to advance and drive the exhausted enemy over the Pyrenees, and pursue them into their own France. It was, in short, the fatal blow against Napoleon. To give the Russians their due credit, they were playing the Corsican hot-head a similar trick on the other side of Europe. Napoleon was really one of the most dupable men in history.

In the Peninsular campaign from 1808 to 1814 Wellington gave a display of superhuman capability (physical and mental) such as rarely has delighted the world. From the first battle at Vimeiro he showed that he could beat the French — who had driven almost every other general in Europe off the map. He told Croker before he set out for Portugal that he was not afraid of his enemy, as everybody else seemed to be. He had carefully considered the French method of fighting in dense columns; and had determined to meet them by an extended line only two deep, which would expose their flanks to a greater fire. It was a stroke of "genius" — or that common sense which was Wellington's supreme quality.

However, the Peninsular War was not so much a triumph of guns as a victory of one man's mind over the mind of millions. The true history of this six years' campaign is much more a story of psychology than of military affairs. The battles might almost be dismissed as insignificant incidents. Wellington beat the French out of Spain not merely because he knew more about war than the best French generals did, but mainly because he knew infinitely more about the minds of men. He handled Spaniards and Portuguese until they did what he wanted, even if it was sometimes only to do nothing; whereas the French generals had no method of governing them except by killing them. It was, in short, the essential difference between Wellington and his rival, Napoleon. One was a gentleman who believed in intelligent kindness; the other was at heart a cad, who was more ready to shoot his opponents than to argue with them.

If ever a human soul was inspired, it was Wellington's in Spain, though it was not the kind of inspiration that would have been obvious to the theologian. He spent his spare time not in prayer, but in fox-hunting; which was part of a deliberate plan to keep fit. When most of his officers went home on leave, or brought their wives out to Portugal, their chief never left his post until Napoleon was beaten to the ground. He had one or two very reliable men to carry out his orders; but the Peninsular War was as much a work of personal art as a Corot landscape or a Beethoven sonata.

Wellington in Spain had moments of military triumph which suggest the miraculous. There was, for example, that great living chess match with Marmont in 1812; when both sides were playing a desperate game, with everything at stake. Marmont was pressing Wellington very hard indeed, and it seemed that he had surrounded the English army. Then came that tremendous act of great drama, at the battle of Salamanca. Wellington was eating his breakfast, with the French shot falling all round him, when a messenger brought tidings of a new move on the part of the enemy; and Wellington, galloping to an observation post, in one glance saw that the Frenchman had made a fatal blunder at last — he had left a gap in his line. "*Mon cher Alava, Marmont est perdu!*" was Wellington's curt comment to his Spanish friend at his side. He gave a few rapid orders; and, with his greatest victory within his grasp, he turned to Fitzroy: "I am going to take a rest; when they reach that copse, near the gap in the hills, wake me." Then, in Sir Herbert Maxwell's words: "He lay down in his cloak on the heath, among the sweet gum-cistus flowers, and was fast asleep in a minute." It was all over an hour or two later; forty thousand Frenchmen had been utterly defeated in almost as many minutes. The whole affair savours of the supernatural — this uncanny soldier who could see a great victory by one sudden confident glance; and then lie down and sleep like a child until the moment came. Human creatures of the common stock have not eyes and brains and nerves of that kind.

To get the picture of this man into the right perspective, it must always be kept in mind that all the while he was fighting the French, he was also almost absolute ruler of Spain and Portugal, as far as any one can be said to rule peoples who usually follow their own desires. The Spaniards were the first people in Europe with enough pride and independence to resist the insolence of Napoleon. Being thus full of genius and intelligence, they have always been a problem for rulers. Wellington's skill in handling the anarchy of the Peninsular populations, making them at least a half-organised mob, was a greater feat than beating the French armies. He was always a diplomatist first: a soldier only when the intellect was powerless before the attack of fools who were too stupid to reason.

The military brilliance of the Peninsular War is only a background in a miniature portrait of this man. It is in the finer civilian details that his delicate quality comes out. When he had driven his enemy out of Spain and had crossed the French border, beyond the Pyrenees, his first determination was that none of the invaded people should suffer as the Spaniards and Portuguese had suffered from Napoleon's reckless savagery in the Peninsula. At last he had made the

British soldiers — recruited from drunkards and criminals, as he himself had said — into an orderly army, to whom the French population soon flocked with delight as purchasers, almost as friends. When some French peasants shot a British soldier who was attempting to plunder them, Wellington congratulated them on their courage; and at once shot another plunderer whom they had brought in as their prisoner. An officer of rank was ordered home in disgrace because he had allowed his men to touch the official documents of a French commune. The Spanish troops that Wellington had brought with him showed signs of taking their revenge for the years of French invasion and tyranny. They were immediately ordered to return home, at a moment when Wellington wanted every man he could find. But if he could not fight as a gentleman — then he preferred to be beaten. As he wrote curtly to the Spanish General: "I have lost 20,000 in this campaign; but it was not in order that General Morillo, or anybody else, should come in and plunder the French peasantry. . . . It is a matter of perfect indifference to me whether I command a large army or a small one; but whether great or small, it must obey me, and above all, it must not plunder."

It is possible to argue that he did not really care for the sufferings of the French, and was only considering how most easily to persuade them to allow him to advance rapidly on Paris. But the whole of Wellington's career, with innumerable proofs, is unanswerable evidence of his determination to save unnecessary suffering, and to protect the civilian population from the effects of his military operations. He had refused to capture the great convoy of French civilian followers who were retreating from Madrid within his easy grasp. There is, also, that remarkable fact, quite outside his army career, which must have struck his harder contemporaries with astonishment: namely, that in later years he ceased to preserve game on his estates, because one of his keepers had been killed in a poaching affray. Gleig tells how the tender-hearted Duke then begged a reprieve for the murderer; and he ended the incident by declaring: "I would rather be without a pheasant on my lands, than that such scenes should occur again." Such was the value that the greatest soldier of his day put on human life; while Napoleon had callously drenched Europe with blood rather than surrender the hope of getting his maddest whim. It was the difference between a decent human being and a criminal. War, to Wellington, was not an end in itself. As he told the politicians of Europe, when the time came to make terms, his end, he said, had been to restore peace to the world and give it freedom from the burden of armed forces — not merely to conquer the French and wring out of them an indemnity. Wellington, as we have seen, had early realised that peoples are only the helpless pawns of their rulers. He may even have asked himself why France should be so heavily punished just because an Italian had tried to conquer the world at the cost of French blood.

Wellington had an innate sense of the rights of man as something much bigger than the rights of nations. He was much more international than patriotic. He never lost his head after his victories; he never rushed off, like Prince Rupert's troopers, to raid the baggage wagons. He calmly continued to pursue the fundamental end which he had in mind during all these years in the Peninsula; namely, to make it impossible that Napoleon, or any other man, should impose his tyrannical will on the peoples of Europe. Blücher and his Prussians wanted to sack or burn Paris. That would have been, in Wellington's long view, an act of childish petulance. He desired to stop destruction, not to do more of it. In this deep instinct of humanity, Wellington had a worthy colleague in Castlereagh. When the kings and statesmen of Europe were clamouring for the spoils of victory, like the crew of a pirate ship, Wellington and Castlereagh calmly insisted (as far as they were able, in a chattering crowd of diplomatists and worse) on giving them, instead, a peace more worthy of civilised men.

II

Waterloo will probably always be the great event in Wellington's biography. It was not so in reality: for it was only his most spectacular moment. Nevertheless, the spectacular has a way of forcing itself unjustly on a careless world, that too often has the "film" mind of the child and the intellectually immature.

Waterloo had, indeed, all the gigantic outlines of the most impressive panorama; and it is noteworthy that Wellington dominated it all in a very personal sense. So few generals retain their individuality throughout the turmoil of a great battle. Most of them disappear from view, until fate — without much assistance from them — has given one side the victory. But if ever a commander held his grip throughout a battle (and before and after it also), it was Wellington during the three days' battle around Waterloo.

It has been charged against Wellington that at Waterloo he was hopelessly surprised and outmanœuvred by Napoleon; and that if he won the battle at all, it was by a sheer fluke which he owed either to the stubborn courage of his men or to the unexpected arrival of Blücher and his Prussians.

The truth is that the Waterloo campaign was the final triumph of his military system. He planned, to a decimal point, what he had to do, and he carried it through with complete success. It is not surprising that there have been misunderstandings of the military and political position which made the Waterloo campaign necessary in the form it took, for probably Wellington was the only man in Europe who clearly grasped the essential facts; and it was not until near the end of his life that he put the whole problem into

DUKE OF WELLINGTON
From a portrait by Count D'Orsay National Portrait Gallery

words, in a memorandum for Lord Ellesmere's guidance when the latter was writing an article on the subject in 1842. By reading this memorandum one can understand the vast scope of Wellington's mind; how he was merely a soldier by chance, having infinitely greater powers as a statesman. Many men might have won the Battle of Waterloo; but there was not another man in Europe who appears capable of having written this masterly memorandum explaining why he acted as he did. In it the military position becomes a mere detail in a massive design of the political structure of all Europe. It was the work of the most brilliant diplomat of his age — and of most ages.

Had he been an upstart adventurer — playing for his own hand — Wellington would have planned this campaign in a very national and even selfish manner, considering his own reputation and perhaps his own nation. But he had the cosmopolitan mind which considers the good of all other nations as well. He was not intent on beating Napoleon off his own bat, as the cricket phrase runs. He conceived his duty as being to hold him in check until the allied armies, following the Prussians, arrived to administer the conclusive blow. His whole campaign of Waterloo was constructed with that end in view. He accomplished it with such perfect precision, according to plan, that he was able, by his own forces alone, to annihilate Napoleon, with merely the assistance of the Prussians at the end of the day; though it is only fair to add clearly that the faithful Blücher's army was always an organic part of the Waterloo campaign. The Prussian had given his word that he would be there at all costs. Wellington knew the promise would be kept — as it was — and made his plans with the Prussians as part of the final blow.

In this memorandum, Wellington proves conclusively that he was not surprised by Napoleon, before the British army could concentrate; but, rather, that he was playing his cards with scientific skill, when he refused to assemble his forces at one spot until the last moment. He had to take the risks of that hesitation; and he took them up to exactly the right minute. It is child's talk to babble of surprise, when we find that Wellington had all the time he needed to assemble his army at precisely the place where he had always intended to fight, if Napoleon foolishly allowed him to concentrate there. To listen to this chatter of surprise one would imagine that the English general had been caught on an open plain in the midst of his march. Whereas, the enemy found him on the exact spot that he had chosen and had minutely examined, weeks before.

There were, of course, some of the symptoms of surprise that would be likely to catch the journalist's eye. For example, Wellington seemed to be frivoling at the Duchess of Richmond's ball in Brussels on the night — even the early morning — before the preliminary battle of Quatre Bras. Had they known it, they might have discovered Wellington lying on the floor, playing games with children, only the day before; while the greatest terror of Europe, Napoleon, was within striking distance. To the small mind, fast bound by the conventions of mediocrity, such conduct may seem folly. But, in fact, it was one of the chief factors in Wellington's greatness. His mind was so superbly normal and of such balanced sanity, that he never allowed the small matters of life — which are really the important great ones — to be overwhelmed by those assertive public demonstrations which are too often considered as all-important affairs. It is the small man who gets life out of proportion, who imagines that it is more important to beat Napoleon than to play with clamouring child-friends. Whereas, deep in the heart of life, it is not so at all. For the play of children is one of the urgent necessities of a normal world; while the roaring marches of upstarts and bandits of the Napoleonic kind are merely passing and trivial, though disagreeable, incidents.

Wellington had a perfect sense of the proportions of life; he never allowed the fundamental facts of normal human affairs to be disturbed by the abnormal accidents. Napoleon was almost an accident in his view of life; and he treated him and his armies as such.

Now, it may seem that this verdict must be erroneous, seeing that Wellington had a stern sense of duty, which he never disobeyed throughout his career. It has been already noted that he never took leave to go home all through the Peninsular War. Before that, he had been many consecutive years in India, on service without a break. After Waterloo, to the end of his life, he was a slave to his public duties — until at last he once, almost petulantly, asked if the Duke of Wellington was the only man in England who was not allowed to rest or do as he pleased. Yet he did please to spend many of the hours before Waterloo in the most playful of play, as if the fate of Europe did not tremble in the balance which he held in his own hand. The important fact to note is that when it came to the supreme struggle at Waterloo, between the simple man who liked playing with children and, on the other side, the man who was consumed with a fierce desire to conquer the world — which left no time for the domesticities of life — when these two were locked in mortal fight it was the idle player who won, and the fierce worker who was beaten.

Wellington held his position at Waterloo for hour after hour of the most savage attack that Napoleon ever made on his enemy. The English were almost a raw army of recruits; the Duke had scarcely a staff officer with whom he had worked before, and there was only one of them unwounded when the day was over. Wellington was everywhere in the thick of the fighting; so far as the command went, it was a one-man battle; and the commander in chief gave most of the orders in a very direct way. It was not a case of a "G. H. Q." miles away; Wellington's responsibility was at his elbow, and his enemies were often only on the other side of the hedge. If blunders were made, there was no excuse for this chief, for he was always on the spot itself.

Wellington did exactly what he set out from Brussels to do — stop Napoleon until his allies arrived. He succeeded so completely that he had enough in hand to turn his wall of defence into a charging line of attack. He not only held Napoleon up at Waterloo, he charged at him with his whole army; and the French were not merely stopped but broken into an utter rout.

III

It was only after Waterloo that Wellington had a reasonable chance of showing his real self. So far he had wasted his precious youth and early manhood in the negative work of destroying thoughtless people who believed that the important affairs of this world can be settled by physical force. The whole theory of war is a denial of the dignity and power of intellectual reason. After the final destruction of the anarchist, Napoleon, Wellington had never any necessity to go to war again; and he began to live that life of civilian statesmanship for which he was so much more suited than a military career.

His first great diplomatic work was to make the peace of Europe secure after his victories in the field. The soldiers in arms — the poor dupes of the political adventurers and profit makers — were killed or scattered; but the Napoleons and Czars, the Talleyrands, the Metternichs and Cannings, the Fouchés, and all the rest of the professional ruling class of many nations (who so often make their living by stirring up social disorders) had to be restrained, if possible, by some kind of international law. It has been overlooked by most people that it was Wellington who took the chief part in this civil settlement, as he had taken the chief part in the military victory. Like Julius Cæsar and Alexander the Great, he was both statesman and soldier.

It had not, in truth, needed supernatural ability to beat most of the generals who had led their armies against him; for men of brains are somewhat rare in the military profession — just as men of delicate artistic tastes rarely become rat catchers. But in politics and finance — the trades where Wellington was now to compete — the ranks were filled with men who had all the quick mental agility of the card sharper and the professional rogue. It was a field of action where Wellington was handicapped by the gravest of disabilities — honesty. In war he had shared with his enemies the superb human virtue of physical courage; and by throwing his brains into the scale he had turned it, and won. But he shared nothing in common with these new opponents, these ministers of State and their bankers. Many, perhaps most of them, were grasping men, seeking their posts and their profits at all costs; and generally regardless of the welfare of their own nation or of anybody else.

After Waterloo, Wellington's position was almost supreme. Emperors and kings treated him as if he were nearly divine. He had saved their empires and kingdoms, and they clung round him as children cling to any one who pulls them out of a pond. The great British soldier proved as efficient in peace as in war. He calmly restrained the foolish creatures who were clamouring for revenge and spoils; he did his best to give Europe the only thing for which decent men fight battles — that is, peace.

Now this peace was not a vague sentimental affair which could be settled by pretty, soft words. It was a most technical problem of finance, where Wellington was to prove himself as great a master as in war. He was made the head of the Arbitration Commission. Sir Herbert Maxwell has put the position vividly:

"From this point his despatches become simply bewildering in their numbers and the intricacy of the calculations. . . . Not only did he succeed in consolidating the claim against France into one manageable sum . . . this was a large reduction from the aggregate of claims . . . to enable the French Government to make their payment, Wellington negotiated a loan for them with the leading financiers of Europe." Wellington's own words are very suggestive of his task: "Since Baring left me, as I generally spend the greatest part of every morning now with money-changers, Rothschild has been with me."

One of the chief ends and objects of the war had now been revealed — the bankers and profit-makers were reaping their harvest, and it fell to Wellington to save Europe from the money-changers as he had saved it from raging men-at-arms. Of course he was not so completely successful; for he was not allowed (by the rules of this new financial war) to shoot down the money-lenders, as the military code of war had allowed him to kill the soldiers who did not agree with him. One of the most remarkable things is that he, with all his inexperience, should have been chosen for this very technical task. The reason is very plain: Wellington was the one man of the ruling class whom every one knew to be an honest man, and also a clever one.

For the rest of his life — almost half of it — he served his country (and all Europe) as a statesman. After the more spectacular tumult of his military triumphs, Wellington's civil career has been underestimated by the historians; whereas, it was really more distinguished than his career in war. Perhaps it would be truer to write that it was mainly distinguished in the high plane of theory, rather than in accomplishment; for the odds against Wellington in politics were too heavy for a complete practical triumph such as he had won on the battlefield. His virtues made complete success in politics an impossibility. For he had two qualities, honesty and straightforward simplicity, that were almost as useless in political life as a bolster would be in a cavalry charge.

But it was because of these two virtues that this man is so distinguished above the ordinary in English politics. Wellington has been strangely misunderstood by careless historians; he has been mistaken for a reactionary despot, who was against all reform or democratic welfare. Nothing could be farther from the truth. Wellington was certainly not a democrat if such be one who believes that every adventurer who tickles the fancy of the mob is necessarily devoting himself to the service of the people who elected him. For example, he knew too much about history and current affairs to be deceived into a foolish opinion that the men who had made the French Revolution were democrats. For had he not spent his life, hitherto, in crushing the chief product of that "democratic" Revolution — to wit, Napoleon Bonaparte, who was so far from being a democrat that he was a military tyrant. Wellington's realist mind soon analysed that sort of "democracy." Likewise he could never have understood the rhetoric of Mr. Canning, who put most of his "democracy" into his speeches and his middle-class conservatism into his actions. All which subtle sentiments Wellington's simple mind was quite unable to understand, except with contempt. He had none of the politician's platform tricks. He could only quietly perform the immediate duties of his office, and take the next inevitable step. He was very little interested in such a politician's window-dressing as the Reform Bill of 1832; and when he saw that it might mean street riots if it were not passed, he considered the whole matter so insignificant that he at once gave way and persuaded the Lords to accept it. When it was made an Act, the Chartists agreed with the Duke that there was little democracy about it.

Wellington once wrote to Lord Redesdale (January 28,

1838): "There is nobody who dislikes, so much as I do, and who knows so little of Party Management. I hate it; because in my opinion it is the cause of all that we are suffering at present."

Wellington was one of the most complete realists that history has known, and he was, therefore, by his nature unable to apply false sentiments to a political situation; just as he had never wasted a moment in idle fancy on a battle. He had won his battles because he could detect a hard fact quicker than any other general in Europe. So likewise, when he came home into politics, he instinctively ignored all the party rhetoric of the politicians, and applied his mind whole-heartedly to the facts. It was one of the very rare cases where this has happened in political life.

He had shown this realist mind in the first political office he held — the Chief Secretaryship of Ireland in 1807. For when the politicians were attempting to raise party capital out of the tithe agitation, Wellington curtly told them that the real cause of unrest in Ireland was high rents — a statement which to-day would class him with the extreme Socialists. He then added that canals should be cut; and also, that the clergy should be sent to live in their parishes. With such a persistent instinct for simple common sense it is clear that the great Duke of Wellington could no more breathe with comfort in the political atmosphere than a man can breathe in water. So Britain had to lose the advantage of much of the good he might have done. Had fate made him a despot, he would undoubtedly have governed England with quiet efficiency; and less time would have been wasted on the brilliant rhetoric of Canning and the clever manœuvering of Peel. Wellington once held in his own hand almost all the chief offices of State for a few weeks in 1834, while Sir Robert Peel was hurrying home from Italy to form a government. The Duke alone did the business of all these combined offices; and when he handed them over to their new ministers he had not only completed all the current work, but had also wiped out the long arrears with which they were clogged. He was able to do this because never in his life did he waste a moment over the innumerable things which do not matter — which are the chief concern of the small minds.

A Prime Minister who did his business, instead of talking about it, would have made a revolution in English history. Nothing had been seen like it since William Cecil and Robert Walpole had been in power generations before. No event in his life was more typical of this man, who was a miracle of hard work and efficiency. Little wonder that the politician's historians have tried to blacken him as a reactionary. For if Wellington had had his way, the men of windy rhetoric would have disappeared in a political catastrophe not unlike the annihilation of Waterloo.

The events of the Duke's career in political life are not very exciting in their details; and this was because he stood outside the full current of ordinary party politics. In the pages of Greville's diary — one of the most illuminating of the historical sources for this period — Wellington appears as a monumental figure, looming behind and above all ordinary men; strangely and impressively alone in his simple habit of attempting to get the national business done with the greatest efficiency and the least disturbance. Greville did not agree with the Duke in politics, but he was continually fascinated by the selfless patriotism of the man. Again and again he comments on the way in which Wellington was sinking his own interests in the wider good of the whole community. Wellington's first principle in politics was that the king's government should be assisted to do its work whenever it was acting in the interests of the State; and he was almost entirely indifferent whether he himself was in office or not. This conduct, of course, was unforgivable in the opinion of the professional politician; but since Greville, the diarist, was not a politician, but a gentleman like Wellington, he continually records the Duke's action with astonished joy.

Thus he wrote on July 11, 1831:

The Government are in exceeding delight at the Duke's conduct ever since he has been in opposition, which certainly has been very noble, straightforward, gentlemanlike, and without an atom of faction or mischief about it. He has done himself great honour; he threw over Aberdeen completely on that business about foreign policy . . . and now he is assisting the Government in their Lieutenancy Bill, and he is in constant communication with Melbourne on the subject.

On August 20, 1833, Greville reveals the political mind of Lyndhurst against the gentleman's mind of Wellington:

The Duke of Wellington has continued to attend in the House of Lords day after day, proposing alterations and amendments to all the Bills, evidently reading hard, and preparing himself for each occasion, always loaded with papers. Lyndhurst said to somebody, 'I shall attend no more, what is the use of it? The Duke comes down every day and tries to make the Bills *better;* if I could make them *worse*, I would come too!'

Greville, who was, after all, a man of a very cynical world, and did not weary his soul by too eager hopes of meeting saints in Whitehall and Westminster, naturally had many moments of suspicion that Wellington could not really be as good as he seemed. For example, on March 26, 1832, when the Reform Bill was at the crisis of its career, he wrote:

"I expect, and I beg his pardon if I am wrong, that the Duke will make as mischievous a speech as he can, and try to provoke declarations and pledges against the Bill." But in the next day his diary records: "I did the Duke of Wellington an injustice. He spoke, but without any violence, in a fair and gentlemanly manner, a speech creditable to himself, useful and becoming. If there was any disposition on the part of his followers to light a flame, he at once suppressed it." With his political prejudices so often running contrary to the Duke, this finely balanced observer was continually admitting that the Duke of Wellington was a model of fairness.

The Duke's attitude to the Reform Bill struggle of 1832 is entirely typical of his political position, both in the way he fiercely opposed the Bill at the beginning, and also in the way he surrendered, and helped to pass it at the end. The whole episode is a summary of Wellington as the statesman and the key to most of his civil career.

But so little of what a man says or does in public is reliable evidence of what he is really doing or really thinking. It is necessary to get behind the scenes, into those more intimate nooks of the human soul, where alone the public behaviour can be measured at its true value. So many great reputations have been made because the real man has been able to hide himself as discreetly as a warship was hidden by smoke screens during the recent war. But there is endless evidence of Wellington's inner mind. On the occasion of the Reform Bill, for example, one can at once find a typical piece of evidence of this stubborn honesty which hampered his whole political career.

Mr. Gleig had written to the Duke, suggesting the possibility that Lord Brougham — who does not seem to have had any principles that would not give way to an acceptable offer of value — might be persuaded to join with Sir Robert Peel in resisting the Reform Bill. Mr. Gleig was a clergyman, and therefore accustomed by his profession to worldly compromises and easy give-and-take in points of principle; but even he added apologetically (in this letter dated from the Athenæum Club September 9, 1831): "I am aware how painful it must be to a mind like yours to entertain the thought of acting with such a colleague; but if with so much at stake there be no chance of breaking up the present Cabinet, except by encouraging them to betray one another, even your high sense of honour might, I think, come under the influence of necessity." It was a daring proposal to suggest to the Duke of Wellington that he should play tricks with his principles — for the simple soldier has rarely the subtle logic of theologians, ready in self-defence, when they are found out. The reply from the Duke is one of those revealing documents which are more valuable to the historian than international treaties or orations in Parliament. It is dated September 17, 1831, and ran:

> I have two objections to the course you propose. The first is one of conscience. I could not deceive any man. I prefer another to Lord B., whether as a debater in Parliament, an officer in a court of justice, or a colleague, or an honest man. The second is that if there was no such preference, I could have no confidence in that gentleman. I cannot pretend that which I do not intend. All this may be very foolish. I may not be equal to the difficulties of the times, but I cannot help it. I believe that in these times, or at all times, honesty is the best policy, and adherence to principle the only true guide for one's conduct.

All of which, as the professional soldier teaching the theologian the elements of morality, is not without the subtle humour of the great masters of irony.

From this solid base of an honesty that was almost rustic in its simplicity, Wellington conducted his political campaign — as he had based his military ones on the impregnable lines of Torres Vedras. His treatment of the Reform Bill was very logical when once one realises his elementary principles. He was convinced that the Reform Bill was the beginning of the same process that in France had ended in the Reign of Terror and the guillotine. It may be easy to prove to-day that he was wrong; the dullest wits can prophesy when they know. He had not realised that the "mob" in England had never done anything much rasher than pull down a few railings of Hyde Park. When the fanatic Cromwell cut off Charles Stuart's head, the mob had to be kept back by armed mercenaries from rescuing their king. The English dislike disorder even more than tyranny.

If Wellington was not an historian, he had an instinctive genius for seeing and understanding the full significance of what happened before his eyes: and after the widest experience in all Europe he wrote thus to Gleig on April 6, 1831:

> In a short time, and that a period approaching nearer to be counted by months than by years, nothing will remain of England but the name and the soil. . . . The question reduced to its simple terms is this: Shall we continue to have a Government capable of protecting our lives, properties, and institutions, or shall we not? Or rather, shall we incur the certain loss of all these — the happiness, and prosperity, and greatness of our country, in order to follow the example of the delusive theories of our neighbours?

Some hasty people have jumped to the conclusion that the Duke of Wellington was one of those who are mainly concerned in saving their lands and goods from the clutches of a rising democracy. Such a judgment is an error. He certainly believed that a respect for the just rights of neighbours was a necessary basis for a civilised society. He had probably never studied the laws of the orthodox political economists — having always avoided tedious nonsense — and the latest arguments of modern economics had, of course, not been put before him, or any one else, at that time. But if Wellington was not a professional economist he was a shrewd observer of human behaviour; and a course of many years' encounters (on the battlefields and in the council chambers) with "reformers" of all sorts and nationalities, had convinced him that instead of being anxious to restore the lands and goods of the aristocrats to the people, most of the reformers showed a still greater earnestness in filling their own pockets.

What other opinions could any sane man have come to when faced by the results of the French Revolution? Any one who was still innocent enough to imagine that Napoleon was the saviour of democracy would have mistaken the tinsel monarch of a fancy-dress ball for the real royal line. Since Wellington believed that "reform" in England might come to the same ridiculous end that it had reached in France — a military tyranny instead of a democratic paradise — it is little wonder he tried to stop the Reform Bill. He knew by experience that social disorder always ended in the strong and the brutal getting the prizes. The success of the French Revolution had been the triumph of army contractors, tenth-rate lawyers, and half the rogues in France; and Wellington had a certain conviction that a revolution in England would likewise mean the triumph of the strong and not the salvation of the weak. As he said to Lady Salisbury: "If there were a revolution in this country, it must end by a military dictator"; and when he was told that the Duke of Bedford had announced that they must choose between despotism or anarchy, Wellington commented with biting humour: "I can tell Johnny Bedford that if we have anarchy, I'll have Woburn" — the Russells' family estate.

Such being his reasons (good or bad) for resisting the Reform Bill, they were also, paradoxical as it may seem, his reasons for giving way and even assisting it to pass. The wealthy middle classes had tricked the discontented poor into an agitation for an enlarging of the parliamentary franchise; and were able to organise a sufficiently powerful (or at least, noisy) party for "Reform." Rioting began — which is generally the work of professional political agitators, and rarely the deed of an unorganised mob — and it became clear that if the parliamentary vote were not given to the new industrial classes they would take it by force, just as the Puritans had seized power by arms in the seventeenth century. Now, Wellington had a horror of one thing above all others. He dreaded war; and above all else he hated a civil war. More than any one in Europe he realised its inevitable

The First Duke of Wellington 39

atrocities while it lasted, and its futility when it was won. Rather than risk a revolution, he was prepared to stand on one side and allow the Reform Bill to be passed. Being a supremely sane man he knew that nothing worth having was gained by force.

His dread of war was one of the main principles of Wellington's foreign policy also. His rigid rule for British diplomacy was never to interfere with the affairs of any other nation, if it could possibly be avoided. Wellington was as anxious as anybody to put down cruel despots and make nations happy; but he refused to march armies about Europe in this desirable crusade, because he knew that the evils of society can no more be cured by armies than the Atlantic can be dried by a mop. He knew, by experiments in the laboratory of life — as distinguished from theory — that the opposing sides in civil war are usually as indistinguishable as two peas. When he was asked his opinion of the rival parties in Spain he replied: "I would not give a toss for the choice between Don Carlos and Marotto, the Queen and Espartero. They ought all to be hanged on the same tree, to avoid the injury which might be done to a second." It mattered nothing to the Duke whether a civil war was for a queen or a republic. He thought the most righteous reward for rioters — royalists or democrats — was a rope.

It would not be very profitable to go through Wellington's political life in detail; for it was only the logical result of the root principles already mentioned. Honesty is so much more monotonous than crime. He had too great an experience of the world to believe for a moment that reforms could be won by any hasty changes in the laws; still less had he any belief that "reformers", as they named themselves, were at all likely to honour their promises. Besides, he was rarely convinced that the reforms so enthusiastically advocated would have any beneficent effect. Thus, when Peel, who was a very nervous creature, lost his head when confronted by the calamity of the Irish famine in 1845, Wellington never for a moment was so stupid as to imagine that to open English ports to corn was the quickest way to feed the Irish! As he told Croker, he was totally unprepared for Peel's sudden change of policy: "nor do I comprehend how the repeal of the Corn Laws can remedy the potato famine in Ireland, where the want is not of food but of money to buy it." Lord Stanhope has recorded that directly he spoke to Wellington of the Irish famine, the Duke began to consider the precise economic facts bearing on the production of the potato in Ireland — whereas Peel discussed how to get corn for England! It was the difference between a sane man and a half-witted sentimentalist.

The Duke's realist mind had already applied itself to the danger of famine in Ireland. He had written a letter on that subject to the Duke of Northumberland in April, 1830. He saw the injustice of English landlords drawing rents from Ireland, and spending them elsewhere, so he said:

If we cannot enforce residence in Ireland we must at least endeavour to encourage it . . . by prevailing upon the King to adhere to the rule of granting Irish offices, honours and distinctions only to those resident in that country. I have invariably adhered to that rule.

On July 7 he wrote again:

The annually recurring starvation in Ireland . . . gives me more uneasiness than any other evil existing in the United Kingdom. . . . The proprietors of the country, those who ought to think for the people, to foresee this misfortune, and to provide beforehand a remedy for it, are amusing themselves in the clubs in London, in Cheltenham, or Bath, or on the Continent, and the Government are made responsible for the evil, and they must find a remedy for it where they can — anywhere except in the pockets of the Irish gentlemen. Then, if they give publick money to provide a remedy for this distress, it is applied to all purposes excepting the one for which it is given; and most particularly to that one, viz.

the payment of the arrears of an exorbitant rent. You may rely upon it that you have judged correctly in refraining from giving the publick money to relieve the existing distress. The Irish gentlemen of all ranks must be made to feel, or we shall never have a permanent remedy.

It is difficult to understand how a man who wrote in this stern manner of the social and economic sins of absentee landlords could ever have got into the historical textbooks as a harsh Tory. By some misfortune (which, in view of the unending evidence against the theory, is almost inexplicable) Wellington has usually appeared in history as the man who refused to permit any reforming change which would shake the position of the privileged governing class, of which he was one. It is a theory without substantial facts to support it. Wellington certainly thought that the democracy of England had not the practical knowledge of affairs that entitled them to seize power and govern in the place of the owners of rotten boroughs. But it was hard common sense, not class feeling, that made him prefer the existing government (bad though it was) to a rule by still more inexperienced persons.

He was the most businesslike man in England. His correspondence (even the most trivial) was answered with the most rigid punctuality; he kept his appointments to the moment. Except in the hours of exercise and relaxation (which he systematically enjoyed with the enthusiasm of a wise man) he was a hard worker and a student and reader from morn to night. For those who did their work less strenuously than himself he had impatient contempt. When Marshall Beresford once complained to him that the members of the British Government had neglected their duty in some way, Wellington wrote to console him: "The omission to which you advert, unaccountable as it is, must be attributed to that kind of neglect and slovenly mode of doing business which is too common among public men in England."

Wellington cannot be precisely described by any of the conventional terms by which men are grouped into classes or parties. None of the political party names will cover his qualities and opinions. He was neither Tory nor Whig, Conservative nor Liberal. Neither was he aristocrat nor democrat. He had one of those minds which seem to stand outside events and look on with a superb impartiality. He once wrote from Seringapatam in 1805, when he was still young enough to be prejudiced: "I have no confidence in my own judgment in any case in which my own wishes are involved." The man who wrote that was clearly unsuited for any party, for to be a party man means the triumph of self-interest over truth. The nobles and gentlemen who thought the Duke was their friend and political ally perhaps rarely guessed how fragile was his belief in their cause. On January 17, 1834, he wrote to Lord Aberdeen: "There is a good deal of alarm about the Church . . . my friends the country gentlemen don't seem to me to think much about that or anything else excepting their homes and foxes." Wellington only tolerated such brainless creatures because he distrusted the self-termed "reformers" still more. He had the wise man's horror of all disturbers of the peace — whether emperors or Robespierres.

There is a theory (held by those who are always looking for "great" men instead of stable peoples, and finding their generalisations in their dreams instead of searching for them in the record of facts) that disturbed times produce the strong geniuses who are capable of handling them. Wellington knew too much of life to listen to such an empty fallacy. "Look," he said, "of late years to Spain, Portugal, Italy, Belgium — they have been ransacked through and through, and whom have they produced? Third-rate and fourth-rate men at most." When asked whether France had not been an exception, he replied, "I think not. Bonaparte is a man apart; you must not put him into the common scale. . . .

But except him, the French Revolution has not produced very superior men. Talleyrand, I don't reckon — he belonged to the ancient régime." When pressed again with the suggestion that France did produce some great figures at the time of the Revolution, Wellington calmly asked, after the manner of Socrates, "Where are they?" And before that simple question so much of the vague "great-man" theory of the history textbooks fades away. So many of the Revolutionary figures are only famous because they did mad or ridiculous deeds in a very noisy manner. But noise is not a scientific standard of value in history. Wellington possessed one of those well-balanced, calm minds that are not deceived by the shrieks of rhetoric or the rattle of revolutionary drums. So when pressed to acknowledge the great men of the French Revolution he asked, "Where are they?" It was entirely typical of this careful thinker. He had come across so many "great men" in his career — and had come to think that the common men were saner.

For the closer it is examined the clearer it appears that the basic fact about Wellington's mind was its power of getting at the facts which were the root of a problem. He ignored the sentimental trimmings that did not matter, except for concealing the truth. That was why he detested politics and politicians, as he once said to Madame de Staël; who almost passionately replied "*Parler politique, pour moi c'est vivre.*" To talk politics in Wellington's opinion was waste of time, because politicians rarely discussed facts. Indeed, he had a considerable suspicion of talkers of any kind. Gladstone, when a young man, first met the Duke at Peel's house. He recorded how everybody rose when the great man entered the room, and then he added with evident astonishment, that he "appears to speak little, and never for speaking's sake, but only to convey an idea commonly worth conveying." Whereas Gladstone made words his life's hobby! When Wellington attended the House of Lords, which he did reluctantly, it was in the hope of getting something done which would be of more use to the nation than a fine speech. He once told Stanhope that in one session he had drafted and moved amendments to twenty-five Railway Bills. His suggested amendments were to prevent monopoly and mismanagement which would damage the State. But the politicians were not interested in that sort of thing — or perhaps they were more interested in railway shares — and the amendments were rejected. It was for this reason that the Duke never became a popular statesman. He was always considering facts and ignoring the rhetoric which made the reputation of men like Canning. It may be argued that Wellington had such a simple brain that he was unable to see the complexities of a subject. It is said that the only people in the world who do not tell lies are the members of a most primitive tribe in Southern India; and the reason for their truthfulness is that they have not enough imagination to think of a falsehood. So, likewise, it may be that Wellington had such a childlike mind that he could not imagine deceits and complexities. If that be so, it was a strange result that it was this simplest of intellects that alone seemed able to stop Napoleon from crushing all Europe.

Charles Greville, the diarist, had been watching the Duke at very close and intimate quarters for many years. He had started, as already mentioned, with the cynical doubt whether Wellington could be quite as perfect as he appeared. On August 30, 1830, he had written in his diary:

He is exceedingly quick of apprehension, but deceived by his own quickness into thinking he knows more than he does. He has amazing confidence in himself, which is fostered by the deference of those around him. . . . He is upon ordinary occasions rightheaded and sensible, but he is beset by weaknesses and passions which must, and continually, blind his judgment. Above all he wants that suavity of manners, that watchfulness of observation, that power of taking great and enlarged views of events and character and of weighing opposite interests and probabilities. . . .

But he watched him for another twenty-two years, still more closely, and when Wellington died, in 1852, Greville wrote in his diary a remarkable funeral oration. The faults have gone almost to the vanishing point; the praise has become monumental:

In spite of some foibles and faults, he was, beyond all doubt, a very great man — the only great man of the present time — and comparable, in point of greatness, to the most eminent of those who have lived before him. His greatness was the result of a few striking qualities — a perfect simplicity of character without a particle of vanity or conceit, but with a thorough and strenuous self-reliance, a severe truthfulness, never misled by fancy or exaggeration. . . . Passing almost his whole life in command and authority, and regarded with universal deference and submission, his head was never turned by the exalted position he occupied, and there was no duty, however humble, he would not have been ready to undertake at the biddings of his lawful superiors. . . . He had more pride in obeying than in commanding. . . . He was utterly devoid of personal and selfish ambition, and there never was a man whose greatness was so *thrust* upon him.

Greville then went on to contrast this figure of stately civic virtue with the character of Napoleon, whom Wellington had destroyed. The comparison is the only way in which to understand the vast outlines of these two figures of history; it is the only way of realising how mean and petty a creature Napoleon really was — and how great was his conqueror. The most complete summary of Napoleon's career was put by his rival in one sentence: "He was not a gentleman." On another occasion Wellington said: "His policy was mere bullying, and military matters apart, he was a Jonathan Wild." Many historians have written volumes on Napoleon and have not got as much of the truth as Wellington could put into these two short sentences —

and they reveal as much of the mind of the Duke as of the Emperor.

The Duke of Wellington had one of the greatest careers in history; and yet it is doubtful whether his greatness can be discovered by the closest research into his military or political deeds. The secrets of his fame may lie in some more secluded place. Reading between the lines of his stately public progress, one sees ever repeated evidence that here was a very complex private soul, which is worthy of the attention of the masters of romantic literature. The man behind the great historical pageant, wherein he played such an amazing part, seems, somehow, greater and more alluring than his monarchs and fellow cabinet ministers may ever have understood.

It is difficult to find any pivot on which that elusive mind turned in its daily round. For a stable centre it must have had; seeing that it was so steadily consistent in all its wide range of life. Wellington was perhaps the most stable man in Europe; his life clearly had a controlling principle; and yet it is not easy to discover it. On the surface it seemed to be the sternest devotion to what he considered his duty. He once said: "I am the servant of the Crown and the People. I have been paid and rewarded and I consider myself retained, and that I cannot do otherwise than serve as I am required, when I can do so without dishonour." But a man needs some mental stimulus before he can accept a lifelong bondage, even to his King and State; and there are indications that even Wellington wearied of the tightness of his chains.

He had the world worshipping at his feet, or hating him — which is a negative kind of worship — and yet he once said: "There is little or nothing in this life worth living for, but we can all of us go straight forward and do our duty." Before he could have faced the towering mountains of work that he levelled so persistently as they persistently arose, there must surely have been some fund of great enthusiasm on which he could draw for refreshment and inspiration. And yet there seemed an icy coldness about the Duke. In theory he worshipped (as we have just read in his own words) his duty to his king and people; but we know how very theoretical was his respect for his kings, and how doubtful was his belief in the merits of the people.

But a mere automaton of duty he could not have been. It was no lifeless machine that met the thousand erratic uncertainties of the Peninsular War, and the daily twisting of later public civilian life. Wellington would not have done what he did in the world if he had not possessed a mind that was capable of registering the finest shades of the men and things around him; the mind, in short, of the artist — which is the highest summit of life. For no man has been truly great who has not had the artist's vision — which sees life as an ever alluring mystery. Certainly, no soldier has been long victorious without imagination. There was, of course, a harshness in the way Wellington often treated his subordinates, whether in the Army or the Government, which seems sometimes to contradict this sensitiveness of perception. Croker wrote to Lord Hertford, on January 24, 1828, that he had just seen the Duke; who had pointed to a pile of official despatch cases and official documents, with the words: "There is the business of the country, which I have not time to look at — all my time being employed in assuaging what gentlemen call their *feelings*." In this instance the impatience had probably a commendable excuse. But there was one darkest blot on the Duke's life; when he taunted a brilliant officer, who had risen from the ranks, on his lowly origin. For once this splendid engineer had failed; at the critical moment of a battle the bridge, which he had been ordered to build, had broken; and the guns could not be moved across it. His father had been a butler, and as the reprimanded son stood behind Wellington's chair at table, in anguish at his momentary (and unavoidable) blunder, the Duke, mad that his battle had been delayed, turned on him with the scornful question whether he was going back to his father's trade. And the officer went out and stood in the line of fire until he fell dead. It is almost the only recorded moment in Wellington's life when he forgot to behave like a gentleman; and it is noteworthy that his victim was a man who had stood for a moment between Wellington and the accomplishment of his duty in winning a battle.

Yet, one still continues to wonder whether this stern thing called duty was the only imperious motive of his life; to which all else must bow. However noble it may be in itself, it never dominates the great man unless there be a still deeper desire which is its driving force. Wellington must have possessed this greater creed, if we could but find the key; for duty without conviction is the vice of a slave. In Greville's diary, when he was recording the Duke's death, there is a sentence which might have given some clue: "His nature was hard, and he does not appear to have had any real affection for anybody, man or woman, during the latter years of his life, since the death of Mrs. Arbuthnot, to whom he probably was attached, and in whom he certainly confided." The only creature that Wellington cared for in all that adoring Europe must be carefully considered; for she could have told us more about him than we can gather even from the history of the Peninsular War. But since she did not speak, the tantalising screen of his public life still stands between us and Wellington's deepest thoughts. It was perhaps her complete discretion that attracted this most discreet of men. Her husband was his greatest man friend, who went to live with Wellington when Mrs. Arbuthnot died. It is all very strange. It is possible that if these two — and the woman — had spoken what they knew, they might have satisfied the inquisitive world that Wellington was more than a figure of austere service to his country, cold as a

Grecian statue. All the world knew that the Duke was an incorrigible flirt, and there were many affairs where that dainty term was probably not serious enough to do justice to the facts. But all these flirtations, and more, were only the trivial and smaller spoils of a very attractive soldier's adventurous life. Mrs. Arbuthnot was on another, and far greater, scale. She might have told us of those very rarest subtleties of the human soul which alone could give any convincing explanation of the amazing successes of her friend's career. His deeds denote a more profound knowledge of life than can be revealed in despatches. The man who planned and won the Peninsular War and the campaign of Waterloo was certainly a great soldier and a greater statesman; but his life — in the sum total — demands for its final word still something more than military and political judgments. That his greater qualities so rarely appeared on the cold surface may be proof of how deep they were planted in the foundations of his heart — where Mrs. Arbuthnot may have found them — when Sir Robert Peel and General Picton and the rest of them may never have suspected. The mind of this man was not open, so that all who passed might read.

There was something in Arthur, Duke of Wellington, much more valuable to his country than those military victories which saved it from conquest by Napoleon; more priceless than his political compromises which perhaps saved it from civil war. There is nothing constructive — but only destructiveness — in war; and Wellington as a Tory Prime Minister would have faded from the page of history in a few generations. But his soldiering and his statesmanship were only a fragmentary part of his career — indeed it is not a paradox, but the plain truth, that both wars and politics he held in deep contempt. The chief service he did for his countrymen was to endeavour to teach them that the qualities they should demand from their public servants are a rigid respect for the common good of the State (before any class or individual interests whatsoever); and that supreme quality of common sense (or the facing of hard facts) which means a hatred of rhetoric and insincerity and unnecessary trivialities. So far they have not listened very attentively to his advice; which may be because there have been few signs that any one has appeared who is qualified for such ideal devotion. The first Duke of Wellington has been, so far, unique in English history.

GEORGE CANNING
1770–1827

GEORGE CANNING

1770-1827

GEORGE CANNING was as unlike the Duke of Wellington as a very tall yellow-haired colonel in the Guards is unlike a very short, dark African pigmy. In other words, except that they were both men, they were at the two poles apart. Wellington hated the life — or death — of politics; whereas it was Canning's whole existence from his boyhood to his end. Like the Younger Pitt and Sir Robert Peel, he had set out from his school days to become Prime Minister of Britain. He had one distinction from the two other professional politicians just mentioned; for both Pitt and Peel were almost forced into the parliamentary life by their admiring fathers, who trained their sons in all the arts and crafts by which success is most quickly won in a political career. But Canning's father died on his son's first birthday; and, if he had lived, would have been more concerned in keeping his family out of the workhouse than in settling a son in the House of Commons. The training for the premiership was entirely the younger Canning's own idea. It was altogether typical of his alert, restless mind, and gives us the key to his career. Some statesmen become prime ministers because an admiring country calls them to the national aid. Canning became chief of the State because he coveted that post, and in spite of the fact that very few men would willingly have trusted him with anything to which they attached the slightest value. The letter-writers and diary-keepers of his day used quite a large amount of their space in saying how much they distrusted George Canning; they were continually explaining to each other and themselves how this perpetually intriguing person was concocting another plot — which was usually believed to be for his own selfish ends.

However, it is necessary to be more impartial than his contemporaries; and to withhold judgment on this mysterious man until one knows the main facts.

The Cannings were a very representative family of the English social system. They had spent several hundred years of recorded history in qualifying for a firm position in the upper middle class. They had been landowners since at least the beginning of the fourteenth century, in Bishop's Canynge, the Wiltshire village which gave them their name. On the continent of Europe, where they were always likely to be invaded by an enemy from a neighbouring land, there was plenty of fighting to keep all the families of the "gentle" folk in the very ungentle trade of arms. But in England, safe behind the sea and thus securer from war, it was the general custom of later mediæval life for the young sons of the squirearchy, not being able to find a living as soldiers, to go into the bigger towns and set themselves up as merchants. It was for this reason, among others, that there was never that hard line between the "gentlemen", whose chief business was to kill people, and the merchants who made a safer living by taking their customers' money instead of their lives. For some reason, never clearly explained, the former manner of life has always been considered of greater gentility than the latter.

The Canning family was a perfect museum specimen of this type of the British human fauna. A son of the landowning family of Bishop's Canynge had set up as a trader in Bristol during the reign of Edward II. He prospered, and founded one of the great merchant families of that town which in their time was the second commercial city in England after London. It was a common event for a Canning to be mayor of the town; the most famous of them being William Canynges, 1399–1474; but his grandfather, the elder William, a rich cloth merchant, had been already mayor six times, and had represented Bristol three times in Parliament. The younger William, adding foreign trade and shipowning to the family activities, became a national figure during the Wars of the Roses; and entertained King Edward IV when he visited Bristol after he had won the throne. It is worth remembering, as a proof of the erratic strain in the family blood, that this great merchant finished life as a priest of the Church of Rome and dean of the College of Westbury.

The brother of this figure of romance was the Thomas who added to the family adventures by becoming Lord Mayor of London in 1436; and it was this branch of the family that married back into the landed class by an alliance with the heiress of the Le Marshals of Foxcote in Warwickshire. It was a son of this house of the Cannings of Foxcote who did another very typical thing in the social history of his class of Englishmen; namely, he obtained from Elizabeth or James I, at the beginning of the seventeenth century, a grant of the manor of Garvagh in Londonderry, Ireland. It was quite the correct thing for a younger son, who could not get a sufficient share of an English estate, to go to Ireland and (on more or less flimsy excuses) seize the lands of the Irish. The Wellesleys and the Stewarts (of Castlereagh's family) had acquired their earlier fortunes in this way; indeed, almost the sole cause of the Irish problem in British history is because Englishmen have got possession of lands in Ireland which, according to the normal codes of ethics, belong to Irishmen. Whereupon, having, by the natural course of events, made Ireland an impossible home for its unscrupulous intruders, the next turn in the wheel of events was for the invaders of Ireland, after some generations, to re-invade their older home and return to England, where they again had to make their fortunes as new men.

This was just what happened in the Canning family. Stratford Canning of Garvagh had two troublesome sons, one of whom, George, was the father of the politician who is the subject of the present essay. As in the case of his brother, Stratford, there was a love affair of which the parents did not approve. So both sons came to England to make their fortunes. It was a work for which George Canning, who went to London in 1757, had no qualifications. He is usually described as being of very liberal views; but in his case this was perhaps only a kind way of saying that he had no views of any importance. If he could have once got himself established on the first safe steps of the political ladder, this peculiar form of liberality of thought would have been an advantage rather than a drawback; but in everyday life it is as well to have some kind of principles; and if George Canning the elder had any, they were not of a marketable kind. He would seem to have been a peculiarly inefficient minor member of the British ruling class, which has not established its place in history with any marked reputation for culture or skill. Its greatest distinction is, perhaps, its obvious superiority to the plutocracy which has now succeeded it.

The elder George Canning tried law at the Bar, political poems and pamphlets at Westminster, and, finally, a wine trade in the City. But they were all beyond his modest powers of creation and control, and only a paternal allowance of £150 a year kept him out of the streets. The Cannings were usually rash; and, as a last attempt on fortune, this desperate member of the family married. As a way of increasing the excitement of the adventure, he chose a lady without a penny in the world; though Mary Anne Costello came of his own class of Irish gentry, with Sir Guy Dickens of the English diplomatic service as her resident grandfather. The marriage was in 1768; it was not unsuccessful as a romance, but as a financial possibility it utterly failed. The unfortunate husband could not stand the strain, and discreetly died in 1771 at the age of thirty-five, leaving a son of exactly one year old to try the adventure of life which his father had found so difficult. The estate of Garvagh, which had been his by right of entail, had been passed over to a younger son as the price of the payment of George Canning's debts; the allowance of £150 died with him; and the younger George started his career with the affection of a mother, who had nothing in the world except her beauty, as his only heritage.

It has been worth while considering this prenatal history of the famous politician, for it gives a correct perspective to his life. We can see at a glance the family position; half landowners and half merchants; half English, half Irish; adventurers that were wanderers by instinct; and probably, like most people of that sort, not overscrupulous. The elder George Canning's failure may have been because he was more particular about his ethics than were the many other more successful members of his race.

There has been a great deal of discussion concerning the great Canning's earliest years. During those days his mother was endeavouring to make a living on the stage; and the more conventionally minded people were very prim about such things and said that it was altogether improper to allow the son of an actress to become Prime Minister of England. The stage was a form of social impropriety that was beyond apology or excuse; and since Canning was so much distrusted by almost everybody who had anything to do with him in public life, they made the most of this trivial social stain; being only too glad to find an excuse for a dislike which they could not very well define. It was a very marked quality of Canning's career that hardly anybody trusted him, yet it is difficult to say why. So the old rumours of a childhood that had been passed in the lodging houses of a third-rate travelling theatrical company gave some kind of plausible excuse for so doubtful a colleague at a Cabinet meeting. Of course it was only stupid prejudice; nevertheless Canning's unreliability was by no means idle rumour; and an actress mother was almost a sufficient explanation for the duller unscientific people who can rarely trace an effect to its right cause.

Mrs. Canning seems to have been a woman with a brave heart and attractive character; and her famous son paid her grateful homage all his life. She was not a great actress, one gathers; for although it is said that the Queen pressed her engagement on Garrick, who himself acted with her in 1773 at Drury Lane (when she took the name part of "Jane Shore"), yet she played it for only six nights. She then drifted into a struggling provincial career on the boards, during which she married two more husbands; one of whom, Reddish, was of a very unsavoury reputation and many loves; the other, Hunn, at first a well-to-do linen draper, who became an actor when his drapery business failed.

But all this while the other unruly son of the Garvagh family, Stratford, who also had come to London to seek the fortune which evaded him in Ireland, had been doing well for himself. He was now a partner in a flourishing firm of merchant bankers. He had allowed his brother George to go to the dogs, without help; but when it was put to him that his nephew seemed a bright boy, who was on the brink of worse than a Bohemian life, he decided to take him to live in his house like a son and to educate him and set him up in the world. The family at Garvagh relented, and allowed the younger George £200 a year; and he left the provincial lodging houses for the very select home of Stratford Canning. He was sent to a preparatory school to be made ready for Eton, which was to be followed by Christ Church, Oxford. It was a startling change; for, if those two great places of teaching did not succeed in giving more than a mere smattering of scholarship, they did guarantee to provide their pupils with a trademark or passport that would admit them into the "best" circles.

In the days before the Reform Act of 1832 transferred the election of Parliament from the aristocrats and freeholders to the plutocrats and shopkeepers, the Eton and Christ Church hall marks were more than halfway to a government post. In these homes of learning the pupils met the sons of the peers who owned rotten boroughs, and the nephews of Ministers of State who had offices in their gift. It is true they did not teach much except Latin verses, and only a mere glimmer of anything that would make a pupil fit to govern England. But it was obviously better to know the man who could give one a parliamentary seat or an official post, than the schoolmaster who could only train one to fill it with success. Canning knew the right people, instead of labouring to learn the right knowledge. Which was a wise decision, seeing that he was more anxious to get on than to do good.

His educational career taught him to be rhetorical and superficial: and, when it was finished, his chief gift was the power of writing rather flashy essays and very light verse. This capacity for tinkling poems was perhaps the foundation of his success; for they got him discussed and dreaded for his powers of ridicule. He had won a reputation for Latin and English verses even in his preparatory school; but his first public platform was the weekly *Microcosm*, which he and a small group of friends produced at Eton for almost two years. It was such a success that they were able to sell the copyright to a professional publisher for fifty pounds. It may seem paradoxical to attach importance to such an apparently insignificant occupation; but nevertheless, the accomplishments of the grown man were only the tricks of the youth, repeated on a much larger plan. To be trivial on a great scale is not necessarily more praiseworthy than the modest attempt. But it is more profitable.

It is not far from the truth to say that if Canning had not passed his youth in learning to write unimportant verses he would probably never have reached the premiership. They got him talked about in the world of fashion; and it was in the drawing-rooms of great ladies and the smoking rooms of select clubs that the ruling classes of those days discovered their instruments of government. In one of his Eton essays Canning made fun of the manufacture of such literary frivolity; he proposed the granting of a patent for the making of wit; and the applicant tells how: "I have already laid in jokes, jests, witticisms, morceaus, and bons mots of every kind. . . . I have epigrams that want nothing but the sting. Impromptus will be got ready at a week's notice." He may have seen the ridiculous side of his fun; nevertheless he made the idea the practice of his life.

The "Slavery of Greece" was a chief poem of his Eton days. It repeats all the sentimental thoughts by which an enthusiastic nature can cover its ignorance. There is all the usual common form phrasing: "Thou nurse of heroes, dear to deathless fame"; "the stern spirit of the Spartan soil"; "the maddening battles' loud career." Anything that he wrote about Greece might have been written by any schoolboy who had skipped through a first pictorial history of the classical period. The rhetoric of the future Foreign Secretary is already in germ in the lines:

> This was thy state! but oh! how changed thy fame
> And all thy glories faded into shame.
> What! that the bold, the freedom-breathing land
> Should crouch beneath a tyrant's stern command!
> That servitude should bind in galling chains
> When Asia's millions once opposed in vain.

Canning's early verse was a complete thing of its kind; for it contained every platitude which is suitable for poetic form. It remained one of the chief weapons of his political craft.

There was something uncannily precocious about Canning's boyhood. One would have imagined — even hoped — that the son of two such impulsive parents, so bravely callous of their future, would have left some trace on their child. But he was, in spite of the worked-up passions for Greece, as cold an iceberg of calculated self-seeking as ever sat on a school form. He took scarcely any part in games; he did not even take much exercise; he had no light pleasures. He already thought of life as a miser counts his coins: how much can be made of them. Life was something from which he was to extract honours — not a time in which he could do service. It might have been priggish if so young a mind had thought of the latter possibility; it is certainly repulsive that the boy Canning should so persistently have kept in view the former desire.

During his first year at Oxford, Canning set out his hopes of life in a letter to one of his intimates. Of course the House of Commons was the high heaven of his dream, "the only path to the only desirable thing in this world — the gratification of ambition." One is convinced that he visualised this "Power" as a somewhat gaudy figure with laurel crowns and the other stage properties of the Academy pictures of the period. Canning throughout his life continued to think in such conventional terms and symbols. In this letter he then explained that, as a seat in Parliament was not yet available, the Law was the second best. "It leads to honours, solid and lasting; to independence, without which no blessings of fortune, however profuse, no distinctions of station, however splendid, can afford a liberal mind true satisfaction; to power, for which no task can be too hard, no labours too trying." Canning examined the world ahead of him as a robber of banks examines the safes in their strong rooms. Life was something to burgle — not in which to invest one's riches.

But Canning did not worry the Law, beyond putting down

his name as a member of Lincoln's Inn and living at Number 2 Paper Building in the Temple. When he left Oxford and came to London, he had already written many light verses to his friends and to the journals; had made many speeches in school and college debating clubs; and had even written a prize Latin poem, and recited it in an effective manner that did credit to his childish days with a provincial theatrical company. He had spent his holidays from Eton at his uncle benefactor's house, where he met the great Whig leaders; and if, at the end of his Oxford career, his knowledge of scholarship was very limited, he had the greater worldly advantage of being intimate with politicians. Charles James Fox and Sheridan had taken him to Devonshire House; and for a rising statesman it was more important to know the Duchess of Devonshire than the theories of Aristotle. His knowledge, after the united labours of Eton and Christ Church, Oxford, would probably not to-day get him through any matriculation examination in Europe.

But he knew how, in fairly neat verse, to thank fashionable ladies for presents of shooting breeches, or to chaff Mrs. Crew on her theory of appetite. And all these ladies and their relations scattered the news that George Canning was a very smart and very coming young man. He had been trained as a Whig, as became the nephew of Stratford Canning; and, as his colleague friend, Lord Holland, records, had been a most revolutionary speaker at the college political debates.

Whatever may have been Canning's opinions, his practices took a sudden change of direction. Within a year of coming to London, after leaving Oxford, he had become a Tory Party man. It is not right to assume that this conversion was insincere — for the sake of personal convenience and political advancement — for the year 1792 had seen enough of the French Revolution to change a good deal of political theorising. Canning may well have asked himself whether "reform" was worth such social confusion, or, indeed, likely to be realised by such tactics. Nevertheless, the worst of the Revolution had not begun to show itself by the end of 1792; and there is no sign that Canning was clever enough to guess what was coming. So it is more likely that his change from the Whig to the Tory political company was not altogether due to the reaction from Parisian madness; but rather the result of natural conservatism — and personal convenience.

There was a sensational story told long afterwards by Sir Walter Scott, who said that the extreme Radical William Godwin (who had married Mary Wollstonecraft) had asked for an interview with Canning; at which he announced that the English admirers of the French Revolution intended to have one of their own in London; and that they wanted Canning to be their leader. Even at the enthusiastic age of twenty-two, fashionable young poets, however anxious to get into the front line of politics, hesitate when the front line suggested will probably be a barricade in the street. Scott's tale is that Canning was so alarmed by the idea that he rushed off to Pitt and put himself under his safer political banner. Moore gives another explanation by saying that Canning left the Whigs because he was disgusted at the way they had treated Burke and Sheridan — which amounts to the statement that Canning had no faith in a party which did not gratefully reward, by office or money, its literary geniuses!

What is certain is that in a letter of December 13, 1792, written to his intimate friend Lord Boringdon, who was then at Vienna, Canning had announced that if he got into Parliament he would support Pitt and not Fox. His words are evidence of his political mind through most of his career, and worth quoting. He told his friend:

With regard to France, so long as they were struggling for their own liberty, . . . I *wished* most piously and heartily for the total overthrow and destruction of every impediment that could be thrown in the way of their exertions. And *this*, from a thorough persuasion that the right of a nation to choose for itself its own constitution is a right which they claim from *God* and *nature* alone.

The whole thing is reminiscent of the literature in copybooks. Nevertheless it is a commendable opinion and tersely put.

Then Canning continues with a subtler sentence:

I will not deny that in addition to this *motive*, I was actuated also by one other of an inferior operation; I mean a sort of *speculative fondness* which I entertained for the idea of a *Representative Republic;* and a desire to ascertain by the *experience* of a *neighbour* without being at any risk or expense of the experiment *at home*, how far *such* a form of government would increase or diminish the freedom and happiness of a people.

That this young man of only twenty-two years could calmly and coldly sit watching such a blood-stained social experiment in the human laboratory, is a significant quality in Canning's character. It denotes a dispassionate aloofness from the troubles of mankind that is a little inhumane, or very scientific — which may be nearly the same thing. Here at least was a cool head that would not be turned from its course of political reform by the shrieks of the victims; their woes would be remedied — if possible — with the sober dignity proper to great statesmanship.

No fair critic will blame Canning for the decision to which he then declared that he had come in regard to French politics: "When I see the first use made by France of her emancipation . . . is not so much to proceed in the settlement of her own constitution . . . as a wild and wicked attempt to involve all other nations in similar calamities," then, he wrote, he could sympathise with these lawless people no longer. In short, he had discovered that — to put it in political phrases — he was not a Whig, but a Tory. He had watched the experiment of his theory and had discovered, very truly, that the practice was dangerous.

George Canning was not of the robust sort of men who are prepared to carry all their political theories into practice. Being a professional politician, he thought that it was sufficient to talk and write about them. Liberty, for example, had been a very happy subject for a poem on ancient Greece; over the Channel, in France, it was too near to play with indiscreetly. So Canning refused an offer of a parliamentary seat from the Whigs, and accepted one from the Tories instead. We have already heard Moore's statement that Canning had observed the ungenerous treatment of Burke and Sheridan by their Whig patrons; and had come to the conclusion that he himself would fare no better. The Whigs for some years had been watching Canning as a champion who might one day, when a little older, be put into the political arena as a gladiator who could stand up to Pitt. Pitt was flattering enough to think that Canning would be more pleasant as a friend than an enemy. Hence the Tory offer. The advantage of his college friends was soon made clear; for they were all around him, with offers of useful introductions and other first aids in political life.

One of the first people to meet Canning after his compact with Pitt was Lady Hester Stanhope, the Prime Minister's niece. Her opinion of him was very much that which people were to go on expressing until his death: "The first time he was introduced to Mr. Pitt [she wrote] a great deal of prosing had been made beforehand of his talents, and when he had gone Mr. Pitt asked me what I thought of him. I said I did not like him. . . . I did not like his conversation." That was entirely typical of Canning's whole life; nobody, or scarcely anybody, liked him. The "good deal of prosing" is an illuminating remark, for it raises the question what exactly had Canning done that had won him the earnest attentions of the Prime Minister. He was still only twenty-three when Pitt found him a parliamentary seat for Newton in the Isle of Wight. It was a place where the mem-

ber was chosen by the patron and not by the electors —
except in the farce of legal formality — so Pitt must have
had some strong reason for doing Canning this substantial
favour. Why? There is really no answer except the record
of a growing collection of trivial and rhetorical verse; the
memory of some showy and popular speeches in university
debating rooms; and many first-class introductions from the
right sort of people. It does not seem a very stable basis for
a serious Prime Minister's patronage. When the Duke of
Wellington was pressed on the attention of the Government
he had for introduction the fact that he had conducted a
brilliant campaign in India. Wellington's excuse for political office was that he had practically saved India for the
British Empire; Canning's almost only plea was that he
had written some light verses. If any students of Canning
consider this an exaggerated statement, let them produce
some better evidence of why Pitt should have called this
youth to his assistance.

Canning's first speech was considered a great success by
the "right" people. He wrote to Lord Boringdon to say
"how I trembled lest I should hesitate or misplace a word
in the two or three first sentences . . . how in about ten
minutes or less I got warmed in collision with Fox's arguments, and did not even care twopence for anybody or anything . . . how I was roused in about half an hour from this
pleasing state of self-sufficiency by accidentally casting my
eyes toward the Opposition Bench"; when even this self-confident young man was unnerved. However, the cheers
of his friends saved him, and "in less than a minute, straining every nerve in my body, I went on more boldly than ever,
and getting into a part of my subject that I liked, and having
the House with me," Canning sat down with his reputation
as a House of Commons man firmly established. For the
whole of his career he was chiefly famous for his powers of
rhetoric; and he eventually became Prime Minister because

GEORGE CANNING

From a portrait by Sir Thomas Lawrence, National Portrait Gallery

he was the most effective speaker in the House. There seems no adequate reason for this. We must accept the fact, with many other unexpected verdicts of history, on very unsubstantial grounds. Professor Alison Phillips, who has studied this period with specialist care, says: "We read with amazement of the effect produced by Canning's eloquence; of a crowded audience rapt by a phrase into a frenzy of almost uncontrollable emotion. . . . In the speeches as they have come down to us it is difficult to detect the secret of this magic art." Brougham, his contemporary rival in professional oratory, is illuminating on this point; Canning's speaking, he wrote, was "often powerful, always beautifully ornate . . . certainly not of the highest class. It wanted depth; it came from the mouth, not the heart . . . the orator never seemed to forget himself. . . . An actor stood before us — a first-rate one no doubt — but still an actor." Brougham certainly should be listened to as an authority — for he was the other great political "actor" of his age.

This first speech — in support of Pitt's grant of a subsidy to incite the King of Sardinia against the French revolutionists — was followed by other defences of his master's policy and impolicy. Canning, the late schoolboy Whig, said Pitt was right in suspending the Habeas Corpus Act and in refusing parliamentary reform. It was the ordinary method by which deserters gain the favour of their new master. Canning was the more effective, because he had probably never really believed in his first faith. Perhaps he was never, all his life, convinced of anything with certainty — except his own desire to be Prime Minister. In January, 1796, he got his reward, his first step on the ladder of political office; for Pitt then made him Under Secretary for Foreign Affairs, serving under Lord Grenville. Fox had his revenge on the Whig deserter by announcing that the whole matter was a disreputable "job", given to a man who was not capable of

doing the work. But the Tory Government soon comforted
their recruit by giving him still another post, the receiver-
generalship of the Alienation Office; worth £700 a year
salary, and nothing whatever to do except draw his money.

It is necessary not to get the picture of Canning out of
perspective. He had not yet anything like a free hand in
his political career. He was still only a subordinate carrying out the instructions of his superiors; and such he was to
remain until eleven years later, when he became Foreign
Secretary in 1807. Until then, his duty (or his practice)
was to do his work in the way most agreeable to the men
who might help him to rise higher. It is not unfair to state
the position in this way; for during much of his time as under
secretary he was not obeying the instructions of his official
chief, Grenville, but secretly carrying out the orders of Pitt.

Pitt wanted to make peace with the French revolutionaries
as soon as possible; Grenville was convinced that no acceptable peace was possible until the adventurers and madmen
who were in power in France were thoroughly beaten. In
this internal Cabinet war over foreign policy, Canning acted
as Pitt's tool. The work was of a disagreeable, underhand
kind, and needed an elaborated system of "most private
letters", and even a complicated code of secret signs and
names. Messengers from the English agents in France
crept silently through Canning's windows at night so that
Grenville might not suspect. It was all very melodramatic,
and eminently pleasing to the sensation-loving young under
secretary.

It cannot be said that the correspondence which has survived of this period gives the student a very favourable
impression of Canning's ability. Thus, in the Malmesbury
"Diaries and Correspondence" for November 7, 1796, there
is a letter from Canning to Malmesbury in Paris, which
struggles on for two pages of print, without telling the English diplomatist much that could have assisted him in his

negotiations. The end is worth quoting, for it is an example of how Canning loved to string together sentences of no importance even when in a hurry: "It is now," he wrote, "near ten o'clock; your boxes are made up, your messengers wait only for me; and every minute, therefore, that I should add to the length of this letter would be so much more delay in the time of your receiving it and all that accompanies it. You may therefore thank me for bidding you fare well, and you must now believe me, etc. G. C."

The Duke of Wellington, who never wrote or said an unnecessary word in the whole course of his official life, once said to Greville (August 10, 1827) that Canning was "one of the idlest of men" and Greville comments: "This I do not believe, for I have always heard that he saw everything and did everything himself." Wellington would have called the writing of unnecessary sentences idleness! He judged things by their value, not by their length.

There is another letter (July 27, 1897) reprinted in the Malmesbury "Correspondence" which is indexed in a somewhat remarkable manner: "Canning, witticism of, page 439." After wading through tiresomely verbose letters, searching for a pointed statement, one turns to the indicated page with hope. But one hunts in vain for the wit. It raises an interesting question — even an unanswerable problem — how did Canning ever get the reputation of a wit? It is suggested that the only two possible clues given in this letter are not very conclusive: "There is a man in the Strand who has written *stump legs* over his door, which I will take Dr. Leg to see when he comes to town." The other slightly brighter possibility runs: "The Corresponding Societies are to assemble at different places all over England on Monday next, for the purpose of stirring up sedition, and the Yeomanry Corps throughout the kingdom are appointed to meet them." There must be an error on the part of the compiler of the index.

The concise clear replies of Ellis — his correspondent — to Canning's verbosity only make this persistent vice the more apparent. Canning was always thinking of the way in which he expressed himself, rather than of what he had to say. The more critical student will note that it was not often he had anything of the greatest importance to explain. The verbal façade was the greater part of the structure.

But Canning soon got back to the work for which he was more suited than diplomatic negotiations; for the French refused any reasonable terms, having made up their minds that they could do better by fighting. At this collapse of the hope of peace Canning seems to have been genuinely disappointed, and expressed himself in one of his sincerest letters (to Legh, September 29, 1797):

We were within a hair's breadth of it [peace with France]. Nothing but that cursed Revolution in Paris and the sanguinary insolent and implacable and ignorant arrogance of the Triumvirate could have prevented it. . . . It was not any question of *terms*, of giving up this or that — it was a settled determination to get rid of the chance of Peace on the part of the three scoundrelly Directors that put an end to negotiations. Nothing else could have done so.

Canning had more than a touch of the adventurer in his own character; yet he was very different from the type of the "scoundrelly Directors" and their many friends who were the controllers of the Revolutionary Government in France at that time. Canning was not a man who would have driven his fellow countrymen into the agony of war, just to suit his own personal convenience. It is true that he spent far too much time intriguing for office, and perhaps used a very doubtful code of honour. But in this he was merely petty and small-minded; he had not a soul tuned to the deeper and finer affairs of life. But he never sank below a tolerable standard. He had always a fair excuse for declaring that his chief object in public life was to govern his country for its own good. He certainly was convinced that for this national salvation it was all important that he, Canning, should be at the head of the State; yet this was rather a childish conceit than an adult vice.

It was likewise a petty misjudgment, rather than an unpardonable crime, that he should have believed that trivial verses, however witty, were a fit medium for his ambitious political creed and practice. But, after all, since he had been asked to come into politics chiefly on the reputation of his smart poetry, it is not surprising that he tried to do what was expected of him. So, in November, 1797, he and some friends began the publication of the *Anti-Jacobin;* a sixpenny journal appearing every Monday during that parliamentary session. Its object was to laugh the Whigs and Radicals off the political field. It was not as brilliant as the historians (somewhat bored with most of the stiff and pompous persons of the period) have generally imagined. Mr. G. K. Chesterton and Mr. Hilaire Belloc could do the thing a thousand times better, if they tried it again to-day. However, his contemporaries (being bored like the historians) thought the *Anti-Jacobin* good fun — unless they were attacked in it; when they thought it a scandal, and replied as violently as they could. As for the sober people, there is a note in Wilberforce's diary (May 18, 1799) : "Pitt, Canning and Pepper Arden came in late to dinner. I attacked Canning on indecency of *Anti-Jacobin* . . . he and Pitt read classics"; and on the following day he added, "My heart has been moved by the society of my old friends at Pitt's. Alas, alas! how sad to see them thoughtless of their immortal souls."

Canning later on, in 1803–1804, brought out the *Oracle*, as another platform from which he could declaim his verses. Indeed, until 1807, when he became Foreign Minister, parliamentary skits were almost his chief political product; at least it may be said that if it had not been for the verses, the small amount of more serious administration and speechmaking which he did would long ago have been forgotten. Some of the poems were very neat indeed; and, surrounded by their local colour — in the midst of political opponents who were red with indignation, and political friends, rosy with the glow of laughter — these verses at their best must have been very effective. Some of them are of deeper significance. There is the parody of the Church service, by which Canning laughed scornfully at the sentimentalists and loose thinkers who still thought that the French Revolutionary Government was the friend and instrument of liberty. In the following lines it is necessary to remember that Lepaux was one of the French Directory that had refused to make peace with Europe.

> "Couriers" and "Stars", seditious evening host,
> Thou "Morning Chronicle" and "Morning Post"!
> Whether ye make the rights of man your theme,
> Your country libel, and your God blaspheme;
> Or dirt on private worth and virtue throw,
> Still, blasphemous or blackguard, praise Lepaux.
> And ye five other wandering bards that move
> In sweet accord of harmony and love;
> Coleridge and Southey, Lloyd and Lamb and Co
> Tune all your mystic harps to praise Lepaux.
>
> * * * * * * *
>
> Praise him each Jacobin, or fool or knave,
> And your cropped heads in sign of worship wave.
> All creeping creatures, venomous and low,
> Paine, Williams, Godwin, Holcroft — praise Lepaux!

Now that is not only good verse and good parody; it is also a valuable indication of Canning's political basis. He hated the gang of third-rate adventurers who were turning the French Revolution to their own advantage; and he was in like measure contemptuous of the stupid, so called democratic, party in England, who thought the beginning of freedom had arrived in France. Strangely enough, this healthy dislike of self-made governors has been put down to a bias which Canning had against democracy. He certainly had; but it is no proof of this bias that he should have hated the rulers in France who were filling their own pockets by a system of government which they announced was Liberty, Equality and Fraternity. It is little wonder that, when Napoleon made himself supreme, Canning should have written: "It is the galling conviction carried home to the minds of all the brawlers for freedom in this and every country, that there never was, nor will be, nor can be, a leader of a mob faction who does not mean to be the lord, and not the servant, of the people." His suspicion of the "reformer" can be seen in his biting parody of a speech by Erskine to a Whig Club:

He stood here as a man — he stood in the eye, indeed in the hand of God — to whom, in the presence of the company and waiters, he solemnly appealed. He was of noble, perhaps of Royal blood — he had a house at Hampstead — and he was convinced of the necessity of a thorough and radical reform.

Canning had displayed an unexpected capacity for inconspicuous office work when he had been appointed to the Foreign Office in 1796. For two years he scarcely spoke in the House of Commons. We have seen that he was busy intriguing for Pitt, against his official chief Grenville. But he was not happy; probably because he liked appearing on the stage — not receiving visitors on the back stairs. In 1799 he left the Foreign Office and became a commissioner for India. Still restless, he left this post and was made one of the joint paymasters of the forces in 1800. In this year he had one of those strokes of luck for which all adventurers hope. He married Miss Joan Scott, who had a fortune of

£100,000. Her sister became Duchess of Portland; and since her father had made a good deal of his money by gambling, she could scarcely fling her husband's adventurous habits in his face.

Thus, when the long Pitt administration broke up in 1801 and was succeeded by the Addington Cabinet, Canning could now well afford to surrender his office and go out with his dear friend Pitt. If his purse had not been filled he would probably have swallowed his principles and his pride and stayed on in office under the new premier. If it had happened so, history would have lost the most lively time of his career. For he devoted himself to new verse making; and London danced with amusement, and Addington writhed with pain, as Canning lashed him and his followers with every sparkling, bitter line that a reckless and remorseless — even brutal and coarse — mind could invent. It was not the stuff that great statesmen make; but it was the sort of politics that tickled the ears of the camp followers of the parliamentary leaders. It kept Canning in the public eye, and made the people who hang around political clubs think he was a very clever man; which they would never have known if he had gone on sitting quietly working in his office. It was so much easier (and so much more effective) to tell in tripping lines how Addington was a dull creature who was always making mistakes. It needs a first-class mind to create what is good; second-rate minds — like Canning's — are very neat in criticism of other people's failures.

Addington was certainly tempting game. He had managed to get into politics mainly because his father was the medical adviser of the elder Pitt, Earl of Chatham; and the younger Pitt brought the younger Addington into the House of Commons, and eventually made him the Speaker. His father's advice to Chatham had been to drink more wine — as a cure for gout; and the son's assistance in politics was of equal value. Reverting to the family profession, he advised

George Canning

the king to rest his worn-out mad head on a hop pillow. It was probably the most sensible advice he ever gave him. Anyhow, Canning called him the Doctor, and made him into a figure of fun.

> My name's the Doctor; on the Berkshire Hills
> My father prized his patients — a wise man
> * * * * * * *
> But I had heard of politics and longed
> To sit within the Custom House and get
> A place . . .
> I flattered Pitt, I cringed, and sneaked and fawn'd,
> And thus became the Speaker.

And so on. It is not profound; but it caught the public fancy, like a popular song at the music halls. Some of it was a shade better than the halls' standard. Addington had a brother Hiley, and a brother-in-law, Bragge, who both received important offices of State, one in the War Office and the other at the Admiralty. They gave Canning the points for one of his most famous verses.

> How blest, how firm the statesman stands
> (Him no low intrigue can move),
> Circled by faithful kindred bands,
> And propped by fond fraternal love.
> When his speeches hobble vilely,
> What "Hear him's" burst from Brother Hiley;
> When his flattering periods lag,
> Hark to the cheers of Brother Bragge.
> * * * * * * *
> Each a gentleman at large
> Lodged and fed at public charge,
> Paying (with a grace to charm ye)
> This the Fleet and this the Army
> Brother Bragge and Brother Hiley.

The pompous, dull-witted Addington was a maddening obstacle to the alert, bouncing mind which took the place of a sober intellect in Canning. To him Addington's head was as senseless as a barber's block. When somebody suggested that the British coasts should be guarded from hostile fleets by sunken rocks, Canning leaped into print with the idea that the Prime Minister's head would be just the material for the work; and pictured the members of Parliament going down in a diving bell, to visit "the remains of the late Dr. A——, now for his country's sake converted into a mud bank."

Pitt, all this time after his family manner, kept pompously in the background, while his friend was making these raids into the enemy trenches. Pitt professed not to approve these harassing tactics; but they were all part of his game of getting back into power, as soon as he had succeeded in making poor Addington responsible for at least some of the national blunders and confusion, — for which Pitt was more to blame than anybody else. Canning was hanging round the outskirts of the battle, doing what he could to assist his friend; and working up popular sentiment in his favour. For example, in May, 1802, there was, at the Merchant Taylors' Hall, as Wilberforce wrote in his diary: "a grand celebration of Pitt's birthday . . . 823 tickets and people, — near 200 more asked for . . . Pitt not there." But Canning was there to do the advertisement-agent's work with a song on "The Pilot that Weathered the Storm." It was a really appalling piece of doggerel. Here are two verses out of the eight:

> And shall not *his* memory to Britain be dear
> Whose example with envy all nations behold?
> A statesman embarrassed by int'rest or fear
> By power uncorrupted, untainted by gold
> And O! if again the rude whirlwind should rise,
> The dawning of peace should fresh darkness deform,
> The regrets of the good and the fears of the wise
> Shall turn to the pilot that weathered the storm.

It is difficult to understand how the reputation of the author survived its publication. But the writing of advertisements has always been one of the most profitable forms of literature.

Canning did his work with equal effectiveness by speeches in the House. In the great debate of December, 1802, his advertisement of Pitt was made into an oration of polished rhetoric that often sparkled — like the tinsel it too often was. It can be read as a very typical example of Canning's skill. It must have sounded very admirable at the first hearing; the words fitted so well together that the listeners may have been satisfied with the sound alone: the meaning is so often a drag on an orator; though Canning rarely allowed it to stand in his way. "Look at France, and see what we have to cope with and consider what has made her what she is? A man. . . . I am no panegyrist of Bonaparte; but I cannot shut my eyes to the superiority of his talents, to the amazing ascendency of his genius . . . it is his genius, his character, that keeps the world in awe." It was too much like the quack medicine advertisements, describing the pains and dangers of the sick readers. Then followed the recommended remedy — Mr. Pitt. "For the purpose of coping with Bonaparte, one great commanding spirit is worth them all. This is my undisguised opinion. . . . He cannot withdraw himself from the following of a nation; he must endure the attachment of a people whom he has saved."

It was all quite untrue; Pitt had not saved his nation; for Napoleon was getting stronger every day, and largely because the British politicians wasted their time in listening to such empty verbiage as this. But Canning was not insincere. He really believed that these fine speeches helped things on. He went home to his house in Conduit Street, and at once wrote an urgent letter to Lord Malmesbury: "I thought it indispensable to write down, while my recollection was fresh, the precise words (or very nearly so) of that part of my speech which related to Pitt." He then said that he was taking every step to send these priceless sentences on to Pitt himself.

A short time after there is an interesting passage in Malmesbury's diary:

> On the 12th I saw Canning. He had then no answer from Pitt, and this unhinged and mortified him. Canning has been *forced* like a thriving plant in a well managed hot-house; he has prospered too luxuriantly — has felt no check or frost. Too early in life he has had many, and too easy, advantages. This added to very acute parts, makes him impatient of control ... angry with those who conceive less quickly and eagerly than himself ... and indulging an innate principle of vanity, he underrates others, and *appears* arrogant and contemptuous, although really not so. This checks the right and gradual growth of his abilities, lessens their effect and vitiates the many excellent, honourable and amiable qualities he possesses.

Such was Canning's character drawn by a much older and wiser man who admired his brilliant junior with a fatherly friendship.

When at last the dummy Addington was driven out of office on April, 1804, Pitt returned to the premiership. Canning was, very rightly, annoyed that Pitt did not insist on Fox and his Whig friends being accepted as Ministers by the king. As he said to Malmesbury (diary, May 30, 1804), Pitt might have done more than he did to force King George's hand; and he added that in the circumstances he would rather not join the new Government at all. However, although he thus grumbled, Canning, very characteristically — after refusing to take a Cabinet post, which was not offered him! — asked for the good fat job of Treasurer of the Navy at a salary of £4,000 a year, with another £1500 for his deputy.

George Canning

Canning was one of those restless creatures who cannot sit quiet for more than a few minutes. It was a matter of nerves — and Canning was all nerves all his life. When Pitt asked Addington to join the Government, Canning was naturally embarrassed, for he remembered how he had made fun of him in verse. It was unkind that Pitt had no regard for his friend's feelings, let alone his judgment. So Canning wrote a long, rather petty letter of complaint to Lady Hester Stanhope, Pitt's niece:

A. is (if I understand your letter aright) a Minister, and I am — nothing. . . . I cannot face the House of Commons or walk the street in this state of things, as I am. . . . And now, dear Lady H. do not throw down this letter in a passion . . . there is not one expression of anger, resentment, irritation, or extravagance, nor, I am sure, a witty one (which is the next crime in degree), throughout the whole.

What he pretended to want in this letter was that Lady Hester should persuade Pitt to accept his resignation "as a natural, if not a necessary consequence" of Addington's joining the Cabinet. But he did not resign; and one is tempted to think it was only a restless attempt to get higher office himself.

Then Canning (in April, 1805) unsuccessfully defended Pitt's dearest friend, Melville, from a serious charge of financial corruption at the Admiralty, though he scored prettily over Whitbread, of a brewing father, who was the mover of the accusation. In Canning's lines the brewer dies

> And the angels all cried, Here's old Whitbread a-coming.
> So that day I still hail with a smile and a sigh,
> For his Beer with an *e* and his Bier with an *i*.

* * * * * * *

> My name shall shine bright as my ancestor's shines,
> Mine recorded in journals, his blazon'd on signs.

In December of the same year Canning could find no more serious work to do for his country than to write more poetry on the victory of Trafalgar. It is most inferior stuff of the heroic sort; but the amazing fact about it is that Canning took it all with profound seriousness, and wrote a long letter to Pitt, who was then at Bath, nearing his end. The excited poet — while the fate of his country was being decided on land and at sea — begs the Prime Minister to examine each line with minute care; to judge whether "brave in vain" is better than "vainly brave." He suggests three possible alternatives for the seventh line. And so on. Canning had no sense of the true proportion of things. He thought his seventh line must be considered by his chief like a diplomatic despatch. The whole incident is one of the typical scenes of his life. We thereby understand why so few men could take Canning seriously.

Within a month Pitt was dead. One can even imagine that a shadow of remorse crossed Canning's mind lest it was anxiety over that seventh line that caused this unexpected end — and not the disaster at Austerlitz, as less-informed men believed. Canning then went out of office, because he would not join the Grenville-Fox Ministry; putting his refusal on the ground that the king had not been consulted in the matter; which seems most unlikely to have been his true reason. He himself gave a better one, namely, that "to have the labour of the House of Commons devolve upon me in Fox's absence and (what would be worse) under Fox's occasional superintendence, would, I really think, have formed altogether the most unendurable, the most discreditable, and the most hopeless situation into which any man ever was misguided by an inconsiderate precipitancy of ambition." When Fox died a few months later, Grenville offered Canning a Cabinet post; but he demanded so many other places for his friends, that Grenville was frightened by the proposed invasion. Canning had put his terms too high. But in 1807 the Duke of Portland, Canning's wife's brother-in-law, became Prime Minister, and offered him the post of Secretary of State for Foreign Affairs.

Writing on March 14, 1807, Malmesbury said:

> Canning was with me; entered on a long account of his own conduct, principles, and intentions, his professions of political faith, etc. . . . spoke as if the choice of Cabinet places were to be at his refusal. . . . He is unquestionably clever and very essential to Government; but he is *hardly yet a statesman*, and his dangerous habit of quizzing (which he cannot restrain) would be most unpopular. . . . Canning may be safely trusted, for, I repeat, he is honourable and honest, and if Pitt had not forced him in his hot house . . . his mind would have taken a better bend; but spoiled as he has been — feared and wanted as he finds himself — no place is now high enough for him; his ambition rises beyond this visible diurnal space.

In short, Canning had that most certain sign of a small mind — a swelled head — and the worst of his case was that he had so far done nothing to justify his delusions of peculiar merit.

Canning was now (March 25, 1807) for the first time, at the age of thirty-seven, a minister of the first rank; able to make policy, instead of merely carrying out the instructions of his chiefs. It was an age when young men got high office; but so far, no Prime Minister had seen much use for Canning except in a minor post which did not too much interfere with his chief occupation of poetic journalism. Now, however, Canning must be judged by his success or failure in more important affairs than the quality of his rhymes or his rhetoric. His Prime Minister was an amiable nonentity and seriously ill. So at last Canning's acts were really Canning's wishes. The great period of the struggle against Napoleon was beginning; and his bitterest critics must give this young Foreign Minister credit for taking a worthy part in the turning of the tide of the French flood over Europe.

Canning discovered, by a very smart piece of intelligence work, that Napoleon had decided, by the Treaty of Tilsit (July 7, 1807), suddenly to seize Denmark and with it its fleet. The superb self-confidence of Canning was a merit at last. He ordered off the British army and navy to seize the Danish fleet before Napoleon could get there. It was one of the "strong man" touches in modern history; and although it aroused a violent attack by his political opponents, he proved to the satisfaction of most reasonable men that what he had done was honourable enough in the midst of a Europe where every nation was fighting desperately for its life. Canning offered Denmark a treaty of alliance on condition that the Danish fleet was put into safer British hands until Napoleon was beaten. But time was urgent; Canning could not wait to negotiate; and had to threaten in arms. If Arthur Wellesley's advice had been taken it is probable that the bombardment of Copenhagen would have been avoided; but the politicians were anxious for a more showy method. Anyhow, the British saved the Danish fleet from the French by their new Foreign Minister's rapid decision.

Canning showed still more ability in his handling of the affairs of Spain. If he was not the first to see that the Peninsula was the place where Napoleon could be beaten, he at least was one of the first of the politicians to act with energy there; and the future Wellington began the great Peninsular War under Canning's diplomatic instructions. But it was Wellington who won the war, not Canning. Indeed, if the politician had not been really controlled by the great soldier, there is good reason to think that Canning would, with all his energy — or because of it — have driven the British armies to disaster. It was he who insisted on Sir John Moore marching on Madrid, when he had not nearly enough men for such an adventure. The Battle of Corunna and the death of Moore were the result of Canning's unintelligent impulsiveness. His successes were rarely owing to his brains, but rather to his torrent-like rhetorical driving power.

It is so typical of Canning that although he had got hold of a thoroughly sound idea in the Peninsular War, and might have been the honourable partner of Wellington in that great event, yet he wrecked this career almost immediately he had started. He was already restlessly seeking greater power than he possessed as Foreign Minister. At least, there is no other natural explanation of his persistent intriguing against his fellow ministers. He had made up his mind that Castlereagh was not an efficient War Minister; and allowed no chance of criticising him to pass.

An unsatisfactory and hurried Convention of Cintra had been signed by the British generals after the Battle of Vimiera; it allowed the French far too easy terms and made the outraged and invaded Portuguese surrender their just right of retaking the plunder which the French had seized. Canning wanted to repudiate the treaty. But Castlereagh, being a rigid gentleman, said the treaty was signed and, at all costs, must be obeyed in every detail. He had Queen Victoria's instincts in the matters of honour; whereas Canning could not see such fine points of public morality. It was perhaps the main reason why he did not really succeed in life. For the keeping of one's word is not merely a point of honour; it is also a practical necessity in everyday affairs; since, in the end, no one will make terms with the man whose word is not trustworthy.

Canning at last told the Prime Minister that Castlereagh must be removed from the War Office; but everybody knew that he was a hard worker and sure if slow. So nobody had the courage to ask him to resign. Then, fortunately for Canning, he weakened his position very badly by planning the expedition to Walcheren, which came to such a disastrous end in the autumn of 1809. Although it was a weakening of the Peninsular army, of which he was in command,

Wellington said that Castlereagh's plan of an attack on the French by way of the Low Countries was sound strategy. However, the second Earl of Chatham, to whom Castlereagh entrusted the command, was such a foolish creature that he would have ruined any campaign.

The Canning and Castlereagh quarrel thereupon burst into flame; they fought a duel on September 21, 1809, and Canning was wounded. They had both already resigned their offices; and the Portland Ministry broke in pieces. The whole episode is a very terrible picture of the unstable condition of public life at that time. As Wilberforce wrote in his diary: "Lord Castlereagh and Canning fought a duel early on Thursday morning. What a humiliating thing! In what a spirit must our national counsellors have been deliberating." It was worse than he knew, for the probable root of the whole trouble was Canning's determination to be Prime Minister. Arbuthnot explained what had happened in a letter to Croker written on September 23, two days after the duel: "He (Canning) felt that Perceval having led the House, was the obvious person to become Minister; but he distinctly stated that in the event of such an arrangement he himself should retire. In short, he would not consent to remain in office unless he were Prime Minister."

It was the gravest blunder of his life; for he was not so indispensable as he imagined, and he was brushed aside out of any great office for thirteen years, until 1822, when he again became Foreign Secretary. During these intervening years his rival, the slower, more honourable, more balanced Castlereagh, made himself almost the most powerful and respected leader of Europe. The punishment was very bitter; during that period Canning, but for his insolent pride, would have been the arbitrator of some of the greatest decisions in European political history.

When Perceval was assassinated in 1812, and Lord Liverpool formed a new ministry, Castlereagh, who was still an unselfish gentleman, offered to resign the Foreign Office to Canning; but the latter, being still a conceited fellow, said he must have the leadership of the House of Commons also. His insolent terms were refused. Thus it happily happened that Castlereagh guided England through the whirlpools of the Waterloo campaign, the Congress of Vienna, and the settlement of Europe after the Napoleonic anarchy. It was to the honour of Britain that she was represented by a sober, slow-tongued gentleman who could think clearly, instead of by a flashing man, who talked such brilliant rhetoric that he had scarcely time to think what he was saying.

Canning's long rambling letter to Wilberforce, explaining his refusal to take office, was like his vague, vain mind. He pictured himself sitting in the House as an inferior, by the side of Castlereagh, his chief: "If the troops had wished to salute me Imperator in the field of debate, I must have said, 'Nay, my good friends, *there* is your commander. I have sworn to maintain him such, like him as you may.'" Such colossal conceit is almost pathological. Wilberforce's comment on it all was this: "How will all this busy and tumultuous world appear to have been all one great bedlam when we look back on it from a future state."

The plain, decent man was tired of Canning, and for the next few years he was isolated in politics. One realises what a remarkable position it was when one finds entries like this in Wilberforce's diary (February 11, 1813): "Long debate on Vice-Chancellor project. Canning inimitable in wit and sarcasm." These were qualities for which most political parties will pay their weight in gold and office and honours. But they drew the line at Canning! It was too much like an alliance with a wriggling eel that might slip between their fingers any moment.

When he appeared in debates he was usually perfectly reasonable and often superbly wise. In this session of 1813 he made two great orations: one thanking Wellington for driving the French out of Spain; the other a cry of praise that the tyrant Napoleon had been crushed. One of these speeches contained his famous passage: "The mighty deluge by which the continent had been overwhelmed began to subside. The limits of nations were again visible, and the spires and turrets of ancient establishments began to reappear above the subsidiary wave." The other was graced by a magnificent phrase which might have been an epitaph for Napoleon; who had tried "to extinguish patriotism, and to confound allegiance — to darken as well as to enslave — to roll back the tide of civilisation — to barbarise as well as to desolate mankind." This was only the genius of an orator — yet it was genius of its kind. His glowing language in these two speeches was true in fact, as well as gorgeous in the colour of its words.

Yet the clever, really right-minded Canning could not, try as he might, keep on the straight road of unquestionable integrity. In 1814 he had arranged to stay in Lisbon for private reasons; and, with his usual smart intrigue, persuaded the Government to make him a very highly paid ambassador with a special salary of over £14,000 a year. Bulwer (in "Historical Characters", II. 284, 285) said this was "considered a job, for an able minister, on a moderate salary, was recalled, in order to give the eminent orator, whose support the Government wished to obtain, the appointment of ambassador on a much larger salary." The "Croker Papers" contain (I. 86–87) a letter from Canning begging the Admiralty to put a cruiser at the disposal of himself and family for the voyage home; and if possible a cruise to Gibraltar was to be thrown in.

Canning returned to England in 1816 a somewhat humbled man. He must have felt what an outcast he had been, in Lisbon, during these two momentous years; while his rival — who could only stammer his speeches — had become, after Wellington, the most powerful minister in Europe.

George Canning

He had first to defend himself in Parliament for the Lisbon scandal of £14,000 a year. Then in June, 1816, he accepted the post of President of the Board of Control of India, which gave him a seat in the Cabinet. He was still the member for the very commercial town of Liverpool; and since the government of India was still in the hands of a trading company, Canning was now recognised as peculiarly the representative of the well-to-do merchant class. As such, he did his best to assist his Government in crushing any spirit of democratic liberty which was threatening the privileges of the old corn-growing aristocrats and the new manufacturing and shipowning plutocrats, in which last the member for Liverpool was peculiarly interested. But in the department of domestic affairs Canning did not take a prominent part; and that part was probably based on no more profound a principle than a desire to avoid all radical changes, and keep the favour of the trading classes. Canning was still — as he had always been — more an orator than a thinker; and his fluent tongue and rich adjectives still continued to be his chief asset in the House of Commons; and Greville, writing in his diary for March 5, 1819, noted: "Last night Canning moved the thanks to Lord Hastings, and they say it was the finest speech he ever made, in the best taste, the clearest narrative, and the most beautiful language."

The presidency of the Board of Control was not success, but rank failure for Canning; for his rival was handling the greatest affairs of Europe. So he grew restless again. This time his excuse was that, as a personal friend of the Queen, he could not assist King George IV in divorcing her. The King was broad-minded and told Canning that he would not take this opposition as any reason for dismissing or quarrelling with him; and, after all, the President of the Board of Control had — thank heaven — no official duties in the controlling of Queen Caroline. So she was probably only an excuse, and merely some kind of first step in an intrigue for higher office. Anyhow, he left England in order to be out of the disagreeable divorce affairs; and yet, when it was all over and he returned home again, he resigned his post in the Government, Castlereagh sending his evidently sincere regrets and many thanks "for the kindness with which you have assisted me, in the department for the conduct of which I am more immediately responsible."

The great Canning, the most brilliant orator of Parliament, was once more homeless, in the political sense. In the more domestic world of unmarried clerks, one can imagine that he would have been the kind of man who is continually giving notice to his landladies. There was a persistent smallness about him. The Prime Minister certainly soon tried to entice him back again; but the King had sworn he would never have anything more to do with such a fellow. Then the governor-generalship of India was proposed as a suitable post for a man who had been controlling that country for several years — and it would be so much pleasanter for his colleagues to have him in Calcutta instead of Westminster. It was a terrible problem for Canning to decide. It meant the end of all his gorgeous political dreams and his boundless conceits. Croker explained the situation in a letter of December 20, 1821:

Canning has been shuffling about India, yes, no — no, yes. The King *will not* have him at home. Canning hopes this disgust is, like all the King's dislikes, placable and temporary, and he therefore accepted India when it was *not* vacant, as a kind of rope *to hold on to* the Administration by, but *unluckily* old Moira has had a double rupture, and is perhaps already on his way home: this would clench Canning for an Indian exile, and he is therefore punctilious about accepting poor Moira's place, before he knows that it is vacant — so folks talk; and there is, I believe, some truth in their talk. I am sorry to be obliged to confess that all Canning's conduct gives a handle to this sort of imputation. . . . If he does not take care the Canning bonfire will soon burn itself out.

It was a very forgivable indecision; but at last poor Canning decided that India was his only future hope, so he accepted the governor-generalship. Then, almost as in the pages of a tenth-rate novel and the best melodramas, his problem was solved for him. Castlereagh, his rival, committed suicide. Liverpool determined that Canning must succeed him at the Foreign Office; and Wellington promised to make the King accept him. This was the occasion when it is said that George told the Duke that he was pledged never to take Canning as his Minister of State: "You hear, Arthur, on my honour as a gentleman"; to which the Duke made the startling reply that he was not a gentleman, but "the Sovereign of England, with duties to his people, and that those duties rendered it imperative to call on the services of Mr. Canning." And the King "drew a long breath and said, 'Well, if I must, I must.'"

In this manner was the illustrious Canning who had so long thought himself indispensable to his king and country — and almost to the world — reluctantly readmitted to office. As Greville wrote: "Lord Liverpool's proposal to him was simple and unclogged with conditions — the Foreign Office and the lead in the House of Commons." The new Minister's comment on it all has the sad ring of bitterest pathos. His ambitious heart was never quite contented with anything; and the exciting years of great events in diplomacy seemed gone beyond recall: "Ten years have made a very different sort of world to bustle in than that which I should have found in 1812. For fame it is a squeezed orange. . . ." "Bustle in" was a significant term from the pen of such a man: one cannot imagine the serious Castlereagh using such a trivial verb; but it exactly fitted the life of Canning. His diplomacy was a "bustle" rather than an affair of statesmanship.

The contemporary comments on Canning's behaviour at this great crisis of his life are of biographical importance.

The Whigs had hated him as a traitor who was always pretending to be a Liberal but was continually in the Tory voting lobby; and they said bitter things when they heard that he was going to give up English politics and go to India. Lord John Russell wrote to Thomas Moore: "Canning is, I suppose, to bury himself in India: he is a fool for his pains, but it is a fine moral on the value of character in this country": and in another place Russell put it thus: "It is the character of party, especially in England, to ask for the assistance of a man of talent, but to follow the guidance of a man of character."

Of course, all this from a man of Lord John's petty, selfish character sounds very priggish. But yet he only said what better and wiser men were feeling. Canning, they thought, has made a disaster of his scheming life; he has had to give up the game in Europe and go, almost in exile — even if Governor-General — to India. Hobhouse in the House of Commons had made a savage attack on him in April, 1821, and his audience purred with delight as he whipped this rhetorical adventurer who could only have got into an unreformed assembly, elected by corrupt boroughs; when Parliament was reformed, he said, there would be no place in it for "a talent that was without morality." Lord Eldon sarcastically wished him a happy journey wherever he cared to go; while Lord Manners wrote to Peel: "We are very proud of your stout resistance to Mr. Canning's motion. . . . He is a terribly restless, ambitious, and treacherous fellow, and I heartily wish him a prosperous voyage, and a permanent residence in India."

However, as we have seen, they were all disappointed; and Canning remained in England as Foreign Secretary and leader of the Commons from 1822 to 1827. It was the triumph of a rather vulgar, showy man over the better sense of his resisting, but powerless fellows. One part of his duty he accomplished with great success. He turned the

King from a violent enemy to an almost embarrassing friend. He accomplished this doubtful triumph by typical methods: amongst others he made Lord Francis Conyngham, the son of the King's mistress, his secretary: and by January, 1823, Miss Copley wrote to Creevy: "Lord F. Conyngham's appointment gives great disgust. . . . The King is quite delighted with his Secretary of State, and was seen the other day at the Pavilion walking about with his arm round Canning's neck." But it must not be too hastily assumed that this appointment was merely to please his royal master; for Canning had great difficulty in getting any one to work with him at the Foreign Office, where the under secretary at once resigned; and Canning had to offer the post to four others before he could persuade one of them to accept it. Honest men hesitated over Canning, as one would be cautious about sleeping with a rattlesnake.

Now, at last, Canning had almost a supreme power in his hand, and whether he was a great man, or only a rather petty one, is more capable of a just decision. The closer one examines his actions the clearer it seems to be that he had no very original ideas of his own. If he had climbed to power at last, and held it until his death, it was not because he had anything new or very valuable to offer his nation. His secret of strength was what it had always been — the craft of a most effective rhetoric and a sparkling flow of words. For example, there was the famous oration of March 19, 1824, the speech of the "heavy Falmouth coach." It was all delightful fun, which would have been admirable in *Punch*, but beneath its intellectual standard. Yet this is how Wilberforce writes of it:

Lord John Russell's notion about the French evacuating Spain. He made no hand of it. Canning invincibly comic . . . drollery of voice and manner were inimitable; there is a lightening up of his features, and a comic play about the mouth, when the full fun of the approaching witticism strikes his own mind, which prepares you for the burst which is to follow.

Now all this is undoubted evidence of a very charming person; but the qualities denoted are those of a first-class after-dinner speaker, rather than a great statesman. Mr. Temperley, who probably knows as much about Canning as any one else, has summed him up as concisely as possible: "His differences with Castlereagh's policy were rather of shade and of emphasis than in fundamentals, and of method and exception rather than of principle." In other words, if we would study the foreign policy of Europe at this period it should be done in a life of its creator, Castlereagh, rather than of Canning the imitator. There was an all-important matter where he, in a very fundamental manner, reversed Castlereagh's policy. Castlereagh had the "Continental" mind; he said that sooner or later Europe must agree to coöperate instead of fight; and he tried to keep the Holy Alliance — much though he disliked its autocratic ideal — as an instrument of this international coöperation. Canning had no such vision, and he has himself summed up his pettiness in a sentence: "For 'Alliance' read 'England', and you have the clue of my policy." This exposure of his smallness is so conclusive that it needs no comment. Canning's diplomacy in detail with Russia, Greece and Turkey, and with Spain, France and Portugal, is, of course, most interesting and important; but it was not really great enough to find space in a miniature portrait. Probably Canning's influence over it all has been exaggerated; and we shall get nearer the true value of this man if we dwell, as we have done here, on his glibness of speech in the House of Commons instead of considering too minutely his work at the Foreign Office. Nevertheless he was a great man on the stage of his day; and Charles X of France allowed him to dine at his table, a privilege which that last of the Bourbon kings firmly denied to any one except of royal blood. However, one cannot but remember that kings have always had a partiality for jesters and clowns.

But there was one great event, the most famous in Canning's diplomatic career, which must be prominent in even the most miniature sketch. It was the recognition of the South American peoples as independent States. The facts are fairly simple; and they are a test case in the problem whether George Canning was quite as distinguished a diplomatist as he and his biographers have sometimes led the world to believe.

It appeared a possibility that the French and Spanish monarchies might come to terms, and accomplish Louis XIV's long-ago dream of a united Bourbon Empire. With the aid of the French army the absolute king was again in power in Madrid; and he asked the European states to discuss the question of the Spanish colonies in South America, which had cast off their allegiance to Spain. Canning thought that the French might offer their army for an expedition against the rebels; which might be the beginning of strong French influence in South America. So in October, 1823, he threatened that if the French went to the assistance of Spain in an attempt to recover these colonies, then Great Britain would recognise their independence as free States. His real interest in South America was that British capital had made large investments in that new continent, and was developing it as a market for the goods produced by the new industrial England. Canning was the political leader of the trading classes. It was useless, and beneath his pretended democratic and nationalist policy, to appeal to other European powers in this matter; so Canning did something original, at last. He appealed to the United States. He suggested that the two nations should unite in a joint guarantee of the Spanish-American rebel colonies against any attack by Spain or France, or by the Holy Alliance as a whole.

Never was any diplomat so completely overthrown by his own scheme. President Monroe of the United States came to the assistance of the South American colonies, as Canning had asked; but not in the manner that the slow-thinking quick talker had foreseen. On December 2, 1823, the President announced that the United States intended to resist any interference by any European power whatsoever in the affairs of either North or South America. In other words, Canning was contemptuously driven off the field of controversy, along with the Holy Alliance. Great Britain, as well as the rest of the European powers, was ordered to keep hands off America. It was one of the worst diplomatic defeats in the course of history.

The way in which Canning met this national disaster is an exceedingly illuminating searchlight on his character; and also reminiscent of the best farces in the literature of the stage. By this time he had become very skilful in handling the newspaper press; a useful support to which his intriguing mind had turned from his early days. Indeed Lady Hester Stanhope had even declared that whatever her dear Uncle said to Canning in confidence was immediately passed on to the journalists. Anyhow, in the present difficulty the press obeyed his instructions; and announced that the Monroe Doctrine was the acceptance of Mr. Canning's terms! It was perhaps the biggest bluff in the history of official journalism. But it succeeded, and England and Europe read, and were almost all convinced, that the great and clever Mr. Canning had scored another wonderful victory. Whereas he had crept home like a whipped boy.

His nerve in a matter of this sort was worthy of the great heroes of romance — and some of the most skilful charlatans. When on December 12, 1826, he made his most famous speech, in which he defended his policy in the Peninsula and in South America, he carried on the bluff with a courage that was worthy of a better lie: "If France conquered Spain, was it necessary that we should blockade Cadiz? No! I looked another way: I sought the materials of compensation in another hemisphere. Contemplating Spain, such as our ancestors had known her, I resolved that, if France had Spain, it should not be Spain with the Indies. I called the New World into existence to redress the balance of the Old." People who were present have told of the amazing effect of this eloquence on the members of the Commons: "It was as if every man in the House had been electrified. Mr. Canning seemed to have increased in stature, his attitude was so majestic. I remarked his flourishes were made with his left arm; the effect was new and beautiful; his chest heaved and expanded, his nostrils dilated . . . all the while a serenity sat on his brow that pointed to deeds of glory." Thomas Moore wrote in his diary that: "When he said 'I thought of Spain and the Indies,' it was in a sort of scream."

In the midst of the whirling flow of this deluge of oratory was concealed the disagreeable fact that instead of creating a New World to protect us from the Old, Canning had been ordered off the premises as a beggar is turned off a doorstep. He recognised the independence of the South American colonies when the whole matter had been snatched out of his hands. Such was the man. He was able by the skill of his tongue and the art of his acting to make people believe that black was white — which is the art of diplomacy.

George Canning, not George Washington, was the real founder of the United States as a world power. He suggested to President Monroe the plan of annexing the Western Hemisphere. Washington only fought for the liberty of a few States. One can go into the smaller details of Canning's diplomacy and find much that is interesting. But the Monroe Doctrine was his greatest success. It would have annihilated the reputations of smaller men.

The other famous field of his diplomacy was Greece and the

Near East. There is not room to discuss it in this place; but careful examination will soon convince the student that it was adopted from Castlereagh, as far as it was good; and his mishandling of it only led to the naval action at Navarino immediately after his death. As M. Élie Halévy remarks: "*Elle était un échec pour cette politique d'équilibre qui était le secrèt de Canning: car elle déclenchait la guerre russe que, depuis 1822, Canning par un moyen ou par un autre, travaillait à rendre impossible.*"

But less amiable critics will say that it was the sign of the entire failure of his diplomacy in Greece and Turkey and Russia. A battle is usually conclusive proof of the failure of diplomacy. It needed the calm pacifist Duke of Wellington to pull the British honour out of the ruins.

All through the days of his supremacy we can hear the continual buzzing of dislike and distrust of this brilliant man, in almost all the contemporary documents. Thus in April, 1823, Creevy was reporting: "Canning, with all his talents and superiority, had no support . . . no one of any party with him." Beneath all that flashing exterior the critical eye could detect a mind that seemed very small after Castlereagh's large though clumsy soul. Castlereagh never forgot that he was a European, and even owned service to mankind. Canning was content if England could look great and bring profitable dividends to his plutocratic supporters. He was, indeed, almost vulgar enough to be called a "Jingo", having much of the selfish man's taste for sensational wars which others would fight, while he stayed safely at home. Thus, he wrote to Frere in January, 1823: "I do not deny that I had an itch for war with France, and that a little provocation might have scratched it into an eruption."

But in spite of suspicions and dislikes, Canning grew in power mainly because he was a clever controller of the Press and a glib talker in the House. Whatever the reason may have been, when Lord Liverpool collapsed in 1827, Canning seemed the inevitable successor to the premiership: and Greville wrote in his diary, April 13, 1827: "Canning, disliked by the King, opposed by the aristocracy and the nation, and unsupported by Parliament, is appointed Prime Minister. . . . This morning the Chancellor, Peel, Lord Westmorland and the Duke of Wellington resigned." Wellington was a simple unambitious man who was ready to serve his country in any honest administration. But he drew the line at Canning! The Duke was perhaps a little hasty in this case; and Canning, having been commissioned by the King, was undoubtedly in command of the field, while the Duke may have been unreasonable in details.

But it was all of little account, for Canning was already a physical wreck; and within four months of his reaching the premiership he was dead, August 8, 1827. It would be unfair to criticise the four months' office of a dying man. He was only fifty-seven; but he had led a nerve-wracking life. Having so many enemies and so few great talents, he had to work very fiercely to get himself into power, and to retain it when it was won. His life was such a continual struggle that he never had the peace which is so necessary for the doing of lasting deeds. He had so much trouble in the destruction of his opponents that he never had time to think out the construction of a better world — which is the essential work of statesmen.

Canning has been one of the most misjudged of the figures of political history. He was not so bad as his enemies said; but neither had he one half of the abilities that his friends have claimed for him. His faults were very much on the surface; and, at heart, his rather slow mind probably always believed that his own success was the chief end of political life. All around him were men (like Wellington, Perceval, Castlereagh) willing to sacrifice their own advantage for the public good; while Canning, without for one moment desiring or realising it, was demanding the centre of the stage — like any third-rate actor-manager.

However, it will always remain very difficult to discover the real Canning amidst the glitter and noise of his life. Greville, who had the instinctive desire of a gentleman to be fair, and had also large opportunities for knowing the truth, wrote down what he thought of Canning, within a few hours of his death. He had also the advantage of learning the opinion of the Duke of Wellington. They made a composite portrait which is probably somewhere near the the truth. Greville wrote:

Canning concealed nothing from Mrs. Canning, nor from Charles Ellis. When absent from his wife he wrote everything to her in the greatest detail. Canning's industry was such that he never left a moment unemployed, and such was the clearness of his head that he could address himself almost at the same time to several different subjects with perfect precision. . . .

It is a quality which he shared with many famous performers on the music-hall stage, though they handle many balls instead of several diplomatic despatches. Greville continued: "He wrote very fast, but not fast enough for his mind. . . ."

The Duke of Wellington's opinion is also of value:

He said his talents were astonishing, his compositions admirable, that he possessed the art of saying exactly what was necessary and passing over those topics on which it was not advisable to touch, his fertility and resources inexhaustible. He thought him the finest speaker he had ever heard . . . he would patiently endure any criticisms upon such papers as he submitted for the consideration of the Cabinet, and would allow them to be altered in any way that was suggested. . . . It was not so, however, in conversation and discussion. Any difference of opinion . . . threw him into ungovernable rage. . . . He said that Canning was usually very silent in the Cabinet . . . but when he did speak he maintained his opinions with extraordinary tenacity. He said he was one of the idlest of men.

This — adds Greville — I do not believe, for I have always heard that he saw everything and did everything himself. Not a despatch was received that he did not read, nor one written that he did not dictate or correct.

Reading along, and between, the lines of such first-hand evidence, one can see something of the truth — and also the remarkable difficulty of reconciling contradictory evidence. On the question of his idleness or industry, Mr. Temperley's high authority has decided in favour of Canning. Yet one must repeat that the common-sense mind of Wellington would think a man idle if he laboured hard over unnecessary things — and looking back on Canning's labours so many of them would seem to have been much ado about nothing.

There is another contemporary character sketch of Canning, by William Hazlitt, one of the most brilliant thinkers and writers in English literature. He looked on his subject in a more detached way than the political and historical critics, who sometimes give very technical judgments — as a judge is sometimes bound by the technicalities of the law. Hazlitt was a great artist who looked on the world and men with a sweeping glance of wide comprehension. He was likely to see truths above Canning that were not revealed to secretaries of State.

This is some of what he wrote:

Mr. Canning was the cleverest boy at Eton, he is, perhaps, the cleverest man in the House of Commons. . . . He has merely engrafted a set of Parliamentary phrases and the technicalities of debate on the themes and school exercises he was set to compose as a boy. . . . He has been all his life in the habit of getting up a speech at the nod of a Minister, as he used to get up a thesis under the direction of his school-master. . . . It is his business and his inclination to embellish what is trite, to gloss over what is true, to vamp up some feeble sophism. . . . His language is a cento of florid commonplaces. . . . He has no steady principles, no strong passions, nothing original, masculine. . . . There is a feeble, diffuse, showy, Asiatic redundancy in all his speeches — something vapid, something second-hand in the whole cast of his mind. . . . He is a mere House-of-Commons man. . . . He may be said to have passed his life in making and learning to make speeches. . . . He has overlooked the ordinary objects of nature, the familiar interests of human life, as beneath his notice. . . . Truth, liberty, justice, humanity, war or peace, civilisation or barbarism, are things of little consequence, except for him to make speeches upon them. . . . Mr. Canning has the luckless ambition to play off the tricks of a political rope dancer, and he chooses to do it on the nerves of humanity. He has called out for war during thirty years without ceasing, like importunate Guineafowls, one note day and night. . . . This is what makes such persons as Mr. Canning dangerous. Clever men are the tools with which bad men work.

Hazlitt should be read in full. Whether Canning deserved all this fire and brimstone will be debated with passion; and though the evidence is in favour of the prosecutor, the tenderer heart of human compassion may find an excuse for mercy. But one is tempted to believe that Hazlitt was right — for he had almost all the facts on his side.

THE SECOND VISCOUNT MELBOURNE
1779–1848

THE SECOND VISCOUNT MELBOURNE
1779–1848

CLIO, the Muse of history, would seem to have a fickle taste; she must have variety. It may be that the popular fancy, having discovered the weaknesses of one political leader — they have always weaknesses to be discovered — turns in disgust and with fresh hope to some one who is utterly different from the last experiment. Whatever may be the reason, or lack of reason, the next important Prime Minister to succeed Canning (after Goderich, who was a nobody; Wellington, who was altogether too stubbornly honest for this wicked political world; and Grey, who was so full of Whig ideals that he finally buried himself and his party under them) was of a very different sort. The successor to the intriguing orator Canning, whom nobody trusted or loved, was William Lamb, the second Viscount Melbourne, who had no ambitions, never intrigued, and would have been trusted by his greatest enemy — if he had ever made one.

The pedigree of Lord Melbourne is an instructive and concise summary of a large part of the history of English government during the three hundred years that preceded him. He was, in the main, the product of the blending of two families, the Cokes and the Lambs, and the result was just the sort of mixture that produced the governing class of Melbourne's transitional period.

The Cokes had already been lords of the manor of Trusley in Derbyshire for four generations, when they produced Sir John Coke, who was born in 1563. He was an honest and capable servant of King Charles I and served that dull and incompetent Stuart sovereign as a commissioner of the

Navy under that erratic creature, George Villiers, Duke of Buckingham. Clarendon says this Coke was covetous; at least he did well for himself, and acquired the possession of the manor of Melbourne, which was in after days to give the family its title. His two sons, as in all wise families, were of different political views in the first Civil War of the seventeenth century; and his grandson, John, was one of the first members of Parliament to dare to protest against the illegal actions of James II; for which courage he was sent as a prisoner to the Tower. His answer was prompt defiance; for when he came out he gathered together a regiment to assist William of Orange in driving James out of England.

His son, another Thomas, prospered under the new monarchy; he married first a daughter of the Earl of Chesterfield, and secondly, a court beauty; set up a house in London; held the office of vice chamberlain to both Anne and George I; and, in short, made himself a well-established member of that governing set that controls the strings behind the marionette show that simple minds call politics. He was a man of wealth; and his heiress was a daughter Charlotte, who in time succeeded to all the variously accumulated possessions of the Coke family. It was this daughter and heiress who married Matthew Lamb, as we shall now see.

These Lambs, the other main line of Lord Melbourne's ancestors, were of new and more rapid growth. The first to raise his head above the common level of affairs was the Matthew Lamb of Southwell (in Nottinghamshire), who was a very flourishing attorney in that country town. He was the legal agent for the surrounding gentry, and did exceedingly well for himself, as no doubt he did for his clients. For it was a profitable profession to attend to the business of the badly educated, hard-riding, country squires who misruled England during much of the eighteenth century. The foolish rich have always been a source of profit to the lawyers. His brother, Peniston Lamb, went up to London and made a large fortune, likewise by the law, as a member of Lincoln's Inn. Both brothers died in 1735; Peniston, being a bachelor, left his wealth to his nephew Robert, Matthew's elder son; while Matthew divided £100,000 equally between Robert and the younger Matthew. Robert had gone into the Church, the other profitable governing class profession of the eighteenth century, where he had flourished exceedingly and become Bishop of Peterborough. When he died a bachelor, his share of his father's fortune, plus the fortune he had received from his uncle Peniston, all went to his younger brother Matthew the younger, who thereby became for those more modest days a man of great wealth.

Southwell was too small to hold him; and he too went up to London, as his uncle Peniston had done with so much success. He became a perpetual solicitor to the post office, and the legal advisers of great lords in town, instead of smaller gentry in the country. His career henceforward entitled it to a place among the heroes of the most optimistic romantic fiction. Of the old family of the Cokes, whom his father had modestly advised at Southwell, the daughter Charlotte survived, and Matthew married her in 1740. When her only brother died, seven years later, she was left sole heiress of the Coke estates — and Matthew through her came into one more fortune. In 1755 he became a baronet, which then, as now, was the reward for getting a larger share of the wealth of the world than seemed to be one's right. In 1768 he died; and his son Peniston found himself one of the richest men of his day. The Industrial Revolution had not yet made the millionaire almost a commonplace in society; so young Lamb, with his £500,000 in land, and another half million pounds sterling in other investment, was worthy of serious social and economic attention.

The Lambs had almost arrived; they had at least laid

the foundations of a governing class family. Matthew, the baronet, was the parliamentary member for Peterborough, of which town his brother was bishop. His son married Elizabeth Milbanke, the daughter of a fifth baronet of an ancient race of courtiers; while his daughter became Lady Belasyne, and the daughter-in-law of Lord Fauconberg. The alliance between Land and Church had been the foundation of the British constitution since the Puritan Revolution had (for the moment) failed in its attempt to make the City merchants supreme. There was one thing needed to crown the Melbourne palatial structure — a peerage; and this was only a matter of time and proper attention to the necessary details, which the slight intellect of young Sir Peniston was quite unable to accomplish. Not having brains of his own he did the first right thing: he married both brains and beauty. In alliance with extreme wealth, they are together irresistible; and Elizabeth Milbanke, the daughter of Sir Ralph, was without any doubt the brightest spot in the Lamb history. Without her amazing skill in handling the social problems that faced a new family, it is probable that even the million of money would not have succeeded in carrying the somewhat trivial intellects of the Lambs into more graceful circles. For they had, after all, only excelled so far as quibblers over petty points of law. Elizabeth Milbanke was to raise them, for a brief moment, into the higher spheres where men quibble and squabble over political principles; and William her son, the subject of the present essay, was to become the most successful, and the most pleasing, product of her delicate art.

One uses the feminine possessive adjective with some precision. For the relations of Sir Peniston and his wife were of a peculiar kind which would be a fitter subject for a great novel than a historical discussion. They were certainly not a suitable match; nature — unassisted by a fortune of a million — would not have considered it for a moment.

The Second Viscount Melbourne

The mere sight of her charms — combined, of course, with her husband's servile silence in debate and consistent voting in the government lobby, ever since he entered the House of Commons — won him an Irish barony in 1770; and in 1781 he rose to the rank of an Irish Viscount. Then came a long social struggle of over thirty years, before the millionaire became an English peer, with the right to sit in the House of Lords; and by the time that earthly coronet was won, a large part of the million had disappeared. The Lambs were a new family, and established society demanded a high price for a share in its enviable advantages.

Sir Peniston Lamb, now Lord Melbourne, was a spendthrift and a libertine; so it was not a tedious task for him to spend his fortune too freely. Since he was not a man of distinguished brains, the fortune might easily have disappeared without any very tangible result. But his wife had a mind of a very different order; perhaps not of the highest class, but a perfect instrument on which to play all the airs and graces that raise social amusements to the rank of the arts and sciences.

Melbourne House, which stood off Piccadilly (where the Albany now stands in its converted form of many sets of chambers), was purchased from Lord Holland by Lamb in 1770, about the time of his marriage and first Irish peerage; and it remained the London home of the family until 1791; when the Duke of York took such a fancy to its many charms — which by Melbourne's money and his wife's taste had been lavished on it — that they agreed to exchange it for the Duke's house in Whitehall. In one or the other of these two successive homes, Lady Melbourne paid — and more than paid — for her footing in the best society by a generous flow of gorgeous entertainments which made her one of the most famous hostesses of her day.

The society of Melbourne House was very frivolous and wasteful, and of the nature of riotous living; but there was a deeper purpose running beneath all its wild energy. There was, of course, as already noted, the more selfish reason of making this lavish hospitality the foundation of the Melbourne family as a great social institution. But Lady Melbourne was more than a pleasing society lady. At the back of her mind, perhaps very far back, was the hope that the Melbournes might serve their country in politics, as well as themselves in rank and honour. She made her home famous as a centre of the Whig Party. Her friends were of that tone of mind which considers that it is superior to its neighbouring minds in liberality of thought and generosity of intentions. These Whigs, or Liberals or Radicals, have rarely had all the unselfish virtues which they have claimed, and sometimes sincerely believed themselves to be the possessors. But there has often been something, however vague, in the claim; and Lady Melbourne and her guests must have some credit for their political labours, even if they sometimes made them not unlike frivolous pastimes.

The social façade of Melbourne House made a gorgeous spectacle for the public view; and behind the private curtain it was as dainty and select in its charms as wit and beauty and literature and art could well make it. Lord Melbourne himself was of no account. Doctor Dunckley, one of his biographers, has summed him up very concisely: "a dawdler in politics, a dawdler in art, a dawdler even in play. Languid, insipid, aimless, illiterate to an almost inconceivable degree." He must have been almost a figure of fun in the bright Melbourne House set, except that one does not laugh too openly at the man who signs the cheques. But the more one is convinced how dull Lord Melbourne was, the more remarkable becomes the success of his wife.

Lady Melbourne's followers and admirers were (as society judges such things) of the first order. The Prince of Wales was easily attracted by such a glitter; and, as Wraxall has recorded in his "Historical Memoirs", "she might well challenge such a preference. A commanding figure exceeding the middle height, full of grace and dignity, an animated countenance, intelligent features, captivating manners and conversation; all these and many other attractions, enhanced by coquetry, met in Lady Melbourne." Lady Holland drew another picture and added an element of criticism which really increased the charm of the figure: "Lady Melbourne is uncommonly sensible and amusing, though she often puts me in mind of Madame de Merteuil in 'Les Liaisons Dangereuses.' The Duke of Bedford is attached to her: he is almost brutal by the roughness of his manners." The Duke was one of the Whigs, but the Duchess of Gordon, of the Tory Party, had made it quite clear that she would do everything possible to marry her daughter to the Duke of Bedford, and thereby perhaps shake his political allegiance. There was therefore almost a virtuous reason why both Lady Melbourne and her bosom friend, the Duchess of Devonshire, should place their *beaux yeux* at the disposal of the threatened Duke. By such happy accidents was the salvation of the Whigs turned into a less fatiguing labour than a pure problem of political science. The Duke loosened the strain of the situation by discreetly dying; which may be regarded as martyrdom for his party; for it is difficult to know how he could have been pulled out of the Tory fires without endangering the souls of Fox and Grey, who were both adorers of the Duchess of Devonshire and on terms of close friendship with Lady Melbourne. Her influence with Canning, another intimate friend, was used in the other direction; for in his earliest days this friend, with his fickle want of balance, was threatening to become too liberal even for the Whigs; but she was far too level-headed for any such anarchy of thought, and he had to write reassuring her of his safe orthodoxy. However, Canning, as we have seen, soon got altogether beyond the control of the most attractive of hostesses.

To discuss Lady Melbourne and her friends would be the work of a biographical history of her times; but there is one short note which Lord Byron wrote of her in his diary on November 24, 1813, which tells a lot of the story in a few lines: "The best friend I ever had in my life, and the cleverest of women. I write with most pleasure to her, and her answers are so sensible, so tactique. I never met with half her talent."

It may be thought that Lady Melbourne's friends should not intrude unduly in a character sketch of her son; but it is the Melbourne House guests that give the key to his life. There was one friend of his mother who is of peculiar interest in the life of her second son. The first child had been born within a year of her marriage. Then nine years passed without another child until William, the future Premier, was born in 1779. The husband and wife had long ago discovered that their marriage was not a success as an affair of the affections. The ceasing of children after the first must have aroused, or confirmed, comments. There is of course no direct evidence; but when many years afterwards, in 1848, Greville in his diary recorded the death of Lord Melbourne, he noted, as though it were a matter of accepted and common knowledge, that he resembled "in character and manner, as he did remarkably in feature, his father, the late Lord Egremont."

It is a remarkable statement, but Greville was not a man to write a word he did not believe, and did not have good grounds for believing, to be true. His record cannot be ignored, although biographies of Melbourne have been written which have not quoted this piece of evidence; just as standard biographical dictionaries leave out the notoriously admitted fact that Egremont left many illegitimate children. Lord Egremont was a man whom Greville often mentioned in his diary, and always with very affectionate respect. He was certainly one of the most attractive men of his period. George Wyndham (born 1751, died 1837) became the third earl of Egremont and the owner of Petworth in Sussex. Greville is never tired of telling of the many virtues and forgivable faults of the man whom he said was Lord Melbourne's father; how he hated ceremony and affectations, just as Melbourne did; was honourable and frank — which was also characteristic of both. Here is one of Greville's sketches of him: "No man probably ever gave away so much money in promoting charitable institutions and useful undertakings. His understanding was excellent, his mind highly cultivated . . . his manner blunt without rudeness and caustic without bitterness." Except for the philanthropy, it might be a portrait of William Lamb. Still more charming is Greville's picture, drawn from life on the spot, of old Egremont in May, 1834, giving a huge feast to the poor around Petworth; four thousand had been invited:

but as many more came, the old Peer could not endure that there should be anybody hungering outside his gates, and he went out himself and ordered the barriers to be taken down. . . . They think 6000 were fed. . . . Nothing could exceed the pleasure of that fine old fellow; he was in and out of the windows of his room twenty times. . . . There was something affecting in the contemplation of that old man — on the verge of the grave, from which he had only lately been reprieved, with his mind as strong and his heart as warm as ever — rejoicing in the diffusion of happiness and finding keen gratification in relieving the distresses and contributing to the pleasures of the poor.

No one could consider it a disgrace to have the energetic and generous Lord Egremont for a father, instead of the dull creature who was officially married to Lady Melbourne. There is naturally no certain proof that Egremont was her lover and William his son; but the portrait of Egremont that hung in one of the rooms at Brocket, one of Lord Melbourne's country homes, was so like its owner that it was the universal wonder of visitors. The story received its most definite denial when, in later years, Melbourne was taking Sir Edward Landseer, the famous animal painter, round his house. Landseer, like so many others, had impulsively turned to compare his host's face with the portrait; and Melbourne curtly asked, "You have heard that story, have you? But it is a lie, for all that." But even that denial is not altogether sufficient to dismiss the rumour. When Melbourne thus repudiated his illegitimate father he was the leader of his party, and even he could not altogether disregard the public conventions. It is beyond dispute that William Lamb had spent a great part of his childhood at Petworth House; he had been one of the last people who had been called to Egremont's bedside when he lay dying, and the elder man had followed the career of the younger with unusual interest from its beginning to his own end. If we seek for a father for this famous boy, it is Peniston, Viscount Melbourne, who requires an explanation and proof, rather than the brilliant Earl of Egremont, who was in almost every detail a living likeness of the young man.

William Lamb had a somewhat haphazard early education. His father, who was devoted to his eldest son, cared nothing for William — surely a circumstance of some suspicion — while his mother was all affection and care for the second son, who was her favourite. But husband and wife were both consumed in society turmoil. In 1783 Lady Melbourne persuaded the Prince of Wales (who at that moment thought she was the most attractive woman of his life — he was just twenty-one years old) to make her husband a lord of his bedchamber. In 1790, aged eleven, William went to Eton, where he performed the usual duties of his class by mixing with the sons of the right people and mistaking Latin verses for a proper education. However, this learning was sufficient to make its pupils qualified for the highest posts in the State, and Lamb's schoolfellows became archbishops, marquises, lord chief justices and famous fox hunters. William Lamb had no taste whatever for games, or the killing of animals, which Englishmen consider a peculiarly manly sport; and his spare time at Eton seems to have been the foundation of his life-long habit of reading of all kinds. He became one of the best informed men and the most interesting talkers of his day; not because of any education he got at Eton or Cambridge, but because both scholastic institutions gave him so little instruction that he had plenty of time to educate himself.

In 1796 he went to Trinity College, Cambridge, where he does not seem to have startled that quiescent backwater of learning by an unseemly intellectual activity, though he worked hard at the classics according to the conventional practice. His greatest effort gained him a prize for an essay, which he declaimed in oratorical form, "On the Progressive Improvements of Mankind." It was one of those youthful works in which there is a great deal of confident sentiment and not very much certain fact. But the son of a Whig family was expected to contribute some of this amateurish, philanthropic, political philosophy to the general stock. It was hopeful evidence that he was going to carry on the work of his predecessors — and trick the governed people into a continued belief that the governing classes knew their trade of ruling.

It was proof, if any were needed, that Lamb had political intentions, when he wrote some verse in defence of Fox and his party against the attacks of the Canning gang which had appeared in the *Anti-Jacobin*. Lamb's lines were of the current sort of personal satire on his opponents which was the habit of that period. But his lean talent of this kind was nipped in its half-opened bud by a somewhat crushing reply in the *Anti-Jacobin;* which is considered, in part at least, to be from Canning's own pen:

Bard of the borrowed lyre, to whom belong
The shreds and remnants of each hackney's song,
Whose verse thy friends in vain for wit explore,
And count but one good line in eighty-four.

But it was already being noticed that William Lamb had talents of some kind. "Monk" Lewis met him in 1802, when they were both fellow guests at Inverary Castle; and wrote to Lady Melbourne:

You know it would be impossible for William not to do everything better than anybody else. To tell you the truth . . . I have some difficulty not to be of the above opinion myself . . . I did not think it necessary to congratulate you on Pen's [her eldest son] election success . . . but I own I should have said, as the Dissenter did to Frederick, "Truly, Sir, we should have liked your second Brother better."

It had been proposed that William should enter the Church — which has always been a recognised method by which younger sons acquire a share of the national wealth. But Lord Egremont, his mother's closest adviser, said no to this proposal; and, indeed, Lady Melbourne had set her heart on politics as his career. The law was made a first step, and her son entered as a student of Lincoln's Inn, in 1797. It was the correct thing to do; and the Melbournes were not yet sufficiently established to ignore the conventional rules. It was also considered good form to spend a few terms at Glasgow University, in the hopes of picking up some of the wisdom which had dropped from the table of Adam Smith and his solemn colleagues. Smith's works had just captured the shallow intellect of the younger Pitt; and persons with political ambitions then "went north", as Scotsmen with financial hopes "came south." So William and his brother Frederick went to Glasgow in 1799; and worked at history, law, and (of course, in Scotland) metaphysics; and learned to debate in the University Club.

There is no official record of his presence in Glasgow; and all we know of him at this period is a delightful correspondence with his adoring and adored mother, who was the confidential friend of both these sons. William's letters are clear evidence that this youth of twenty-one had ability, and that his character — or want of it, some would say — was already formed. In one letter of January 6, 1800, he wrote of a friend: "I hope you will contrive this winter to rub off a few rum ideas which he contracted in these philosophical colleges, and to divest him of rather too minute and scrupulous a morality, which is entirely unfit for this age." It was entirely the tone one would expect from a boy who had spent his holidays in the saloons of Melbourne House, with the Prince of Wales and Fox and their friends as his mother's guests.

This society had naturally influenced his politics as well as his morals — which are the basis of politics — and a letter of January 14 discussed with Whig fervour a proposal of peace from Bonaparte. He asks indignantly how the Government could abruptly reject so reasonable a proposal.

If I did not know that one always exaggerates the events of the day, I should think it must either lead them to the scaffold, or make them the perpetual, absolute tyrants of this country. . . . The whole transaction leaves the odium of the war entirely upon us, and Bonaparte laid a snare for us with the utmost art. . . . The Aristocrats here are said to grumble, but they are most of them manufacturers, and there is no reliance to be placed on their discontent. If they should become really alarmed and displeased the system goes to pieces that moment; but they will bear more taxes yet.

Early letters are usually better evidence of the writer's real mind than those composed in political maturity — for a Prime Minister often writes to conceal the truth rather than to reveal it. Lamb's opinion of the political system he was one day to govern is put with energy in this same letter:

The King will maintain at all hazards the Ministry; they themselves are too old in their trade to be frightened by petitions or mobs; Parliament is composed of their bondsmen; the majority of electors throughout the country are either bought or frightened. What is to move this weighty fabric, built upon influence, power and interest, defended as it is by an immense military force? If they hold together and resolve to stand out to the last it is impossible to conceal from oneself that nothing can overthrow them but the greatest and most important event, such as the failure of the funds, or the rising of the mass of the people.

Then follows another letter of ardent approval of Bonaparte:

Every line he writes carries with it an air of greatness and sincerity. . . . We are fixed in bigotry and prejudice. We think there is no liberty but our liberty, no government but our government, and no religion but our religion.

This letter was written in the midst of a war; and in an advanced modern "democracy" would probably put the writer in the hands of the police. But the State in Melbourne's day had not invented so many instruments of oppression. One gathers that Lord Egremont had been getting anxious about the influence of Glasgow; for William wrote to his mother on February 8:

I daresay Lord Egremont is right enough about the disputatious disposition of these men who have been so unfortunate as to have been at Millar's [the professor with whom the Lambs lived in Glasgow] . . . the truth is the Scotch universities are very much calculated to make a man vain, important and pedantic. This is naturally the case where there is a great deal of reading. You cannot have both the advantages of study and of the world together.

In a letter of March this youthful cynic asked his mother to tell him what was happening to Lord King and Sir Henry Parnell, who had both been at Cambridge in his time: "I am afraid they are half mad, and only eager to overthrow the Church and put up the Dissenters." Then he goes on to criticise a sermon of Hall the Baptist, who had, naturally, offended Lamb's liberal tastes; and he launches forth in a scathing attack on all such sects: "Because Bolingbroke was a debauched man, they say all atheists are debauched; because Mirabeau was a rogue, they say all atheists are rogues." Then follows a passage which reveals more of the future Prime Minister's mind than we shall get from any official despatches:

I do not like the Dissenters, and this Hall is one. They are more zealous, and consequently more intolerant, than the Established Church. Their only object is power. If we are to have a prevailing religion, let us have one that is cool and indifferent, and such a one we have got. Not that I am so foolish as to dread any fires and faggots and wheels and axes, but there are other modes of persecution. Toleration is the only good and just principle, and toleration for every opinion that can possibly be formed.

This letter is much more valuable than the writer's great speeches. For one can say what one believes in a note to a dear sympathetic mother, while the House of Lords would be weary if it heard half the truth.

After parts of two winters in Glasgow, he came back to London, and read for the Bar with considerable energy. He was "called" in 1804; but it all ended with one complimentary brief. He had more serious work on hand than reading law. For the greatest merit of William Lamb was that his university was the world; he was too liberal in his taste to tie himself to law or politics or religion or any of the sectarians' parts of life. He was a man of the world — a limited world perhaps — but not a pedant. A sentence from Lady Airlie's (his descendant's) valuable book, "In Whig Society", well expresses his next university: "His days after he left Glasgow were spent in desultory reading and his evenings in the delightful society open to him at Melbourne House, at Devonshire House and Holland House, where all the talents and the wit of the day were gathered."

His mother, Lady Melbourne, was the chancellor of the "university" where her son learned the greater part of his knowledge. If the world of fashionable wit could teach him anything it was at his disposal in his mother's drawing-room.

It was not the world of affairs itself, but the smaller world where clever people talked about affairs. Wellington was in the field in India, already more informed about the practice of life than any statesman of his time; and he was soon to go to the Peninsula where his knowledge of mankind was to become still more profound. William Lamb was only to learn about the world from the after-dinner conversation and at the late theatre supper parties at Melbourne and Devonshire and Holland Houses. It is a proof of his cleverness that he learned so much.

In 1805 the Melbournes' eldest son, Peniston, died; and William, the second, became the heir to the family title and estates. His father was heartbroken and only allowed the new heir £2000 a year instead of the £5000 Peniston had received. However, in 1805, after the manner of the period, he bought his son a seat in the House of Commons; the law was finally put on one side, and the Melbourne House Whig smart set began to consider how to make a career for the new heir. He seemed a promising pupil. In 1806 he married Lady Caroline Ponsonby, the Earl of Bessborough's only daughter; and when Lord Minto met him a few weeks later, at the house of the bride's father, he reported that William Lamb "seemed to be a remarkably pleasant, clever and well-informed young man." His marriage had several material advantages for a political career; his wife was a granddaughter of the first Earl Spencer, and the niece of Georgiana, the famous Duchess of Devonshire. It was thus almost as if he had bought up several valuable shares or plots in the Whig political estates.

But the man who married Caroline Ponsonby was gambling heavily in the stock markets of life. It would have been as safe to marry a volcano. She had learned all the best parlour tricks of her class — and more: French and Italian, and some Greek and Latin; painting and sparkling conversation; and a thousand and one other vivacities, and perhaps madnesses, which were going — as we shall see — to make her husband's life a very restless affair, as far as any one could disturb the cynical calmness of such a man. It was a double marriage day in the Melbourne family; for at the same time his sister, Emily, married Earl Cowper, a great Whig peer. It was another link with the Whig Party; it put the Melbournes at last beyond reasonable chance of social disaster, and well set in the ranks of the English aristocracy. They were, of course, only a young branch; but, then, the younger Pitt had made the House of Lords a rather new and cheap institution; and blue blood was not so closely analysed as it once had been. Englishmen were beginning to learn that a hereditary aristocracy had been, on the whole, an expensive luxury in their history. They did not yet realise that aristocrats were much cheaper for the nation than plutocrats were going to be.

The interesting characteristic about Lord Melbourne's political career is that it came just at the moment when the aristocratic rule of the eighteenth century was gradually merging into the plutocratic rule of the nineteenth. William Lamb himself, with his mixed — even doubtful — parentage, was a very typical example of the transition period. He was not altogether of one class or the other; if his mother supplied an old family, her husband supplied the money. There was more of the aristocrat than of the plutocrat about William; but then Greville's story of his parentage is more likely to be true than false.

Within a few months of Lamb's entering the House of Commons, Pitt died. He was the end of the eighteenth century, and another evidence that Lamb was in a transition period. In a few more months Fox was dead also. The political situation, when these two old rivals passed off the stage, was necessarily very confused. Lamb's formal entry into the work of the House was the honour of moving the Address in reply to the King's Speech; it was just the professional political recognition that one would have expected to be given to the son of Melbourne House. But of greater interest is the first note of his opinion on the business of the Commons. A bill had been introduced to make freehold estates liable for the debts of their dead owners. That the landed class had been so long able to escape this obvious duty was an injustice which Lamb — although his own fortune was personally concerned — recognised very clearly. He said in this diary that he had "the fullest intention of speaking . . . but my resolution always failed me." He indignantly added that the Bill was rejected "sixty-nine to forty-seven — the majority having in it many landed proprietors, either in possession or expectancy; a most disgraceful division, and one which really hurt and mortified me deeply. . . . I never can think that they ought to prevail against the glaring injustice of the law as it stands at present." It was evident that Lamb had entered Parliament with the idea of considering other interests than his own and those of his class. It was a sign that his career might be unusual.

Then a month later, in April, 1807, he made another speech which showed his independent courage. He seconded a resolution that declared that it was "highly criminal in any Councillors of his Majesty to fetter their own discretionary power of offering advice to the Crown." This was a protest against the King's demanding, and the Ministers' giving, a pledge not to propose Catholic emancipation again. It required courage for the son of Melbourne House to stand up against the unconstitutional orders of the Crown; for the Prince of Wales was the family patron. Lamb's record of one speech in this debate is interesting: "Mr. Canning made a speech of some ability, but pettish, querulous, and little, beyond his usual pettishness, querulousness, and littleness . . . with the most evident arrogance, entirely unsupported by any dignity." His further comment is useful evidence of the amount of democratic conviction that made the political principles of the Whig mind of this period; for after adding that Canning finished his oration "by saying, that, even if his Majesty should be condemned at the bar of that House, it was still some consolation that from that sentence lay an appeal to the people, which, under certain circumstances he should think it his duty to make", Lamb continued: "The indecency of this threat produced a long and indignant clamour in the House."

It is not entirely obvious to the more modern mind why it should be "indecent" to ask the people to judge their "representatives" in Parliament. But Lamb was born at the end of the eighteenth century, when the Whig and Tory families had almost convinced Englishmen that it was their duty to obey their members of Parliament and not to criticise them. The Melbourne House folk never really believed in democracy; they only talked of it with much generosity. But it would be entirely wrong to imagine that Lamb was insincere: he believed in things even more important than democracy. Thus it was at this early stage of his career that he mentioned in his diary a very fluent speech by the new orator, Mr. Milnes. It had been a great parliamentary triumph but Lamb wrote: "it wanted that which is the nerve and soul and marrow of a speech — real truth and integrity" — both more eternal qualities than that high-sounding thing called "democracy" — which, after all, may be only a phrase invented by debating clubs. Certainly it was a matter which could scarcely have entered the head of a politician of that period — except to give colour to a peroration. So we find Lamb writing (May 13, 1807): "I left London for Brocket Hall, having settled my election for the borough of Portarlington in Ireland"; it being the candidate who settled the election, not the electors.

Lamb had one of those detached and thoughtful minds which could judge a question without any apparent national or class bias. For example, he wrote in his diary what he thought of Napoleon's methods of governing a conquered people. He was clearly searching for facts, not rumours:

> I have never met with any correct information upon the conduct of the governments which Bonaparte substitutes in the place of those he subverts. . . . I much suspect that the improvement is so great as to be very sensibly and gratefully felt. . . . He gives his soldiers plunder in the moment of victory, he levies contributions, which fall with the greatest weight upon the highest orders; but on the other hand he suppresses all disorder, he administers prompt and satisfactory justice, he does away with the enormous and galling privileges of the nobility and clergy.

Now, in most of these conclusions Lamb was probably entirely wrong; nevertheless, the passage is a valuable proof of his impartial and inquiring mind. It was the same when he had to try to be a party politician. It was evidently a difficult task, for he wrote:

> The Ministers very fairly offered all the information necessary for full inquiry upon all the contested points — by the Convention in Portugal, the campaign in Spain, and the negotiations with America. I foresee a session of much uninteresting debate. The fault of Opposition is a determination to make differences of opinion where, in fact, there exist but few, and those trifling.

When the Duke of York was charged with corruption, in the notorious Colonel Wardle and Mrs. Clarke case, Lamb voted for Lord Althorp's motion; in which, in defiance of his leaders, that simple, honest soul condemned the Duke's conduct in the severest words. Here again, a stubborn determination to be scrupulously just made Lamb disregard the personal advantages that would have led a smaller-minded man to remember that the Duke of York was the King's son and the close friend of his mother.

Lamb showed other qualities than this primitive sense of rigid truthfulness — which is often a gift that goes with a rather dull mind. For in February, 1809, he made an estimate of the value of the future Duke of Wellington: "Sir Arthur Wellesley has about him everything that gives promise of great military genius and of the character of an enterprising and successful commander." So far the character might have been drawn by any fairly shrewd observer; but it was in the further comment that Lamb showed his penetration: "but it is also evident that from his habits he is better fitted for chief commands than for subordinate situations." That went to the very heart of Wellington's character.

So far Lamb had chiefly demonstrated his unsuitability for party politics. A cynic, as he was, might have fitted into its eccentric habits; but an honest cynic was a creature out of the main stream of political life. Sinecures, or offices with salaries but no duties to perform, were the pivots of the whole system — for how could members be persuaded to vote, if they got no rewards? So disrespectful and careless of this system had Lamb already become that he made a speech in favour of a wild, reckless suggestion that these desirable sinecures should be abolished. Political stupidity — and moral principles — could go no farther.

So Lamb began to show signs of disgust with political life, and he went to Parliament little, and spoke less. It is impossible to ignore the obvious comment that perhaps this lack of interest was not altogether disconnected with the very remote chance of the Whigs ever getting into power and office. For when the Prince of Wales became regent (and practically king from 1812 onwards) he did not put his earlier Whig friends into power; and the Whiggish game seemed hopeless. During the Regency Bill debate, when office seemed so possibly near, Lamb was more subservient to the Prince of Wales; and, on behalf of the Whig Party, moved an amendment to save the regent from restrictions on his power. And Lamb, with even more servility, refused to protest against the reappointment of the Duke of York as Commander in Chief, an office from which Lamb had so recently driven him with so much indignation. But one does not expect saints in political circles; Lamb may very well have seen by this time that the Duke was not as bad as he had been painted; indeed, was even a useful man at the Horse Guards. In the general election of 1812 Lamb lost his seat, and was out of Parliament until 1816.

But his life was not left without incident and ever agitated variety — for he was married to Lady Caroline Ponsonby. If the evil spirit of mad mischief and impossible eccentricity were ever made into a picture of beauty and charm, then it was surely the wife of William Lamb. As the husband wrote in his Commonplace Book within a few years of the marriage: "Every man will find his own private affairs more difficult to manage and control than any public affairs in which he may be engaged." In the excitement of parliamentary debates, a man may say many things he does not exactly believe, or that are of little importance whether he believes them or not. But in the secret places of a Commonplace Book a man faces the stern reality — and we arrive at his fundamental theories of life. It is in a sentence that Lamb wrote concerning his marriage that we can get nearer his political philosophy than by anything he said in the House of Commons as Prime Minister of England.

"It is the nature of human things that no man can be free and independent." Then he goes on to quote Euripides: "Alas, there is no man who is free. Whoever he be, he is either the slave of wealth or of fortune or of the multitude of his fellow citizens, or the provisions of the laws constrain him to act in opposition to his own judgment." These are words which help one to understand why Lord Melbourne, even when he was ruler of Great Britain, was somewhat careless of what laws were voted, or rejected, in the Houses of Parliament. The wisest of men are rarely enthusiastic. This wise fellow saw no reason to hope that any legislation would give him a peaceful home.

By 1809 it is clear the domestic wheels were not moving without friction, for Lady Caroline wrote to her husband:

> I think lately, my dearest William, we have been very troublesome to each other; which I take by wholesale to my own account and mean to correct, leaving you in retail a few little sins, which I know you will correct. . . . Condemn me not to silence, and assist my imperfect memory. I will on the other hand be silent of a morning, entertaining after dinner; docile, fearless as a heroine in the last vol. of her troubles; strong as a mountain tiger, and active as those young savages, Basil's boys, to whom by the way, you will give one shilling apiece. You should say to me, *raisonnez mieux et repliquez moins.*

In another letter to Lamb she wrote of a preacher she had heard on Sunday:

> He takes rapid advances in the Methodistical style; the last time we were "Oh, my dear brethren"; this time we were "Oh, my dear brethren and Christian warriors and hardy veterans", with a great deal about love and souls in torment. He so entirely lost himself at the conclusion in the military simile he had adopted that he addrest three old women in a voice of thunder, which stirred them amazingly, calling them to fight, and strive, and obtain the kingdom of heaven by blood, and loudly addressing them by the appellation of "Ye veteran Christian warriors."

Now this is not a life of Caroline Lamb; and her wild passionate adventures with Lord Byron, or the romps with her page boy and many others of intermediate degree, cannot be told here. But it is as impossible to give any idea of her husband's public career, without some knowledge of this tumultuous domestic tragedy — or comedy, or film play romance — behind the scenes, as it is impossible to understand Wellington's campaigns in the Peninsular War without a continual remembrance of the lines of Torres Vedras, which lay behind all his movements. When earnest political fanatics and ambitious colleagues and designing enemies were clamouring to Melbourne that this was the right and logical thing to do, or not to do, for his party or his nation, the perplexed and hesitating statesman must often have pondered over the intimate experience he had of human nature; and wonderingly asked himself whether right and wrong, and logic and reason, had as much influence over our social affairs as moralists and legislators imagined. When he remembered how difficult and impossible it was to control Lady Caroline, to repeat the process over a whole nation must have seemed a hopeless task. William Lamb started life with the germs of cynicism very active in his blood; and his wife gave him no reason to become an optimist as he grew older. She taught him his deepest lesson in the science of political economy; namely, that the people of this world are not easily reformed by logic, and cannot be persuaded to live peacefully together by calling a committee or a parliament to draft a few rules and regulations. Human nature — like Caroline Ponsonby — must be left in great part to work out its own salvation, or its own ruin. So Lord Melbourne made a pessimistic Prime Minister; seeing no good proof why there was much reason for being hopeful of accomplishing any great reforms.

Turned out of Parliament by a disapproving electorate, and almost turned out of home by the neurotic genius whom the law insisted was his wife, Lamb turned to the society of books. Of course, he also tried the relaxation of shooting animals — the usual refuge of the English "gentleman" who has not often been well enough educated to think of anything more intelligent. But Lamb was above the low standard of his class; and, in the words of the editor of the "Melbourne Papers", "literature was, after all, his chief solace, and it was during this period of his life that he acquired those stores of knowledge which, combined with the original turn of his mind, made his society so delightful." He read with such good purpose that the cynical man of fashion, who seemed to lounge through life, became one of the best informed men of his time. He was not a pedant or a specialist in any department; but he gained a wide knowledge of the world. Which is the first necessity of statesmanship.

When he again found a seat in the House of Commons, in 1816, his knowledge had become too deep to permit him to hope that the pet ideas of the Whigs would do much good to anybody. But he hesitated to change his party. As he put it himself:

> In politics you may serve the cause of wisdom and justice better by remaining with those to whom you have attached yourself, even after you disapprove much of their conduct, and prefer that of their adversaries. . . . Nothing can justify a man in unsettling the mind of others, weakening the force of reverence, authority and example, except a conviction " of overwhelming certainty of error " —

as he explained in the words of a Franciscan friar. Now Lamb could never have been overwhelmed by an absolute certainty in this uncertain world; of which he knew enough to be certain of nothing. He found no clear guidance in the parliamentary debate; for he wrote that in the House of Commons " a torpor of all my faculties almost always comes upon me, and I feel as if I had neither ideas nor opinions."

His father had been made a peer of the United Kingdom in 1815, and thus entitled to a seat in the House of Lords, a privilege which his earlier Irish peerage did not give him. So his son was now heir to a place one day in that assembly, and was consequently a little freer from party chains, He began to fancy the flashing career of George Canning; and his vote began to go to the Tories. Thus against all the vows of the Whig philosophy he voted for the repressive measures with which the Tory Government endeavoured to crush the working-class demand for relief from the starvation and unemployment that followed the Napoleonic wars. He was wise enough to know that anarchy must be suppressed; he had not good enough brains to find any real remedy that would stop the anarchy at the source. He could only help to crush the effect — the usual resource of statesmen who are not efficient in their profession. So Lamb voted for the suspension of the Habeas Corpus Act in 1816, when Lord John Russell — the purest juice of the driest Whig root — tried to protest; and, also, for the Six Acts to crush rebellious opinions in 1819.

He was in a difficult position. "Reform" was in the current political air, but Lamb was not ignorant enough to be sure what ought to be done. If he had known only half what he did, it would have been so easy to decide; instead of which he could only write that he "cannot go so far as to admit, when I am speaking, that the majority of the people are always right." When Russell, full of pious certainty, got up to move that a corrupt borough should be disfranchised, Lamb very pertinently remarked that it was a corrupt borough that had returned Russell himself. He even added: "I anticipate the total destruction of freedom of speech from a reformation of the Parliament, and for this reason." The reason was not a very conclusive one; but we who have lived to see a reformed Parliament a hundred years later, may wonder whether speech is now as free from the lash of the party whips as it was in Melbourne's unreformed days.

A man with this kind of mind was obviously unsuitable for parliamentary life; and he looked like making a failure of his career. He was short of money; for his father and mother had always been spendthrifts, and his wife was as reckless in finance as she was in everything else. By reason of his financial wants in part, but more on account of his fatal political scepticism, he could not stand up to his slashing independent rival, Duncombe, in 1825; and once more he was put out of Parliament by men who had more certain, if not better, minds.

But a sudden change came in 1827 when Lord Liverpool ended his long ministry. He had possessed the qualities of a well-balanced administrative machine, and he was succeeded as Prime Minister by Canning, with whom the idea of balance will never be associated — except at the end of a gymnast's pole. Lamb had long been regarded as one of Canning's unofficial disciples; and he now received the reward of his services. He was given a parliamentary seat and appointed Secretary for Ireland, at that time a somewhat subordinate post under the immediate control of the Home Office in London. Melbourne was now forty-eight years old; it was his first political office; and his old family friend, King George IV, was glad to welcome him as a formal servant of the Crown at last.

In this post Lamb can be studied in his most attractive light. The cultured man of the world, with much scepticism and cynicism — and all the other isms bred in that vast social wilderness — at once became as complete a success in his office as if he had passed his life in a technical training college for the bureaucrat's chair. He proved one more example of the still unrecognised law that the expert often knows less than the untrained. However callously William Lamb may have lounged through his life hitherto, he had always remained a very honest, conscientious gentleman; with a sense of honour that must have been almost an instinctive survival rather than the product of the society of that day.

But the facts are their own best explanation. First, he charmed every one in Dublin by his delightfully frank manners. He was only too glad to receive any one who desired to see him. There were no stiff ceremonies and forms while Lamb was in office. Every one could speak freely to him, and they received the frankest of opinions in reply. In a country which had produced unbalanced fanatics on both sides, as its chief exports and imports for centuries, the sane, well-poised Lamb was just the man to see matters in their proper proportions. Any one who took dogmatic religion very seriously was to him an object of gentle amusement; and unhinged Orangemen and zealous Catholics alike to him were people to be soothed to a civilised state of mind. As the numbers of both fanatical parties together were probably only very limited — far less than the political agitators on both sides endeavoured to make the two nations believe — if Lamb had been given a free hand, he might have worked wonders in that unhappy land. Daniel O'Connell was so delighted with him that he wanted to get him returned as the member for Dublin. As Doctor Dunckley puts it in his biography: "He gave an example of the spirit in which Ireland should be governed. A hitherto proscribed party and persecuted race felt that they had a friend in him."

This late man of fashion was full of energy of all kinds; he drafted reforming bills on all sorts of subjects; on criminal procedure, tithes, public works, and education. He tried to stop the newspaper proprietors' being bribed to support the government. He cross-examined everybody, and searched for the truth wherever he could hope to find it. But it was mostly in vain. The governing set in Ireland did not want reform or peace or happiness for the people — they wanted posts in Church and State, and as much of the peasants' rents as they could lay their hands on; and when the office-seekers had finished with Lamb's time, the officeholders, already in possession, saw to it that cold water was poured on all his efforts to get some hopeful reform given a trial.

Perhaps Lamb himself, with his cynical pessimist mind, was relieved when he realised that he was really only a dummy figure in the machinery of the governing system. He had to do what the Lord Lieutenant in Dublin or the Home Secretary in London told him to do, or not to do; and the former had been six years in office, and was quite convinced that everything was beyond hope in that mismanaged land. The Home Secretary had a sense of detail which Lord Wellesley, the Lord Lieutenant, lacked; and Lamb was full of energy to grapple with all the work that came along. But it all came to nothing; and Lamb's term of office in Ireland was more useful in proving how much sound sense and capacity for work he possessed, than for producing results. When Canning died within a few months of becoming Prime Minister, his successor, Goderich, retained Lamb in office. Even when the full-blooded Tories came into power under the Duke of Wellington, Lamb was asked to hold his post, for the Duke recognised a straight and able man when he found him, and cared little or nothing that Lamb was of Whig origin, the only one in his Cabinet. However, the scheme soon broke down, and Lamb, with all the other Canningite survivors, resigned.

In 1828 Lamb's father died and William became the second Viscount Melbourne; and thus left the Commons for the House of Lords. He had just got back to England in time to see his wife before she died. They had been separated for years, though it had been against the grain of both of them. Once, earlier, when the formal deed of separation was taken to her for her signature, she was found seated on her husband's knee, feeding him with delicate slices of bread and butter. She had gone to live with her father-in-law, and her husband continually visited her there. In her last illness she wrote (by her doctor's hand) a long letter ending, "God bless you, my dearest William"; and he sat by her side as she died. She had asked him to come to her in her last moments; for she wrote that "the only noble fellow I ever met with is William Lamb."

The political air was full of reform; and when the Duke of Wellington, with his usual energy, forced through the Catholic Emancipation Act in 1829, the noisy sort of people, who hate anything new — however good or harmless — made the position impossible for a Tory government that had dared to reform; and the Whigs in 1830 got back into office, which they had not held for twenty years. Lord Grey was the Prime Minister and Lord Melbourne was Home Secretary, his first great office.

It was a rigorous test for the man; for the country was bubbling over with disorder of all kinds; and it was the peculiar duty of the head of the Home Office to maintain the peace. Melbourne's only other official work had been in Dublin; and it was thought that he was incapable of taking his departmental work very seriously. Greville, writing November 21, 1830, reports: "The state of the country is dreadful; every post brings fresh accounts of conflagrations, destruction of machinery, associations of labourers, and compulsory rise of wages." The day before Greville had declared that Melbourne would be useless at the Home Office because he was "too idle." On December 12 he wrote: "The only one [of the Ministers] who has had anything to do is Melbourne, and he has surprised all those about him by a sudden display of activity and vigour, rapid and intelligent transaction of business, for which nobody was prepared, and which will prove a great mortification to Peel and his friends."

England was in a condition of social fermentation. The position after the Napoleonic Wars was extraordinarily like the social and economic position after the Great War of 1914–

LORD MELBOURNE
From a portrait by Sir George Hayter

1918. Page after page of the two histories, separated by almost exactly a hundred years, might be read indifferently of one or the other. There was the same problem of a swollen currency; the same problem of unemployment; the same colossal war debt; the same ignorance of the ruling classes, unable to find the right remedies for the scores of evils, or perhaps the same indifference and the same determination to cling to their own wealth at all costs. The whole picture belongs to the general history of the times; and now it is only necessary to insist on the fact that a false move, a little want of tact, some petty indiscretion on Melbourne's part, and the social structure might have been badly torn. There had been a terrible tearing in France within living memory; and in 1830 there had been a political outburst in Paris which, for all the outlookers could judge, might again end in massacres.

It was this most delicate condition of society that the cynical and lazy Melbourne — so rumour described him — had to handle; with no experience of public administration except his short time in Ireland, when his chief official duty had been to do nothing. At the Home Office he made a success that was little short of miraculous. It was a triumph for honest common sense, when the most experienced official might have come to disaster because he knew too much about administration and not enough about men. Any success that Melbourne had in politics or administration was in spite of the fact that he knew very little and cared less about either. He applied to both sets of problems the simple rules that would naturally suggest themselves to the mind of a graduate in the world of common, simple men.

To-day a Home Secretary is in a very different and less difficult position. When the Government of a few years ago was faced by the General Strike, it had a large, specially trained police force behind it, to carry out its orders; and, if necessary — as a last resource — there was, still farther in the background, a large disciplined army. Melbourne had only a fraction of these forces behind him. Peel had certainly just founded the Metropolitan Police force, but it was in its childhood and untried; it could not even stop the mob from breaking windows. The King, William IV, as recently as November, 1830, had been invited, with his Ministers, to be the guest of the Lord Mayor in the City of London. Every kind of protective force had been suggested to guard them: in Greville's words: "All the troops that could be mustered were prepared, together with thousands of special constables, new police, volunteers, sailors and marines." But the Duke of Wellington said he did not want to be massacred and refused to go! It is not hard to value the power of the law, if its best was no safer than that. All this was in London. The rest of the country was far less protected.

Melbourne relied, in the main, on tact and justice — even if it were of the somewhat limited kind that could alone get into the brain of a governor of the early nineteenth century. He quickly decided on the general lines of his policy. On January 11, 1831, he explained to Lord Derby, who was worrying about the safety of his district: "The two remedies of which the resolutions of the magistrate demand the application are new laws and a large military force" — which are always the first demands of the governing class when it has not enough skill to meet an emergency. Melbourne goes on to explain that "many of the evils arise not so much from the inadequacy of the law as from the difficulty of enforcing it; and as for the second, you must be aware that it can only be employed for a time, that it can produce but a partial and uncertain tranquillity, and that after all it is a most unsatisfactory way of maintaining order and preserving the public peace." Then he goes on to give the local terror-stricken gentlemen a nasty rap over the knuckles: "Surely it is a disgrace that the great county of Lancashire, with its opulent, populous, and commercial cities, with its numerous nobility and gentry, with its respectable and enlightened inhabitants of every description, agricultural, manufacturing and mercantile, should be unable to enforce the law within its own limits. . . . What is the cause of this state of things? Is the magistracy defective?"

As to the need for new legislation to meet the emergency, there is an amusing reply of Melbourne to a letter from the King, begging his Home Secretary to devise some drastic law against labourers' unions. Melbourne called his Majesty's attention to the fact that governments had been making laws of that kind since the time of Edward I; and only recently these had all been repealed and replaced by a revised act: "Since the passing of this Act the evil has undoubtedly shown itself more manifestly and increased, but whether entirely in consequence of the passing of the Act it appears to Viscount Melbourne to be impossible to presume with confidence." It is not often that a Minister has the pluck or wisdom to tell his sovereign that his laws and regulations are a very clumsy and ineffectual method of social reform.

He gave evidence of his freedom from class prejudice in the matter of these riots; for he asked: "Are these disturbances and attacks upon machinery encouraged by some of the masters whose interest it is that improved machinery which is being erected, to the prejudice, of course, of their inferior factories, should be destroyed? All these causes have been suggested to me, and I should be anxious to profit by your lordship's superior information." The Duke of Northumberland got some more straight opinions for his district: "I learn that there is a great want of system and concert among the magistrates, and it is reported to me, I know not with what truth, that some who are in the commission for the county of Durham have acted with great indiscretion and irresolution, and in such a manner as rather to foment and encourage than to repress and terminate tumult and disorder."

Not that Melbourne was afraid to hit. When the labourers of Hampshire were marching about, destroying farms and their machinery and demanding money, then he asked the War Office to send troops; and ordered the judges to hold special courts that convicted a thousand prisoners. But when the Sussex authorities could not put their hands on the rioters who were burning so many hayricks, Melbourne refused to allow any improper traps to be set to catch them; and when a magistrate suggested using a spy as an *agent provocateur* he got a reply that must have made his conscience blush. For Melbourne told him that:

> The danger of employing spies and accomplices has always been found to be that, in order to further their own interests they are too apt, first to bring forward false accusations; secondly, to excite and encourage to the commission of crimes, in order that they may have the honour of informing against and detecting them; and I beg leave to recall to your recollection the transactions of the year 1817, when there is too much reason to suspect that the rising in Derbyshire, which cost the lives of three men on the scaffold and the transportation of many more, was stimulated, if not produced, by the artifices of Oliver, a spy employed by the Government of that day. . . . I am sure you must feel that in our anxiety to discover the perpetrators of these most dangerous and atrocious acts we should run as little risk as possible of involving innocent persons in accusations, and still less of adopting measures which may encourage the seduction of persons, now innocent, into the commission of crime.

The Home Secretary who could write such a letter at such a period of danger and panic was a memorable figure in the history of his time. When it was proposed that something should be done to break up the labour unions, Melbourne merely replied that he and his colleagues had considered whether "these unions, their meetings, their communications, or their pecuniary funds, could be reached, or in any way prevented, by any new legal provisions; but it appeared upon the whole impossible to do anything effectual, unless we proposed such measures as would have been a serious infringement upon the constitutional liberties of the country, and to which it would have been impossible to have obtained the consent of Parliament." For Parliament had not yet been "reformed", and would not yet do what the Government whip commanded.

Soon afterwards, he protested against the newspaper cry for a general arming of the people, as a national guard. Melbourne again kept his head: "There does not appear to me to be so great a degree of danger as to justify the training to arms of all those who may be desirous of preventing tumult and protecting property," for, he went on, "arms, placed in untrained hands, only produce accidental, unintended, and unnecessary bloodshed."

In answer to a question from the Duke of Wellington, whether a local union of labourers was legal, Melbourne replied that "I am not aware of any law which renders their existence illegal whilst they continue separate and independent," and even if they acted with other similar bodies, and so made themselves an illegal body, yet the justices should not prosecute "except in a very clear case and upon very sufficient and unquestionable evidence." He then made a sly dig at the Duke by adding: "The concessions which were made to violence in the year 1830 [when Wellington was Prime Minister] have, I fear, had a permanently bad effect upon the character of the agricultural population." Lord Melbourne taunting the Duke with democratic weakness is a comedy of history which could be examined with interesting results. It is probable that Wellington and Melbourne were the most democratic statesmen of their period; though that is not the opinion of most historians — who have disregarded the facts. In 1834 Melbourne was asked to give his opinion on the actions of the farmers in refusing to engage union men. His reply was remarkable for a Home Secretary. He naturally had not arrived at the convictions of most modern statesmen, that trades' unions are a necessary part of the social machinery; so he said he was glad that the masters would not engage union men; but he was strongly against any coercion by the magistrates in this action; the farmers must do it on their own responsibility. Then he made a very important proviso:

> The farmers should receive every encouragement and support in such proceedings, always taking it for granted that they have themselves acted justly, and have not generally attempted to reduce the wages of the labourers below their fair and natural level. . . . I omitted in my former letter to state that a union for legal purposes being itself legal, it appeared to me doubtful whether a labourer who was thrown out of employment by being discharged by his master for belonging to a union could be refused parish relief.

It would be an interesting problem to discover what would have happened if Lord Melbourne had been Home Secretary after the Great War of 1914–1918, instead of after the Napoleonic Wars.

In the events of this period as Home Secretary we can get as near the real Melbourne as in any part of his public career; and it is not the least important fact to remember that all the while he was administering the details of his office with such worldly and philosophical wisdom, his leisure was still devoted to the classics and theology and to a new-found enthusiasm for Elizabethan drama. The frivolities of Melbourne House had produced a successful if unexpected result.

During his time at the Home Office, great events (so-called) had been happening in Great Britain. The Reform Bill of 1832 had become law. But Melbourne had no enthusiasm for it; he admitted, when he spoke for his Government in the House of Lords in its support, that hitherto he had resisted a "reform" of the House of Commons, and he only gave way now because he saw it was impossible to resist any longer; and he added that since they were going to reform, let it be done thoroughly. There was nothing very reactionary about all this; for Melbourne was not such a hypocrite or a fool as to believe that giving votes to a few hundred thousand well-to-do middle-class people was going to "save the world for democracy."

Therefore, as far as the great Reform Bill is concerned, we may regard the matter as a merely unimportant episode in Melbourne's life; except that as Home Secretary it fell to his lot to keep order in a country which threatened to turn the issue into a civil war. Melbourne, who had a deeper wisdom, probably wondered why people could behave so foolishly. But he had to meditate how badly he was behaving himself; for Greville had a long talk with Lady Cowper, Melbourne's sister, and reported: "Between Palmerston, Frederick Lamb, and Melbourne she knows everything and is a furious anti-Reformer. . . . Palmerston and Melbourne, particularly the latter, are now heartily ashamed of the part they have taken about Reform. They detest and abhor the whole thing. . . . I told Lady Cowper that nothing could justify their conduct, and their excuses were good for nothing." Of course "ashamed" was not the right word for the case; for the serious-minded Greville, who always took his opinions very piously, could not appreciate the subtlety of a cynic's mind: Melbourne did not really think the Bill was so fundamentally important; and even if it were, it could not be resisted without bringing worse disasters than its passing would cause. Indeed, when it came to the final struggle with its opponents, Melbourne showed the greatest determination and courage, and refused to accept any compromise. It is probable that he realised, with the instinctive judgment of a man of culture, that he had no right selfishly to defend the privileges of his own wealthy class, so shame was not the condition of his soul. But the Reform Bill was not an affair that produced heroes of great quality in any party.

When Melbourne took office as Prime Minister in July, 1834, on the retirement of Lord Grey, who had (so reluctantly) put the Reform Act of 1832 on the statute book, he undoubtedly found himself in an embarrassing position as the leader of a political party that was supposed to be clamouring for "reform" of all other sorts as well. Greville's comment is instructive: "Everybody wonders how Melbourne will do it. He is certainly a queer fellow to be Prime Minister, and he and Brougham are two wild chaps to have the destiny of this country in their hands. I should not be surprised if Melbourne was to rouse his dormant energies and be excited by the greatness of his position to display the vigour and decision in which he is not deficient. Unfortunately his reputation is not particularly good; he is considered lax in morals, indifferent in religion, and very loose and pliant in politics." What Melbourne thought about it was concisely summed up in a sentence to his private secretary: "he thought it a damned bore, and that he was in many minds what he should do — be Minister or no."

He decided to be bored. What he did as Prime Minister is not the most vital part of his career. For a Prime Minister is the one man in a country who can rarely do what he thinks right; so his period of power is not often so interesting as the earlier and freer days of departmental office that went before. Except for the few months from December, 1834, to April, 1835, when Sir Robert Peel formed a short-lived ministry, it may be said that Melbourne, in his two administrations, was Premier from July, 1834, until August, 1841. But nothing of a legislative or administrative kind that happened during that time of office is very illuminating on his character. The Municipal Reform Act of 1835 is the most conspicuous measure, but it was in no sense the Prime Minister's child. There was a Marriage Act in 1836, making wedlock more of a civil than a religious act — which must have given the widower of Lady Caroline mixed emotions. More valuable was the reduction of the Stamp Duty on newspapers in 1836, from fourpence to one penny; which certainly allowed the Press to say more, though here again the Premier may have meditated whether quantity was as valuable as quality.

That so little happened during the Melbourne administrations is more typical of their chief than any activities could have been. It may have been mere laziness on his part — as his enemies said — or, more probably, it was his instinctive wisdom that the world could not be made tidy and socially beautiful by Act of Parliament. Anyhow the result was very small. It was a policy of negations, as the politicians measure progress; but it is not at all certain whether any possible activities would have been better for the people than the quiescence. The two great problems of Melbourne's period were the Chartists and the beginning of the Free Trade movement. In 1838 Cobden and Bright founded the Anti-Corn Law League, in the same year that The People's Charter was announced. Melbourne did not give help to either of these demands. But he refused to crush them by force. The Chartists were sitting in London, even appealing to the people to come out on a general strike, and, if necessary, to take up arms. Melbourne announced on behalf of the Government that they did not intend to pass special repressive laws — they were content to rely on the good sense of the nation. Then he did a remarkable thing. He sent for Robert Owen, who was the most dangerous reformer of them all — for his revolution was constructive, and therefore more dangerous and permanent than temporary destructive rioting — and he gave him the honour of a personal presentation to the Queen. The oligarchs of law and property were aghast; but Melbourne cared little about their propriety if his sense of justice was satisfied.

To-day free trade in corn and almost every substantial wish of the Chartists are all accomplished facts, made into laws of the statute book. If Melbourne's ghost could come back to the Parliament where he had once treated all these things with calm indifference, and if he put the brief question: "Well, you have got what you wanted — Has it done you as much good as you hoped?" — would there be any convincing answer that would send the ghost back to its grave in discomforted shame? Would the ghost of the cynic have reason to blush when it passed Mr. John Bright or the Chartist leaders, if those dead men perchance were also taking the air in Westminster Hall? Whereas, if Robert Owen had had his way, England would probably have been a revolutionised land indeed.

But if Lord Melbourne was not wise enough to insist on some deeper reform, which would do more for his nation than the trivialities which aroused the enthusiasm or the hopes of duller minds, he could, and did, teach his countrymen that if their Prime Ministers could not do miracles, they could at least be honest and wise in doing nothing. If he did nothing great, at least he could save other people from being foolish. He could always say something that was full of suggestive common sense — which is a form of wisdom that brilliant statesmen so rarely possess. If he asked for postponement of a settlement, it was in order that reconsideration might bring more wisdom.

For example, when somebody wanted to increase the Navy, he wrote to Russell, November 27, 1838: "It would be better to try if we cannot by negotiation with Russia, make an arrangement respecting her fleet in the Baltic." When somebody else wanted to suppress the trades unions, he replied: "Unions amongst the labourers after what has taken place amongst the manufacturers must be expected . . . but I fear full as much an aggressive and heated mode of dealing with them upon the part of the magistrates and country gentlemen as I do the combinations themselves." When the free traders clamoured for cheap corn he wrote: "I cannot but doubt whether a large labouring population dependent in any considerable degree upon foreign corn, is a safe position." There were moments in the recent Great War when anxious ministers of transport might have said that Melbourne was a prophet and not a reactionary. When the cheap corn orators and plutocrats were persistent, Melbourne added (January 20, 1839): "I am quite convinced and, as far as I can determine it, determined that the Corn Law should remain open. The present outcry is raised evidently by the master manufacturers taking advantage of the present dearness of corn, and with the object of lowering wages." Modern historians may imagine that Melbourne was an old-fashioned Whig landlord; but it is necessary to remember that the contemporary Chartists held the same democratic opinions as the Prime Minister on this point. When at last, all common sense being unheeded, Melbourne had to begin to give way on the Corn Laws, he did it with his customary contemptuous sarcasm. As the Cabinet, which had decided to modify the duties, was leaving the council chamber, the Prime Minister called after his colleagues: "Stop a bit; is it to lower the price of bread, or is n't it? It does n't much matter which, but we must all say the same thing."

If Melbourne could not shine as the father of legislation in which he had no belief, it was his good fortune to be set a national task which no other statesman — except the Duke of Wellington perhaps — could have accomplished with such polished success. Queen Victoria came to the throne, during Melbourne's premiership, in 1837, at the age of eighteen. She had already a very firm, active mind, but these were both virtues which might have become the worst of vices in a constitutional monarchy. It was the duty and accomplishment of Lord Melbourne to get that determined, self-willed young sovereign on the right road of a very lóng and very successful reign. That the duty was accomplished was because there was very fine human material on both sides.

The task began within a few hours of the young Queen's accession. Her diary put the position in a nutshell: "At 9 came Lord Melbourne, whom I saw in my room, and of *course quite alone*, as I shall *always* do all my Ministers. . . . I like him very much and feel confidence in him. He is a very straightforward, honest, clever and good man." Later in the day, Melbourne came again. "I had a very important and a very *comfortable* conversation with him. Each time I see him I feel more confidence in him; I find him very kind in his manner too."

So the royal tutor began his scholastic duties. During the remaining four years of his office as Premier, Melbourne was to make the relationship between himself and his royal pupil into a constitutional duty which had many of the more subtle elements of the grand romances. The position was not without delicacy. The tutor had the reputation of a man of the world who was suspected of many intimate women friends, and almost no morals to sustain him in the wildernesses of his temptations. In 1829 a peer had doubted the virtue of his wife, when she had met the fascinating Secretary (as Melbourne then was) in Dublin. Two courts of law held that there was no sufficient evidence against Melbourne; but since he had become Prime Minister Mr. Norton had charged him with impropriety with the most charming Mrs. Norton. Again he had been acquitted in a court of law; and his chief political opponent, the Duke of Wellington, being a gentleman of honour (and of many love affairs also), refused to allow Melbourne to resign, as he offered.

Now, in spite of legal verdicts in his favour, such is not a record of character which might seem the best evidence that Melbourne was the right man to be the resident tutor of an inexperienced royal maiden. It was, in fact, a character which made him one of the most commendable guardians in history. It is one more piece of evidence that Melbourne's practical character was always in conflict with theory. The lazy man had proved himself a hard worker; the man trained in frivolity had shown himself full of wisdom; and now the man without a moral code that would be recognised by any ethical society with a reputation to maintain, was to prove himself a sound guide for inexperienced feminine youth.

The story of Melbourne's tutorial classes in social and constitutional deportment for royal young ladies must be read in the many memoirs of the time. It began at the first state function, where Greville says: "She went through the whole ceremony, occasionally looking at Melbourne for instructions." The first fact which the most casual thinker must have noted was that this education of a youthful sovereign was in the hands of the leader of a political party, who might have taken most unscrupulous advantage of his position. Instead of teaching the young Victoria to be a constitutional Queen, who would regard all parties with rigid impartiality — according to the somewhat ridiculous and unsatisfactory theory that had held the constitutional field since the fall of James II — Melbourne might have taught his young mistress to be a Whig. However, he did nothing of the sort. His political opponents, such as Wellington and Peel, regarded him as an entirely honest man, in whose hands the honour of the British constitution was perfectly safe. By universal consent of everybody whose opinion was worth considering, Melbourne did not favour his own party in his education of the Queen.

Now, to be entirely frank, this was in his case not such an

astounding virtue as it seemed. Any one who has considered his career with any attention must see that he did not teach his pupil any special political party faith — because he had no particular party faith himself. Melbourne was such a success as a royal tutor because he was neither a Whig nor a Tory, nor a Radical nor indeed anything in any definable political sense. He was, instead, one of the best bred, most intelligent, most impartial, most complete gentlemanly cynics who ever succeeded in persuading Englishmen to make him their ruler — since Charles II returned to his throne after the fall of the Commonwealth. And he had a high sense of personal and national honour, which had been knocked out of Charles during his hard days of exile on the Continent. Melbourne, the man who could never quite make up his mind what was right and what was wrong in political affairs, or whether anything mattered at all, found himself at the end of his career with the ideal post at last — the training of a constitutional monarch, whose official duty it was to accept any policy that was proposed by her Ministers. That Melbourne had a pupil who had too much intelligence to accept any such ridiculous theory with a submissive obedience was not Melbourne's fault. It was indeed his added happiness.

What Lord Melbourne made of his pupil we shall see later when considering her own career. For the moment we are concerned with Melbourne's side of the matter. The arrival of the young Queen Victoria was a sudden break in his life. A lounging man of fashion by early habits and by inclination, in 1837 he was fifty-eight years old, when life would naturally be beginning to lose some of its illusions. The time was rapidly coming when cynicism would be no longer a rather charming, half laughed-at philosophy, but a terrible conviction.

Like a flash, all this was changed. Melbourne found himself the constant, privileged companion of the first lady of the land, who was also a very delightful young woman, frankly admitting by her every action that she liked him as much as a friend as she respected him as a constitutional adviser. Melbourne became an alert creature again. That shrewd, honest observer, Greville — that artist in words — has drawn a very beautiful picture, from the life, of the scene at Court as it passed before his eyes; a picture which has all the stiff formality of the fashionable portraits of its period, yet with a sense of composition that gives restful pleasure to the mind:

> Victoria was transferred at once from the nursery to the throne. . . . She found in her Prime Minister and constitutional adviser a man of mature age, who instantly captivated her feelings and her fancy . . . by a shrewd, sagacious, and entertaining conversation, which was equally new and delightful to her . . . their relations assumed a peculiar character, and were marked by an intimacy which he never abused. . . . His loyal devotion soon warmed into a paternal affection, which she repaid by unbounded manifestations of confidence and regard.

Never was the code of honour more rigidly maintained than by Melbourne when he taught the young Queen the rules of the life which she had before her. As Greville goes on:

> In all that Melbourne said or did, he appears to have been guided by a regard to justice and truth. He never scrupled to tell her what none other would have dared to say; and in the midst of that atmosphere of flattery and deceit which kings and queens are almost always destined to breathe, and by which their minds are so often perverted, he never scrupled to declare boldly and frankly his real opinions . . . and to wage war with her prejudices. . . .

The little Queen sat in her room all the earlier part of the morning, endeavouring to understand, from the despatches placed before her, what was happening all over the vast Empire which it was her hard fate to have inherited. Between eleven and twelve Melbourne would come to add his maturity to her ignorance. In the afternoon a two-hours' ride — generally a gallop — with Melbourne always at her left hand. In the evening, Melbourne still at her left hand at the dinner table; and then the card table until after eleven, "Melbourne invariably sitting on the left hand of the Queen and remaining there without moving till the evening is at an end." It is a picture not without its comedy, and perhaps its tragedy also. For this stately gentleman who had hitherto lived "indolently sprawling in all the attitudes of luxurious ease" was now eternally "sitting bolt upright; his free and easy language interlarded with 'damns' is carefully guarded." But the hardest of the new trials of this royal tutor was that he had "exchanged the good talk of Holland House for the trivial, laboured and wearisome inanities of the Royal circle."

Such was the daily round for months on end; indeed for four years, until the end of his ministry. If there was boredom, it was in the more public part of the royal scene; for his young pupil could never have been dull. She was an adequate reward for his tedium; and he had the satisfaction of success. He came out of this delicate ordeal with complete distinction. As Greville wrote after watching the stately ceremony of this daily ritual: "His manner to her is perfect, always respectful, and never presuming upon the extraordinary distinction he enjoys; hers to him as simple and natural, indicative of the confidence she reposes in him, and of her lively taste for his society, but not marked by any unbecoming familiarity."

Only once during this time of peculiar opportunity did Melbourne play his party's game; and then there was an excuse that no human being could have resisted. His Government had been so nearly beaten on the Jamaica Bill that Melbourne and his colleagues resigned office. There is much more than constitutional information in the answer of his young Mistress to his letter of resignation:

The Second Viscount Melbourne 149

The Queen thinks Lord Melbourne may probably wish to know how she is this morning; the Queen is somewhat calmer . . . she tried to occupy herself and try to think less gloomily of this dreadful change . . . but on waking this morning all — all that has happened in one short, eventful day came most forcibly to her mind . . . she could n't touch a morsel of food last night, nor can she this morning. The Queen trusts Lord Melbourne slept well, and is well this morning.

However, the resignation held, and Sir Robert Peel was asked to form a ministry. Following the usual custom, he naturally asked to be allowed to appoint the chief ladies of the Queen's household, so that they should be of his own Tory Party; but the Queen stubbornly refused to part with her Whig attendants. Peel said he would not be Prime Minister on any other terms, so Melbourne came back; while the Queen wrote to her uncle, the King of the Belgians, telling him of her terrible ordeal at the bare thought of losing "that truly inestimable and excellent man, Lord Melbourne . . . whose character seems to me still more perfect and noble since I have gone through all this."

No official, or even private records, will probably ever reveal precisely just what were the terms of friendship between Melbourne and his royal pupil in this unexpected alliance between the Crown and the premiership. It was too gorgeously mounted, after the manner of a stately dance of the most formal periods of ceremonial dignity. Yet there was in the background of the courtly and official pageantry a very warm human touch which it would be affectation to ignore. When faced by the fact that her half-betrothed lover was coming to England in October of 1839 to make the engagement complete, the young Queen suddenly began to hesitate and declare that her mind was not as sure as she had once thought. She wrote to her uncle in Belgium saying that even if she consented to the engagement, the marriage could not take place for two or three years; and a few days later she was writing to her dear tutor after a dance: "The Queen anxiously hopes Lord Melbourne has slept well. . . . It was very wrong of him not to wish the Queen good-night . . . for she *saw* he did *not* go away immediately after supper. When did he get home? It was great pleasure to the Queen that he came last night." It was a letter which might have made the elderly heart of the well-seasoned Melbourne meditate on its past history.

While its entirely impartial chief was instructing his Queen in her constitutional duties, the Whig Ministry was dragging along in its somewhat undistinguished career. As already noted, it was not a very important part of Melbourne's life; he and his colleagues were not making a great stir in history. Which was so entirely typical of him, for if Lord Melbourne had had his way, the nation would have found its own salvation without much assistance from him — except some witty cynicism to brighten its task. As he told his royal pupil he liked peace and stability. But the essence of politics is continual agitation, even if it is usually much ado about nothing. So, in the course of nature, the Melbourne Ministry came to an end in 1841, and was succeeded by the Peel Government which was to do great deeds — or, at least, make much commotion in the land.

William Lamb's career was over, for all biographical purposes. He lived until 1848, but it was as a failing man. When he had to leave his Queen, she had written him a parting letter to tell him: "She was dreadfully affected for some time after, but is calm now." Then she forgot the formality of royal letters to her Ministers and went on in common prose: "we [for she had a husband now] do, and shall, miss you so dreadfully," just as if the address had been a villa, instead of Windsor Castle. But she ended: "Happier and brighter times will come again."

But they did not come for Melbourne. He went back to try to take up his life at Holland House, where he could

The Second Viscount Melbourne 151

sprawl once more and flow on with his charming conversation, which was so well informed about everything in the world. The Queen never forgot him and there was correspondence which the strict constitutionalist thought was incorrect with an ex-premier. But Melbourne never gave partisan advice that damaged his opponents. Besides, he was too ill in health to have ambitions now in his old age, which was not strange, seeing that he had never seemed to have them in his youth. Melbourne was a man who loved to look on the world, rather than mix with it. All he had to offer, as payment for his board and lodging on this earth, was the honest advice of a very wise man, whom wisdom had made a cynic.

When he died Greville wrote in his diary an obituary notice which has rarely been surpassed for literary draftsmanship of such sombre things; and still more rarely has the truth been so honestly told. It would almost prove that the only wise man is the cynic, and the only moral man is one who has no principles. At least, this is the verdict of the man who was more likely to have heard all sides of the question than any other of Melbourne's contemporaries. This is what Greville wrote:

> He never was really well-fitted for political life, for he had a great deal too much candour, and was too fastidious to be a good party man. . . . He held office with a profound sense of its responsibilities; there never was a Minister more conscientious in the distribution of patronage. . . . He was perfectly disinterested, without nepotism and without vanity; he sought no enrichments for his connections and steadily declined all honours for himself . . . alone undecorated amidst the stars and ribands which glittered around him. . . . His distinctive qualities were strong sound sense and an innate taste for what was great and good.

There were many spots on this figure, as Greville carefully tells; but the final summing up is this: "Taking him altogether, he was a very remarkable man." It would seem an ideal character for the leader of a nation. Only, unfortunately, the very wise and honest and disinterested man has so little chance of a career in political circles. Melbourne's virtues were the qualities that bring a Prime Minister to sterile disaster. He had tried the great gamble of governing and could not pretend that he had found a way of salvation for men. He was once asked to consider some amendments to the Poor Law Bill; and referred the applicant to another official. "I have been with him," was the reply, "but he damned me, and damned the Bill, and damned the paupers." And the disillusioned Melbourne answered, "Well, damn it, what more could he do?" It was a question which the best of rulers have never succeeded in answering with much success — and Melbourne was too honest to take refuge in rhetoric. So he became a cynic. It may be a cowardly retreat; but it has the elements of the picturesque — and is more instructive than the enthusiasms of smaller minds.

SIR ROBERT PEEL
1788–1850

SIR ROBERT PEEL

1788-1850

It has already appeared that English history, wearied with the restless, noisy Mr. Canning, turned for relief to Lord Melbourne, who was in every fragment of his character different from his predecessor. Now once more, in its endless (and ever disappointed) search for perfection in its leaders, Englishmen tried a Prime Minister who was as unlike Melbourne as a November fog is unlike a delicious April day. Every one admitted that Melbourne was a person of charm, however inefficient and unsuccessful as a political leader. No one of taste ever said that Peel had charm of any kind known to the world of art; but most people (especially the dull ones) said that he was one of the most efficient and successful Prime Ministers who ever led the Houses of Parliament. Certainly in every term of art, psychology and political science he was as far from his predecessor as the North Pole is from the South.

It is a noteworthy fact that the men who have led England at the varied periods of its history have usually been, in a very personal way, completely representative of their times. Sir Robert Peel was the leader of Britain near the prime of its success as the greatest industrial power in the world. The manufacturers had turned their island from a land where farmers were the chief factors of wealth and influence into a nation where factories and their machines and their profits were the most dominant power. It was the England which the Industrial Revolution had built on the ruins of the old England of Walpole's day; and the Peels were the most representative family of the new industrial class.

They were, as early as they can be traced, a yeomanry family of Yorkshire; though it is quite possible that (as the name, meaning a baronial stronghold, denotes) they may have once been of higher social rank. But, as discovered records know them, they were Yorkshire farmers who moved to Lancashire in the early part of the seventeenth century. Within fifty years they were successful manufacturers of woolen cloth; though they appear to have remained substantial yeoman farmers as well. They were, in short, one of the families that made Lancashire the most typical county of factory England; as the southern and western counties might be called the typical parts of the older feudal and craft and agricultural England.

For the present purposes it is not necessary to go farther back than the Robert Peel who was both farmer and weaver about the middle years of the eighteenth century. He married, in 1744, Elizabeth Haworth, whose family was of considerable age and rank, in a modest way, and his brother-in-law Jonathan Haworth, who had learned the trade of printing on calico, took him into partnership. They were among the first in the field; and were also pioneers in the use of machinery driven by water power. The workers were thereby thrown out of employment; and naturally saw no advantages in machines which made fortunes for their masters and brought starvation to themselves. So there were desperate riots and smashing of machinery; and the Haworth and Peel firm fled to Burton on Trent, where workers were more docile. The removed business prospered more than ever, and the Peel of that generation left £13,000 each to eight children. He was the statesman's grandfather, and in many ways very like him; simple, hard-working, honest according to the standard of the Industrial Revolution — when men made money without considering the welfare of any one except themselves — and he had a touch of melancholy reflectiveness which gave him the nickname of "the

Philosopher." He was also handsome, tall and strong, all typical qualities of his stable yeoman stock. He was so full of simplicity and moral earnestness in his trade that he often told his friends that "the gains to the individual were small compared with the national gains arising from the trade." It was characteristic of the Peels that they were always convinced that their own success was for the good of their nation.

His third son, another Robert, was very like him in every way, and his most successful descendant. He also went into the cotton trade; and the family fortune grew enormously. He was almost the type specimen of his period in the economic history of England; a museum specimen, as it were, of the men who made England so rich — and so ugly. They covered corn fields with factory towns and coal smoke. His cousin, Sir Lawrence Peel, wrote: "He would rise at night from his bed, when there was a likelihood of bad weather, to visit the bleaching grounds, and one night in each week he used to sit up all night, attended by his pattern drawer, to receive any new patterns which the London coach, arriving at night, might bring down." He made so much money by his hard work and his intelligence that he became one of the wealthiest men in England. His mind was too active to be satisfied with his cotton mills; and he was ambitious to take a hand in national affairs as well. He was the biggest figure the robust Peel family ever produced — bigger than his more famous, more showy son; for people who make speeches usually get more attention than those who do deeds. He was successful in everything he touched; he was an amazing unity of great energy and fertile ideas. The mental fertility was sometimes of a limited and personal kind. For example, in 1780 he wrote an essay to prove that the national debt was a national blessing in disguise; whereas, of course, it was only the rich men, who could invest their money in it, who received the blessing — of a safe investment. The long war with France was another "national blessing", which gave the English manufacturers a monopoly of the new industrial developments — while continental Europe was devastated by marching armies. For this great blessing of war the Peel firm offered £10,000 as a voluntary thank offering to the national exchequer.

In 1790 he became member of Parliament for Tamworth, where his new cotton mills had made that town practically his personal property; and the estate of Drayton Manor, outside it, had raised him to the dignity of the great landlords. To represent it in Parliament was, according to the ideas of the period, almost his right. He had married a charming and wholesome wife, Elizabeth Yates, the daughter of his partner; and she was of a beauty and character suitable for her husband's risen fortunes. Their eldest son, Robert the statesman, was born in 1788. There are more or less authentic tales of his birth; that his father fell on his knees with a vow that he had dedicated his son to the service of his country; and, again, that at baptism there was the more modest wish that this infant would "tred in the footsteps of the immortal Pitt." William Pitt was the father's ideal of all that was sound in statesmanship; and thereby the shrewd manufacturer showed his sense; for if Pitt had any policy at all, it was to increase the riches of the new manufacturing classes. His admirer's convictions were probably confirmed when after ten years of consistent support of the Minister in the House of Commons, the elder Peel was made a baronet in 1800.

It was a dignity he could now well afford to maintain with full honours; for his business affairs were exceedingly prosperous. One of his greatest strokes of genius was the introduction of infant labour into the cotton factories. He brought pauper children down from London, and drilled them into the meritorious habits of making him a fortune. At some of his mills the children were kept at night work for a year without a break; and the hours of labour were sometimes fifteen a day. Peel was full of moral indignation at the suggestion to raise the price of food — which would have made these useful children more expensive to feed. He was also filled with a desire for economic liberty, and opposed any attempt to control the hours of his adult workers. He was, in short, one of the most complete specimens of the energetic, self-reliant, half-witted Englishmen who made their nation — or rather themselves — the wealthiest country in the world.

As his social position grew to great importance, the scandal of overworked children in his mills could not be allowed to continue without an effort at reform. In the words of Mr. and Mrs. J. L. Hammonds' "The Town Labourer": "His mills had been notorious for their scandals, and in 1784, and again in 1796, the magistrates had made complaints." So he persuaded Parliament to pass the Health and Morals of Apprentices' Act, 1802. A happier title would have been the "Morals of Masters"; but in any case nobody took much notice of the Act in the way of enforcing it, so the Peel fortunes were not badly damaged.

The first Sir Robert Peel took the first step in the Industrial Revolution. He and his kind practically bought up England. They dislodged the older landowning classes, so dominant during the eighteenth century, and made themselves the chief economic factor of the new England of the nineteenth. But he was farseeing enough to prepare for the next step; which was inevitable if the new men were to survive as a permanent institution.

He arranged that his son, the young Robert, should become governor of England in a political sense, as his father before him had been the master of it in the economic sphere. The elder Sir Robert Peel had ruled his cotton mills; it was to be his son's work in the world to rule the whole country from Westminster. So from his earliest days the boy was appren-

ticed to the trade of politics. In the more stately language
of his sentimental father, he was dedicated to his country.
As the business of governing was a privileged trade, and could
not be successfully accomplished by merit alone, the father
allowed his son £12,000 a year; and when he died left him
over £40,000 a year in lands and stocks and shares. Beyond
this, he was able to give his five younger sons £250,000
each and his three daughters £60,000 each. So instead of
dedicating his son to his country, it might be almost said
that he bought it for him. In those simpler days the Peel
fortunes were considered very large indeed; and the elder
Sir Robert was said to be the seventh wealthiest man in
England.

Now, it must not be imagined that there was any very con-
scious plot in this ambition of the Peels to rule their nation.
They were not of the sort that had imagination to see far
ahead. They were shrewd enough in judging the next step.
A popular pattern for their cottons, a useful machine, came
well within their vision; but the further future needed a
wider culture and a broader mind than any of them possessed.
Even Harrow and Christ Church, Oxford, could not give Sir
Robert Peel, the coming Prime Minister, an imagination.
So when his father determined to train him up as a professional politician instead of a cotton manufacturer, the
wealthy cotton lord had probably no far-reaching designs
of building up a governing family. It was in the main a
very laudable desire to make his son of public service.

But it is impossible to ignore the half-conscious, half-
instinctive knowledge that the Peel business and also the
businesses of their fellow traders would prosper the better
if their owners kept a firm grip on the national government.
The elder Peel was not an orator or even a ready speaker;
and though he was one of the chief advisers of Pitt on all
matters of commerce and industry, his control over the
legislature was rather remote. It would obviously be far

better if a Peel could be Prime Minister himself. Whatever his motives, it is a definite fact that the elder Peel set out from the very beginning to train his eldest son to be as near a successor of Pitt as that son's ability (and fate) would allow.

The Peels could always convince themselves of their high moral purpose; and the first Sir Robert may have really believed that he was giving his child to his country. But, nevertheless, it is perfectly permissible (and even scientifically necessary) to look at the transaction from the other side, and wonder whether he might not be giving his country to his child. There are two sides to most questions, and the problem whether politicians make sacrifices for their country, or whether the people make sacrifices for their statesmen, has never yet been precisely decided.

We have it on the authority of Sir Lawrence Peel that "as the child grew his father set to work seriously on the manufacture of another Pitt." This was a more difficult task than the manufacture of cotton goods; and somewhat beyond the capacity of the enthusiastic parent. One rather primitive method was to make the child repeat both sermons every Sunday evening. He had in the future a marvellous memory for speeches heard in the House of Commons, so the discipline may have done its work successfully. Since he was always very pompous in his oratory, it is possible that the early sermon may have been responsible for that also. At Harrow he had an industrious, even pious career. Lord Byron, his school fellow, has given us a summary of it: "As a scholar he was greatly my superior; as a declaimer and actor I was reckoned at least his equal. As a school-boy out of school, I was always in scrapes, and he never; in school he always knew his lessons and I rarely; but when I knew it I knew it nearly as well. In general information, history, etc., I think I was his superior." The general impression is that a man of genius has thus recorded the ways of a studious boy of a very uninspired type.

At Oxford, it was much the same. Young Peel did everything that serious study and good brains could accomplish. He almost did more; for he took very brilliant firsts in both classics and mathematics. This was in 1808, the year after classics and mathematics had been made into separate subjects for a degree. In mathematics Peel stood alone in the first class; in classics he had four companions. Except Peel, they were all failures in life; unless the bishopric of Chichester be considered success for one of them.

So far Peel had done well. He had absorbed all the conventional education which had usually been the endowment of the governing class during the last hundred years in his country. He had even learned to shoot and to hunt the fox, almost as indispensable as the classics. Such as Canning and Melbourne and some others had been able almost to omit sport — but then they had something of genius, of which Peel gave no sign. Within a few months of leaving Oxford, Peel was of age; and he at once entered Parliament as the member for the Irish city of Cashel, where he had the honour of representing twelve electors. His father had bought him this seat, so there was no question of political ability on the part of the candidate. Everything was proceeding with polished perfection in his career; and to complete his orthodoxy, he became a student of the Bar by joining Lincoln's Inn.

His father was delighted. He clearly began to hope that everything was working out according to plan; for he wrote (November 13, 1809) to his son: "You have hitherto afforded me unspeakable pleasure in the manner you have conducted yourself, and I have no fears for the future." He was quite right in his optimism. The son of such a wealthy man could not be long ignored in political circles. For the two months of the first session he was modestly silent; but in 1810 he was given the honour — usual for the son of a wealthy man whose money might assist the party — of seconding the formal address to the Crown. We have seen that Lamb, another rich son, had a similar political favour bestowed on him. Peel said he wrote down every word of his speech before he started; and it was a great success in a prim and proper way. His father wept with joy in the gallery, and wrote that the performance was "judged to be, by men the best qualified to form a correct opinion of public speaking, the best first speech since that of Mr. Pitt . . . he was about forty minutes on his legs without being in the least embarrassed." There is one other sentence in his father's letter: "he said nothing that could give offence." No single sentence could better express this characteristic — almost the chief characteristic — of Peel's method. He got his way by conciliating, not by hitting his opponents. Indeed, as we shall see, in all the important events of his life, he won by adopting his opponents' principles, which he had vowed he would always resist. It was not heroic courage, as it is usually understood; but it made Peel a famous statesman.

His old chief at Oxford, Dean Cyril Jackson, of Christ Church, wrote to the young politician a letter of congratulation and advice; he said if Peel would only go on reading Homer diligently, and even learn him by heart, then all would be well, for he (Homer) "alone of mortal men thoroughly understood the human mind." The Dean had been training a large part of the great English statesmen for a generation; and his letter may explain why the governing classes of this time were such a singularly incapable lot.

Peel's first important speech was a few months later, March 30, when he defended the Government for the utter failure — even colossal scandal — of the attack on Walcheren. This speech also was a success; and Dean Jackson wrote with enthusiastic pride: "You surpassed yourself. . . . I suppose therefore you have been reading Homer." Peel had done the correct thing for a young politician: he had defended the Government when it had committed an appalling blunder, leading to terrible loss of life. He got the reward of his discreet servility; and was made Under Secretary for War and the Colonies. Peel had plenty of money supplied by his delighted father; he lived in a fine house next Lord Liverpool, and gave many dinner parties to useful men. Wealth continued to push the Peel family along the road to power. And Homer did his part; for when Peel defended Wellington's policy in the Peninsula he did it in the heroic terms of classical rhetoric that were to remain Peel's method throughout his career. The young orator declared that he cherished "the sanguine expectation that the day would soon arrive, when another transcendent victory would silence the tongue of envy and the cavils of party animosity, when the British commander would be hailed by the unanimous voice of his country, with the sentiment addressed on a memorable occasion to another illustrious character — *'Invidiam gloriâ superâsti.'*" If Wellington had wasted his time in coining such sentences of well-balanced pomposity, it is probable that he would have been driven into the Atlantic. But it is the business of professional politicians, like Peel, to say nothing — and to say it very well.

Percival was assassinated in 1812; and the new Prime Minister, Lord Liverpool, who had been Peel's chief at the War and Colonial Office, made him Chief Secretary for Ireland. The testimonial he sent to the Duke of Richmond on Peel's behalf is of biographical interest:

> He has been under me in the Secretary of State's office for two years, and has acquired all the necessary habits of official business. He has a particularly good temper, and great frankness and openness of manners, which I know are particularly desirable on your side of the water. He acquired great reputation, as you must have heard, as a scholar at Oxford.

So Peel went to Dublin in September, 1812, at the age of twenty-four.

Daniel O'Connell naturally gave the coldest of welcomes to a Chief Secretary who was such a rigid opponent of Catholic Emancipation. "Cold" is, indeed, scarcely the correct adjective for what he wrote of Peel:

A raw youth, squeezed out of the workings of I know not what factory in England, who began his parliamentary career by vindicating the gratuitous destruction of our brave soldiers in the murderous expedition to Walcheren, and was sent over here before he got rid of the foppery of perfumed handkerchiefs and thin shoes . . . a lad ready to vindicate anything — everything!

Peel was Chief Secretary for Ireland for six years, 1812–1818. During his term of office there is scarcely a trace of any attempt to go beyond the dull routine of the English system of government in Ireland, which had been an open sore in the sides of both nations for centuries. There had been feeble intellect or grasping selfishness on the English side and a great deal of pugnacious prejudice and sullen revengefulness on the Irish. Both sides had produced reasonable and honest men who would have been capable of planning a successful remedy for this national hatred; but there were always far more unreasonable and dishonest men who were determined to keep up the scandalous quarrel. It had reached a stubborn refusal to give way on both sides.

Peel was a typical example of the man without genius or imagination who was content to obey the orders given by his superiors, to sit tight and carry out the law as he found it. He was not expected to find new remedies. He had not the mind to think of anything very new. But he was as safe an administrator of the old law as could easily be found; and Lord Liverpool had great faith in him. Soon after his arrival in Ireland, Liverpool pursued him with a letter of reminder that a new Act had been passed, making the buying and selling of parliamentary seats illegal, and asking Peel to be careful not to get involved in such transactions, though he hinted that a good deal could be done behind the Government's back. All that the official life of Peel (sanctioned by his trustees) can say is: "to the usual peculiar transactions in Irish close boroughs officially Peel shut his eyes and stopped his ears." The matter concerned Peel very personally; for his seat at Cashel had been bought for him by his father. This he had to surrender; and as it was not likely that any democratic constituency would elect such a man as Peel of its free choice, he was compelled to find another corrupt borough, and asked his father to make "the arrangements incidental to the elections." So the family wealth again did its duty to this son dedicated to the service of his country. It was unfortunate that his country had to be paid to take him.

In Peel's simple orthodox mind, the Protestant ascendency in Ireland was a great and praiseworthy fact; and the chief object of his administration was to strengthen this English rule by every act in his power. He belonged to the small class that had, as the observant people put it, a stake in the country. The Peel stake was a very large one; and they, more than most, dreaded any upheaval which would overturn the established order. A new political system which would allow a lot of radical agitators like Daniel O'Connell, or worse, to invade the Parliament in London might easily cause havoc in English affairs. There would soon be a Radical majority in the legislature if the Tory seats, paid for (as Peel's seat at Cashel had been) in solid Tory gold, were to be seized by a low-class Catholic democracy when they got their own popular representatives by emancipation. The English anti-Catholics may have been very loud in their Anglican fervour; but a good deal of their passion had a distinctive economic flavour. They may have dreaded Rome for its dogma; but they did not overlook the fact that, for various reasons, Rome might be unsound in economics and politics also. A poverty-stricken

Sir Robert Peel

Catholic electorate might vote unsympathetically against the Peels and their industrial kind.

Daniel O'Connell opposed Peel with a vigorous hatred. He said Peel's smile reminded him of the name plate on a coffin lid. The boisterous Celtic nature was raised to fury at the sight of this prim Anglo-Saxon sitting safely surrounded by all the pomp of law and armed force. He knew his man and goaded him until Peel was forced to send him a challenge to fight a duel. When O'Connell accepted battle, he was arrested; and when it was arranged to fight the duel in France, O'Connell was again arrested on the way. It is not a very bold thing to undertake to fight a duel if you can be sure that your opponent will be arrested before he reaches the field of battle. But whatever the truth of the matter, everybody laughed. Besides, Peel was trying to get a reputation as a statesman, not as a swordsman; and the whole affair was lacking in dignity, especially when in this duelling there was much more talk than bloodshed.

Peel's six years of office in Ireland, continued under three different Lord Lieutenants, was a stubborn resistance to all the fundamental Irish demands. It is generally admitted by his biographers that he was more responsible than most men for the long delay in granting that Catholic emancipation that alone gave any hope of peace between England and Ireland; and which came so late, and so grudgingly, that the Irish canker had been rooted beyond hope of any legislative operation. He was nicknamed "Orange Peel", that is, as one of that most bigoted partisan set that had vowed that there should be no compromise with the Irish people. The Orangemen were the people who meant to rule Ireland as a conquered land and treat its native inhabitants as serfs. And the mild-tempered Peel got the reputation of being their tool.

Of course, there is much to be said on Peel's side. The Irish were most annoying, and it would have needed a government of saints to come to terms with them. Peel seems to have been honestly of the opinion (as he wrote to Croker): "that Papal superstition is the cause of one-half the evils of this country"; and he added that he had "serious doubts whether the half would be alleviated by Catholic emancipation." But a man with a more cynical worldly wisdom — and with less money in danger, as we have suggested — would have allowed the Irish to try their own remedy.

The remedies which Peel applied to Irish discontent were one or two Coercion Acts; and a pious — but not very hard-pressed — attempt to introduce popular education. But his most earnest work was devoted to a strengthening of the police. It was he who established the new Royal Irish Constabulary; just as one of the first things he did, as we shall see, when he got into power at the English Home Office, was to establish the new Metropolitan Police Force in London. Both acts were most typical of the man. He had little constructive ability, few ideas of reform. All he could do was to raise up some reliable force that would suppress the disorder of discontented people. The police forces of Ireland and London were the active expression of his firm determination to save the established classes from the pressure of the disestablished. His substitute for intelligent reform was stronger police.

There was one other great work to which he devoted much energy all through his six years in Ireland, though it was scarcely of a kind to appear in public reports. In order that the case shall not be stated unfairly, it will be best to give it in the precise words of the biography of Peel issued by his own trustee. Mr. Parker there adds a note on the Irish elections of 1818, at the end of Peel's term of office as Chief Secretary. He says that these elections have "left but little trace in letters. Negotiations, doubtless, were conducted more conveniently by words of mouth. Their successful result was due largely to the integrity and singleness of purpose with which for six years past Mr. Peel had used all diligence to apply the patronage at his command as to engage the most political support." In those candid words one can read how the unimaginative, uninspired Peel continued to govern Ireland by the methods that had misgoverned her for generations. His conventional mind saw nothing wrong in this bribery: indeed his official biographer goes on to give in detail many examples of "the principles on which, with scrupulous good faith, he had worked a system now regarded as corruption." It is a eulogy worthy of the ironic pen of Voltaire or Heine.

The examples are interesting; and, in a life of the prim Peel, even very amusing. For this product of the Industrial Revolution and all its horrors had times when he could forget to be pompous and give way to the temptation of humour. Thus in one letter to Lord Whitworth Peel wrote:

> When G. wants a baronetcy he is very rich, and when he wants a place he is very poor. I think we may fairly turn the table on him, and when he asks to be a baronet make his poverty the objection, and his wealth when he asks for office. Lord H. has no sort of a claim. He and his whole family are more overpaid in point of favour from the Crown than any other in Ireland. He has not an atom of influence, and abilities about equal to his influence.

But when the "influence" could be placed at the disposal of his Government, Peel did not whip himself into sarcastic indignation; for in March 8, 1816, he wrote: "It would be good policy to direct the channel of patronage as plentifully as we can towards those who are adhering to us on these pressing questions of army establishment and property tax." On May 29, 1817, he suggested: "As G. has been constant in his attendance and support, and really gives us very little trouble, I think his protégé should be appointed to the Customs House place vacant." Having no ideas on the reform of Ireland, Peel thus preserved the existing evil system by generous bribery and stronger police. It would be unfair to expect any more fertile result from his pious mind. But in the matter he had really at heart — his policemen — he was unbending, for he wrote: "We ought to be crucified if we make the measure a job, and select our constables from the servants of our Parliamentary friends." The firm protection of law and order was the first necessity in Peel's opinion.

In August, 1818, Peel resigned his office as Chief Secretary. There was no very clear reason given. Perhaps his rather timid soul was alarmed at some of the work he had to do. In May, 1817, he had written: "I am quite tired and disgusted with the shameful corruption which every Irish inquiry brings to light." It is more probable that he began to think he was entitled to a more important post. After all, the Chief Secretary was then only an underling of the London Home Office, and, in fairness to Peel, this is a fact to keep in mind when we criticise him for the small results of his work in Ireland. But there is no sign that he kicked against his bonds. He had nothing to propose himself. As to his hopes of greater office, Croker was filling him with rumours that powerful men were talking of the premiership being within his grasp: "Yarmouth told me last night that you might be Prime Minister whenever you would." To which Peel answered: "in the emphatic terms of a reverend Pastor in the 'Vicar of Wakefield' — Fudge. I am thinking of anything but office, and am just as anxious to be emancipated from office as the Papists are to be emancipated into it. A fortnight hence I shall be free as air."

But there is so much evidence that Peel was not an artless, unambitious, modest fellow, as he generally posed in the public eye. He was too timid to be dishonest or to intrigue; but no one can imagine that he resigned his Irish post without the intention of ultimately getting a bigger one; to which he had certainly sounder claims than most of the men in

Sir Robert Peel

public life. In February, 1818, he had written: "I am not a very eager politician, and trouble myself little about that sort of distinction which mere office confers. I have not a single personal object to look to. The only one I ever had, I attained in being elected member for the University of Oxford." The biographer who takes those modest words at their face value will not be a very safe guide to the heart of this man. It will be wiser to believe that when Peel — after retiring from Ireland — went off for a prolonged bout of killing animals on Scottish moors — his favourite hobby — he was merely waiting his chance as the political wheels of fortune revolved. He was only thirty; he could afford to wait; while the wealthy classes could not afford to do without the protection and assistance of the stubborn Tory young man who had won the heart of Oxford University — that home of lost causes. There are many lost causes that are better than the triumphant novelties; but the dead corpses that Peel defended deserved to be buried.

Peel was soon back in parliamentary work; and came for the first time into the front rank by his unexpected election to the chairmanship of the committee which examined the currency problem. It was then almost precisely the same problem which has arisen during the recent Great War of 1914–1918. Seeing that even now there are still two opposing parties of expert financiers who cannot convince each other whether a gold coinage or a paper coinage is the sounder principle in currency, it cannot here be argued at length. It would need a whole volume to attempt to discover whether Peel was right or wrong when he persuaded his committee to report energetically in favour of returning to a gold currency; that is, to compel the Bank of England to pay gold for any of its notes that were presented at its bank counter. He put his case with such convincing clarity that his resolutions were accepted without a dissentient vote; and he was allowed to bring in a Bill to put them into compulsory legal form. This also passed almost unopposed — though in the future the discontented were to curse "Peel's Act" as the foundation of their miseries.

What is more important for our present purpose is to observe that Peel in his earlier days had voted exactly the other way when he opposed Mr. Horner's famous resolution of 1811, which demanded a return to the gold standard, by the compulsory payment of gold for notes. He had apparently done this in obedience to the wishes of his father, who was an ardent believer in a plentiful paper currency which would flood the markets with money to buy his goods. There are many economists at the present day who maintain that a prosperous trade needs plenty of paper money to represent the desires of the consumers. In other words an "inflated" currency is still an open question. But the younger Peel in 1819, when he presented the report of the Currency Committee to the House of Commons, threw over the paper or "soft money" party and his father among them; he said Mr. Horner had been right in 1811 after all, and moved that the bank should be compelled to go back to payments in gold instead of unconvertible notes.

Peel thus began his great deeds in the political arena by admitting that he had made a grave mistake in the past. He was to spend the rest of his life in apologies for other errors. As in the case of currency, so was it to be in the great matters of Catholic emancipation, the corn laws, and, in a degree, of franchise reform. One may call it indecision, or courage in being ready to admit when one had changed one's mind, or, perhaps, mere political expediency to save himself and his party from defeat on the parliamentary battlefield. Probably there was something of all these reasons, and others less definite, in Peel's continual changes of front. Each case must be judged on its merits. The only generalisation that may be made is that if there is any department of human affairs where an absence of rigid fixed principles is a priceless possession, and an ever-present help in time of trouble, it is in the field of politics. It certainly was a distinguishing feature of Peel's career. He was accused of being a stubborn bigot in his earlier days. No one could accuse him of this fault when he had ended. His politics had the frank openmindedness of a weathercock.

After the Currency Committee he still remained out of office for a time. He could not have been anxious to have any official responsibility for the disorder of the nation on all sides. It was the time when the danger of revolution became so urgent that the terrified governing classes — reform being beyond their intelligence — could think of nothing more effective than shooting down the peaceful assembly at "Peterloo"; and putting Sidmouth's (the Home Secretary's) six Acts of repression on the statute book. Earl Fitzwilliam, the Lord Lieutenant of Yorkshire, being a fairminded gentleman, called a meeting to protest against the "Manchester massacre" at "Peterloo", and was dismissed from his office. Peel, being the representative of a new manufacturing family that had made its fortune by oppressing discontented labour, rushed to the assistance of the Government by supporting its stern severity — and was offered, and accepted, Lord Sidmouth's post in January, 1822.

It was not his fault — but his caution — that he did not accept office earlier. He was never a man to take any unnecessary risks; he had not that sort of nerve. The Government had not looked very firm on its feet, or very popular; and Peel all through his life discreetly allowed other men to take the kicks. He himself preferred the prizes. Thus he allowed, and even supported by his vote, the great Poor Law Amendment Act of 1834; but he saw it was unpopular, so he carefully avoided making one speech in its favour. Again, when he was Prime Minister, whenever he found that a budget would show a deficit, he threw the duty of introducing it on some one else, as Goulburn, in 1843; in 1842 and 1845, when he had surpluses to crow over and take credit for, then he himself appeared in the limelight like an actor-manager. These may seem small points; yet this man was made up of rather small things.

In 1820 Peel married Julia Floyd, the daughter of General Sir John Floyd. She seems to have been an amiable and good woman of no particular mental power; but this was altogether a typical choice for Peel. As the Duke of Wellington — who liked clever women — said, Peel did not want a wife with brains. There is no reason to think he was disappointed. Even he hesitated, and asked her whether she would find him too serious a husband, seeing that she was a woman who was so fond of "the world." But she had wit enough to think of the obvious reply: "You are my world"; which Peel thought a very satisfactory answer, being a man of no small self-confidence — which on a smaller scale would be called conceit. It turned out an ideal match for such modest domestic tastes. Melbourne, as we have seen, had taken risks; he had married Caroline Ponsonby, who was adventurous enough to want more worlds than even Alexander conquered. Perhaps Peel was right — genius is a disturbing housemate.

Many letters have been preserved of the correspondence between the faithful Peel and his ever-adoring wife. He was always writing to her when they were separated — and usually of nothing of any profound interest; the number of pheasants he had shot, or some servant he had engaged, or other domestic details that might have happened to anybody who lived in the quietest suburb. These letters are full of the small things of life. There is one of January 22, 1827 (from Strathfieldsaye where he was staying with the Duke of Wellington), which is typical of them in several ways:

My own dearest Julia, I have been very dull from having been a second day without a letter from you. It never happened before.

I might have so arranged it that a coach or a messenger could have brought me one line. . . . I killed 33 pheasants, 8 rabbits, 11 hares, and a partridge. Much more than anybody else.

In the same letter he mentions that matter to which he so often refers in his letters to his wife; namely, the unhappy relations between Wellington and his Duchess. The Duke (on a point of honour, as we have seen) had married a woman who was not of fit intellect for a great man; and merely an adoring nonentity was more than the great mind of Wellington could tolerate as his life companion. So they lived on terms of perpetual friction, which only Wellington's perfect courtesy made possible. Of course, all this shocked the prim mind of Peel very terribly. In this letter he tells how he met the Duchess, full of fears for her husband's health:

As uneasy about the Duke as if he treated her with the kindness which is her due. . . . She burst out a-crying, and such things make me still more hate the sight of those who can find it in their hearts, even if they have no sense of virtue, to usurp her place. . . . What wickedness and what folly to undervalue and be insensible to the affection of a wife! God bless you, my dearest love, and may he ever preserve us in the happiness we have enjoyed.

It was, of course, a very unfortunate affair; but the unprejudiced outsider will observe that it arose because the Duke needed first-class brains in a wife, while Peel had no such lofty standard. The cutting remark about want of virtue just quoted was aimed, of course, at Mrs. Arbuthnot, who was an unending source of moral indignation in Peel's letters to his wife. Thus, in one of 1828: "The shooting yesterday was excellent. . . . I see no signs of the influence of Mrs. A. having abated. She takes her place next him at dinner as if it were a matter of course. . . . But let us leave these odious things. Kiss my own dear children for me."

Peel was of the very righteous kind who pick up their gar-

ments lest they are soiled when they walk near sinners —
and his sinners were so often the people who had most charm
and most wit. He preferred those who were good — and
dull. He walked through life with the greatest timidity.
That was almost his chief characteristic; and we can never
understand his political career unless we realise his nervous
anxiety when he saw Mrs. Arbuthnot sitting next the Duke
of Wellington at dinner. His politics and his morals alike
were dominated by the desire to do what the "best" people
considered right.

It was precisely this physical and moral nervousness
that was the keynote of much of his work as Home Secretary,
to which office he was appointed in 1822; and held (excluding the interval of Canning's and Goderich's short ministries) until 1830, when Melbourne succeeded him in the
Reform Government of Lord Grey. Nothing could be so
unlike as the methods of the two men.

A great deal of Peel's work was very wise; and during his
term of office he made many reforms in the criminal law. He
had not, apparently, that constructive, original brain that
would have thought of these changes on his own; but Romilly and Mackintosh had been advocating the reform of the
penal code for so long that Peel had now only to put their
ideas into formal shape. He did away with the death penalty in many cases of petty offences; but then, of course,
common juries, being more rational and humane than trained
lawyers, had already begun to refuse to convict, and prisoners were escaping punishment. So that this reform was
really in large part a strengthening of the law rather than a
weakening. There is no sign that Peel had a particularly
tender heart. Indeed, there are pathetic letters from King
George IV begging his Home Secretary not to hang so many
condemned prisoners; and replies that Peel could not recommend pardons; and he was sometimes so set on death
that if the King persisted, he, Peel, hinted at resignation.

However, during his first term at the Home Office, Peel did a great deal of useful and necessary work by this codification and slight reform of the criminal law. It was not the stroke of a genius, but the quiet accomplishment of a man with a first-class housekeeper's mind. This domestic mind at its best was Peel's inheritance from his more adventurous businesslike father. He did small things in rather a big way. He never forgot small things. In January, 1828, when he was writing to tell his wife that he was negotiating with Wellington about the formation of a ministry, he devoted almost one third of the letter to discussing the wages question of one of their servants:

> Send for Barnes and tell him I will settle with him about his son's attendance on me shooting. . . . He did live, I believe, with Sir John Shelley. What wages had he there? . . . Is it possible Barnes may have paid something what ought to be charged to my account and not Shelley's.

And so on, with the anxiety of a careful housewife.

Peel's anxiety was very marked at times of crises, when the discontented and badly governed nation was on the verge of rioting. Sir Denis le Marchant said that Peel would then get into such a state of nerves at the Home Office that he sat afraid to open his letters, for fear they brought him more bad news. He was continually begging the local magistrates and masters to stand firm against the demands of agitators. This man of great wealth did not believe that the poor were suffering as much as they said. He told the magistrates that he had carefully considered the question of wages when he settled the pay of his new Metropolitan Police; and he had come to the conclusion that a man might live in comfort and save ten shillings a week out of a wage of twenty-one shillings. Therefore, if cotton spinners could earn twenty-five shillings a week and over, they had no right to grumble. If the magistrates thought they could suppress riots — Peel's nerves were clearly exposed by this proviso — then "I think there can be little doubt that the true policy for the owners of collieries and the masters of mills to pursue is peremptorily and decidedly to refuse concessions which they feel to be unjustly demanded." Doctor Ramsay, Peel's latest and most enthusiastic biographer, comments on this passage: "His warmest admirers will agree that the writer of this letter was using his influence as a Minister of the Crown to support one party to an industrial dispute in a very improper manner." One is glad to know that the magistrate to whom this advice was given refused, with dignity, to behave in so unscrupulous a way. Whereas Melbourne had almost always refused to take sides — except by keeping the peace — Peel used his ministerial power in order that his own class, the masters, should win. Thus, for example, he advised that poor relief should be withheld from strikers, whereas Melbourne, as we have seen, said in a similar case that was referred for his opinion, that he thought it would be illegal to refuse this public aid. It was not that Peel was consciously biased or dishonest: he simply could not see the other side of the question. At the time he gave these decisions and advice, he had just inherited £40,000 or so a year. It distracted his attention from the smaller facts of twenty-five shillings a week. He had no sense of balance in life. In fact, he was a very narrow-minded man.

When Lord Liverpool was stricken with paralysis in 1827, there came a long pause, while Canning and Peel played their cards in competition for the vacant premiership; with the greater figure of the Duke of Wellington on the edge of the ring, rather like a man watching the struggles of ants. Wellington and Peel were united in the determination that they would not serve under Canning's leadership — but for different reasons. Wellington's objection to Canning was the dislike of a gentleman to one whose code of honour he distrusted. Peel was only worried — so he said, at least —

lest Canning should give the Catholics the full rights of citizenship; he said he agreed with Canning on every other material point except Catholic emancipation. There were unkind people who said that what Peel really wanted was the premiership himself. This seems to be a little unfair to him; though it is certainly hard to explain why Peel had worked previously so contentedly and for so long with other friends of the Catholics. He probably saw that the problem of the Catholic relief could not much longer remain in the background, where he could discuss it in the abstract; he would soon have to register his opinion in more definite ways than pious sentiments. But, on the whole, he does not appear to have pressed his own claims unduly; anyhow, Canning was chosen; and Peel, with the Duke of Wellington, resigned office.

He was not to take office again until 1828, when he once more became Home Secretary and this time the leader of the House of Commons under Wellington's premiership; and he himself forced a Catholic Emancipation Bill through the House which he led! It was the first time he had been leader of the Commons; and almost his first deed was to overthrow the firm convictions of his previous career. Perhaps it is not necessary to spend too much time in considering the earnest convictions of politicians. But this was one of the great events of Peel's life. The fact which decided him was his continual dread of a revolution. Timidity was usually the deciding factor in Peel's elastic mind. Ireland seemed on the verge of a rebellion; and as Home Secretary Peel was then responsible for its government. The opposition, in favour of the Catholic claims, must have realised that they had in front of them a government leader who was (in spite of many assertions to the contrary) really only a bending twig, merely painted to look like iron. In 1828, the first year of this Tory Government, he had allowed his opponent, Lord John Russell, to carry a Bill which repealed the old-fashioned Test and Corporation Acts which had hitherto disabled the Nonconformist religious sects. It did not add to Peel's dignity to allow Russell to lead the House of Commons; and the Catholics were naturally excited when they scented religious toleration in the air. It was a blow against the tyranny of the Anglican Church, even though it was on the other side of that ponderous body.

In July the famous Clare election had returned Daniel O'Connell, the Catholic candidate, and swept the government candidate entirely off the field. It was a pungent statement that Ireland did not intend to wait any longer. As the defeated Tory candidate wrote to Peel: "All the great interests broke down, and the desertion has been universal." On July 2, 1828, the Lord Lieutenant of Ireland had reported to Peel that the Catholic leaders "could lead on the people to open rebellion at a moment's notice"; and he added that the rising would be "extremely formidable." Peel's nerves gave way; and in August he wrote to his chief, Wellington: "An attempt should be made by the Government to settle the Catholic question — the settlement should be, if possible, a complete one." In that short phrase Peel was throwing away the convictions of a lifetime. The Duke had, quite candidly, never possessed any dogmatic religious opinions; and in any case he had such a horror of war, and especially civil war, that he was ready to give away any political or social or religious principles whatsoever rather than have anarchy. It was not merely because he was afraid of "property" being upset; it was rather that he had lived through so many wars that he knew nothing good ever came out of them. So, both Peel and the Duke decided that they could not resist Catholic emancipation any longer. The Duke was prepared, as Premier, to propose the necessary Bill; Peel said he would support it in the House of Commons, but only as a private member; for he had opposed emancipation so persistently that it would be now impossible to introduce the Bill himself. It is unnecessary to go through all the manœuvres that followed. It is sufficient to say that Peel at last gave way; and convincing himself that the Duke was the only man who could make the King consent to the measure, he promised not to resign and even to introduce the Bill himself. The King was driven to agree; and Peel got up in the House to confess in public his change of mind. Greville — who being a gentleman was in favour of toleration — wrote in his diary:

> I was in the House of Commons. Peel was very feeble, and his case for himself poor and ineffective; all he said was true enough, but it was only what had been said to him over and over again for years past, and he did not urge a single argument for acquiescing now which was not equally applicable to his situation two years ago.

And Greville goes on to say that after such conduct, so lacking in principle, the reputation of public men would suffer very badly and democracy increase its aggressive power.

Peel's great ordeal came when he had to rise in the House to introduce the Bill. He had already resigned his seat for Oxford University, to which he was pledged up to the hilt to defend the Protestant cause; and when his friends insisted on his standing for reëlection he was beaten by an anti-Catholic candidate. So he spoke as an already whipped man, and he had only been elected for another constituency by the skin of his teeth. On all sides he was being cursed as a traitor. But he had that sort of conceit that almost gets satisfaction from abuse; and when he made his introducing speech, four hours long, Greville wrote that it was "said to be far the best he ever made. It is full of his never-failing fault, egotism, but certainly very able, plain, clear and statesmanlike, and the peroration very eloquent." But this, surely, was too generous an estimate. In his speech on

the second reading he had the calm impertinence — after a
deal of pompous acknowledgment that the credit of the Bill
was not his, but his opponents' — to declare that: "I had no
other alternative than to act as I have acted . . . the course
which I have followed, whatever imputations it may expose
me to, is the only course which is necessary for the diminution of the undue, the illegitimate and dangerous power of
the Roman Catholics, and for the maintenance and permanent security of the Protestant interests." It is not
often that a man has the courage to admit that he has
behaved like a fool for the earlier part of his life; it is still
less often that he has the calm insolence to claim that this
folly has been one of his virtues. The speech was full of
"I" and "my motives", which was most typical of this self-centred man, who was so anxious to prove that he was an
honest man instead of a rogue, as it might seem at the first
glance. There were many occasions in his life where the
proof was perhaps necessary. He was entitled to all the
praise he could get for his courage in introducing the Catholic Emancipation Bill; his useless explanations of his earlier
folly were an unpleasant waste of time.

Two days after the Emancipation Bill received the King's
assent, Peel introduced his Metropolitan Police Bill into the
House of Commons. We have seen that his motive in allowing the Emancipation Bill to pass was to save a revolution
in Ireland. He probably regarded his Police Bill as a defence for the established order in England. We shall soon
see that his Corn Bill was part of the same everlasting fear.
Every one must admit that the London Police force as Peel
found it was worse than useless; and his new system was a
reasonably good suggestion. When Wellington wrote congratulating its creator Peel replied:

It has given me from first to last more trouble than anything I
ever undertook. . . . I want to teach people that liberty does not

consist in having your house robbed by organised gangs of thieves, and in leaving the principal streets of London in the nightly possession of drunken women and vagabonds.

Which was all very true and proper; but the common people had perhaps a sounder instinct; and they dreaded lest "Peel's Bloody Gang", as the street bills crudely put it, might be the beginning of a new tyranny which Peel had so 'thoughtfully placed in his own hands as Home Secretary, for the present, and in the hands of the ruling class henceforward. Paris had its centralised police force; and Chateaubriand's fierce opinion of that was published for Englishmen's warning. There are men of the braver sort who will run risks on behalf of liberty of a deeper kind than policemen can guarantee; but of course Sir Robert Peel was not one of them. Besides, a millionaire can look after his own liberty. So Peel continued with earnest zeal to reform the criminal law — for which work he had almost a passionate eagerness. It was all very necessary; for the economic and political system had certainly produced an enormous mass of social sewage, and Peel clung rather desperately to policemen and lawyers — the last refuge of all bewildered and terrified men.

In September, 1830, the Wellington and Peel Ministry fell before the rising demand for a more radical remedy than the Metropolitan Police Act. Lord Grey (with Melbourne as his Home Secretary to succeed Peel) came into power, and the much debated struggle for the Reform Bill began. The whole affair has been overrated as a period of important history, especially as a step towards democracy. It was a middle-class reform which made the plutocrats safe for another fifty years. Wellington, who had no particular love for the manufacturing classes and their industrial system, which was turning the centre and north of England into factory slums and coal refuse heaps, with his usual candour said he would oppose the Reform Bill to the bitter end.

But Peel played a safer game. He was already conscious that his place in English politics was not among the extremists to either the right or left of him, but as the leader of the middle people, the Middle Classes, from which he sprang. The affair of Catholic emancipation had taught him the lesson that he was not made in the heroic mould of a defender of lost causes. The safe and canny line was his by class inheritance and by personal temperament. He had been playing this safe game since he left office in 1830; and it was proving effective. On December 19, 1830, Greville wrote: "Men are looking more and more to him, and if there is not a revolution he will assuredly be Prime Minister." Only three days before Greville had written: "But who are Peel's confidants, friends, and parasites? Bonham, a stockjobbing ex-merchant, Charles Ross, and the refuse of society of the House of Commons." It was clear that Peel had no chance of becoming the leader of the Tory aristocrats who wanted to drive the Reform Bill out of Parliament without any compromise. He was (a little unconsciously, perhaps) the leader of the Middle Classes who were the only people the Bill would benefit. The Tories of the old school had lived their day; and Peel was the man who was to read their burial service. On February 24, 1831, Greville continued:

> Peel plays with his power in the House, only not putting it forth because it does not suit his convenience; but he does what he likes and it is evident that the very existence of the Government depends on his pleasure. His game, however, is to display candour and moderation . . . while he upholds the Government he does all he can to bring each member of it into contempt.

So when the Reform Bill was introduced Peel played very carefully. Croker, who was a snob, and only liked the opinions of the "best" people, wanted Peel to "pledge himself, like the Duke, against all Parliamentary Reform, but

... he will pledge to nothing. He said good humouredly that he was sick with eating pledges, and would take care to avoid them for the future." Catholic emancipation had taught him never to be a brave man again. Therefore when the Reform Bill arrived, he entrenched himself bravely in the rear ranks of the combatants. It was said that if he had moved the entire rejection of the Bill at once, he might easily have carried with him a House that was certainly dazed — Whigs and Tories alike — by the apparent boldness of its clauses. On the day the Bill was introduced Croker had written: "For the last week every one, Court, City, Ministers, Tories, all agree that the Government holds its seat at the mercy of Sir Robert Peel." It was therefore the more exasperating to the extremists when he was silent until the third night of the debate, and then only spoke with cautious criticism. He artfully argued that instead of being a democratic measure it in reality took away most of the few votes that were still, by chance, left in the hands of the working classes in a few democratic corners where these vestiges of an older mediæval democracy had survived. But as he took no further care to insist that these political stolen goods should be restored, one can only believe that this argument was the ordinary trick of a political debate. He also pointed out that almost all the greatest politicians had been elected to the House of Commons by corrupt constituencies. Which was also true, and a pretty debating point, of which the speaker was himself an example: but it ignored the probability that another political system might conceivably produce even a greater statesman than Sir Robert Peel.

For the moment, the speech seemed a great hit, and Greville reported that: "some said (as usual) that it was the finest oration they had ever heard within the walls of Parliament"; but two days afterwards Hobhouse (who was naturally prejudiced, of course) said "it was brilliant, imposing, but not much in it" — which was not far from the truth. On March 18, Greville was writing that there were bitter complaints of "Peel's inactivity and backwardness in not having rallied and taken the lead more than he has: he is in fact so cold, phlegmatic, and calculating that he disgusts those who can't do without him as a leader." However, his calculation was sound, for the first Reform Bill was defeated. But was Peel really playing for its final defeat? On March 24, Greville wrote: "I continue to hear great complaints of Peel — of his coldness . . . nobody knows what are his opinions . . . nobody feels any dependence upon him. There is no help for it and the man's nature can't be altered."

When their first Bill was thus defeated, the Whigs dissolved Parliament, appealed to the country, and were returned in greater triumph, for the Tories lost more than eighty seats. The Government then brought in the Reform Bill a second time. Whether Peel really meant to oppose the Bill to the bitter end was growing more and more doubtful; and Greville was in despair:

I hear renewed complaints of Peel, of his cold, calculating, cowardly policy; that we are indebted to him principally for our present condition I have no doubt — to his obstinacy and to his conduct in the Catholic question first, to his opposition and then to his support of it. Opposing all and every sort of Reform *totis viribus* while he dared, now he makes a death bed profession of acquiescence in something which would be more moderate than this. All these things disgust people inconceivably.

But the sting about it all was that Greville, and the many people whose opinions he was repeating — that is why his opinions are of such value as historical evidence — knew that Peel was "our only resource, and his capacity for business and power in the House of Commons placed him so far above all his competitors that if we are to have a Conservative party we must look to him alone to lead it."

When the House of Lords turned out the second Reform Bill, the Whigs brought in a third Bill, which also went through the House of Commons; whereupon Peel lost his nerve and became, as usual, very egotistical when Macaulay taunted him for so many changes of policy. The truth was he saw the Bill must be passed and he was tired of the useless fight. As long ago as August 25, 1831, during the second Bill, he had written to his wife: "I have told everyone that I can stay no longer than a very few days, that I must go to join you and abandon the Bill to its fate." The problem was now how to persuade the Lords to accept the third Bill in order to avoid another appeal to the country, which might end in revolution. The Whigs asked the King to create enough new peers to give them a majority in the House of Lords. He hesitated, and the Government resigned. Wellington, whose chief political principle was to form a government if no one else would, told the King he was ready to assist (in office, or without it) in passing the Bill, as a mere act of administrating inevitable public business: he, of course, disliked the Bill, but it was clear that if it was not passed there would be national anarchy. He offered to serve under Peel if the latter would like the premiership; but Peel said flatly he would not assist in any way. He said it would be a "personal degradation to myself" if he, the opponent of the Bill, now turned round and passed it. He was a very sensitive man, and he could not risk any more jeers such as he had received after his change on Catholic emancipation. The Duke had a big enough mind to do what he thought right when the time came or circumstances altered. Without Peel the Duke could not form a government; so the King recalled Grey; and Wellington persuaded the Tory lords to allow the Bill to pass on June 4, 1832.

What part Peel played behind the scenes is naturally obscure. But Greville, who afterwards had very confidential information from the persons involved in the negotiations, came to the conclusion that Peel was all along playing selfishly for his own hand. In February 7, 1832, he had written: "It is clear to me that it is not his real feeling, and that he promises himself some personal advantage. . . . Peel 'loves' himself 'not wisely but too well.'"

On May 17 he wrote:

> Peel, who has kept himself out of the scrape, is strongly suspected of being anything but sorry for the dilemma into which the Duke has got himself. . . . Nothing can be more certain than that he is in high spirits . . . and talks with great complacency of its being very well as it is, and that salvation of character is everything. . . .

In short, he behaved like the prig he was. In the following October, Arbuthnot told Greville many further facts which were confirmed in the main by Lyndhurst in the following January, 1833. From all which evidence Greville concluded that "Peel, full of ambition, but of caution", was trying to get others to take the responsibility for the Reform Bill, while he was to step forward, when all danger was over, and become premier; and he concluded: "All these deep-laid schemes, and constant regard of self, form a strong contrast to the simplicity and heartiness of the Duke's conduct, and make the two men appear in a very different light from that in which they did at first." This contemporary judgment is the more valuable and reliable, in as much as Greville thought Peel was right in refusing to aid the Bill: "Peel acted right from bad motives, the Duke wrong from good ones."

It is doubtful whether Peel had a sufficiently clear and penetrating mind to look into the future and see that the Reform Act of 1832 was the foundation of the middle-class Conservative Party of which he was to become the leader. Until he came back into office in 1841, as Prime Minister, Peel played for safety and committed himself as little as possible. His conduct over the Poor Law Act was typical; he wanted it to go through — for it was necessary for the sake of his wealthy supporters to protect them from the demands of the poor — but he did not venture to speak in its favour: for it was unpopular in many quarters, and even the *Times* was against it. Indeed, he was so cautious about politics that he went off to Italy to spend the winter of 1834–1835. He was called back by an unexpected political crisis, and found himself (by Wellington's unselfish energy) Prime Minister before he arrived.

Then it was that he issued the famous Tamworth Manifesto to the electors. It was the address of a man who was not going to commit himself to anything. It was the common-form statement of a politician who would not do any more than he was compelled to do, rather than the opinion of a statesman who tried to give the nation a lead. It contained all the commonplaces of evasion: "I will never admit that I have been, either before or after the Reform Bill, the defender of abuses; or the enemy of judicious reforms. I appeal with confidence, in denial of the charge, to the active part I took in" the Currency, the Criminal law, and so on. As for the Reform Act, he said he considered it "a final and irrevocable settlement of a great question — a settlement which no friend to the peace and welfare of this country would attempt to disturb either by direct or insidious means." This sentence would alone confirm the dark suspicions that he had never really dreaded the Bill; and that he had only craftily thrown on Wellington the responsibility of letting it pass.

In his opening speech, when he met Parliament, he continued the carefully chosen commonplaces of the political mind: "I offer you the prospect of continued peace. . . . I offer you reduced estimates." Then he mentioned a string of ecclesiastical "reforms" and added: "I offer you these specific measures and I offer also to advance, soberly and cautiously, it is true, in the path of progressive improvement." It was the sort of eloquence that appears in the election addresses of the nervous candidates at local municipal elections. On his position Greville commented with sarcastic shrewdness: "Peel and his Government . . . stand in a false position. As a statesman it must be mortifying to him to reflect that all the great measures which his political life has been spent in opposing have been carried in spite of him, and that whatever danger may have resulted from this cause is in great measure owing to the opposition he was enabled, by his great talents and his influence, or rather the influence of the party which he led, to give to these measures."

Greville thought, afterwards, that this ministry of a "hundred days" was the most brilliant period in Peel's career: "it was during that magnificent campaign that he established the vast reputation." It is difficult to find proof of the truth of this statement. But it is safe to say that during this short time of office, and afterwards when Melbourne again became prime minister, Peel continually demonstrated his skill and power as a parliamentary leader. He had, undoubtedly, a more serious industry than was usual among the dull, careless gentlemen and aristocrats who then made the bulk of the national parliaments. By 1839 a Radical member (of course desiring to throw scorn on the Whig Government) declared in the House of Commons that: "the right honourable member for Tamworth governs England. The honourable and learned member for Dublin governs Ireland. The Whigs govern nothing but Downing Street." Writing in February, 1834, Greville said Peel was "*facile princeps* in the House of Commons. . . . He never was a great favourite of mine, but I am satisfied that he is the fittest man to be Minister, and therefore I wish to see him return to power." During Peel's term of premiership Greville wrote in March, 1835:

"Every day he displays more and more capacity for government. . . . He cannot help being a great man because he lives in an age of pigmies; and he is as great as great talents without a great mind can make anybody."

So when Melbourne fell in 1841, Peel was his inevitable successor as Premier. Scarcely anybody liked him; and the young Queen sent for him with dread — for he had such clumsy manners after his polished predecessor. Besides he had voted to cut down the Prince Consort's allowance by £20,000 a year when Melbourne proposed it in Parliament. But within a year the Queen trusted him completely; and Prince Albert thought at last he had found an English statesman who had a brain capable of discussing statistics and the other heavy matters which made the mental diet of his strong, detailed German mind. Anyhow, if the politicians did not love Peel, they were not clever enough to oppose him with success. So he became the Chief Minister. There has probably never been a chief minister who so completely dominated his whole Cabinet and controlled so tightly all their varied offices. He was so entirely the ablest politician of them all.

The position of Great Britain was very desperate when Peel took office. There had been many economic crises since the Napoleonic Wars had almost reduced Europe to anarchy and destitution. But the winter of 1841–1842 was about the worst. The trade of the nation was in a condition of chaos. The details would need a book to themselves; but in ultimate results it came to this: one in every eleven citizens was kept by the Poor Law; the great industry of farming was done by labourers who could only earn about ten shillings a week; while the urban artisans were clinging to life at $3\frac{3}{4}d.$ an hour — if they were lucky they earned eighteen shillings or so a week; while the unemployed and the starving were the final and frequent proof of the national failure. The Chartists and the Anti-Corn Law League were certain they had remedies; if the Government had none to propose, it was clear that an angry people would become impatient beyond restraint.

Timidity, as we have seen, was the chief factor of Peel's subconscious mind; and he was soon in a condition of shaken nerves when he surveyed the social position before his eyes. He was surely the man who ought to find a remedy for this national disaster; for he was the chief representative of the manufacturing classes who had been making industrial England during the last three generations. They had made themselves rich, certainly, but they did it so recklessly and callously that the Poor Law and the national debt had become two of our largest institutions. The Mediæval Ages had been ravaged by plagues; but these were strange gifts of fate, beyond man's direct control; while this plague of social disorganisation and destitution was the work of the men of the last seventy years — and no men were more directly responsible than the Peels and their kind. Peel was not blind to his responsibility; even if it took the selfish form of a desire to protect the rich rather than save the poor. He wrote to Croker: "We must make this country a cheap country for living . . . landed property would not be safe during the next winter with the prices of the last four years." To Arbuthnot he argued that in one Scottish town, of which he had the evidence, they had the "choice of hundreds dying of hunger, or of a frightful outbreak and attack upon property. . . . There have been 150 bankruptcies among the principal manufacturers of the town. No rents have been paid. . . . My firm belief is you could not have the high prices of the last four years and at the same time tranquillity and security of property."

"Security of property!" The words might have been put on his tombstone as its only epitaph. They were the master key to his political mind; and he set himself with frantic energy to translate his theory into legislative facts. To him "reform" was a question of police and finance. He was a middle-class trader by heredity, and he was convinced that the remedy for all these evils was a rearrangement of the national budget which would make the trading classes prosperous. He would make bad trade into good trade.

There is no doubt that Peel's budgets were very clever performances. His mind was of just the right sort to see that it was folly to put a custom duty on raw and half raw materials coming into a manufacturing country; for such goods were the life blood of our producing trades. He also saw that it was stupid to tax heavily such things as currants and coffee or sugar, which did not compete much with the products of our own farms; and in general he decided that it was madness to tax the food of a nation where so many were starving. By sweeping away such custom duties, literally by the hundred, he did sane work, which benefited almost every one; and, true to his own social set, to no sort of people did these budgets do more good than to the Middle Class. The few protective duties which he also took off were no great loss at that time of our national history, for England had (unlike to-day) no industrial competitors of any importance. So that Peel's free trade finance had scarcely anything to do with protection in the real sense of the term.

There was another great economic deed of Peel's which made a mark in our financial history. He deliberately imposed an income tax — only of seven pence in the pound — which then became a permanent and chief source of the national income. Now in doing this Peel was undoubtedly taking the money out of the pockets of his own class; and, so far, it was what is usually termed an act of democratic politics. There was scarcely any other way of escaping from national disaster; and Peel must have the credit for being longer sighted than the narrower minded Whigs, Lord John Russell and Lord Brougham, who both shrieked against the income tax like a couple of naughty children who are having some of their sweets taken away from them; while the factory owner, Mr. John Bright, had the calm cheek to say that the income tax was an admirable imposition on anything except factories!

So far in his financial policy, Peel was not rousing any substantial opponents. His income tax was an obvious, if disagreeable, necessity if he was to repeal the stupid custom duties which were raising prices without protecting British trade; they were tariffs for revenue, not for industrial protection. So far he was continuing the policy which Pitt and Haskisson had begun. But the most famous of Peel's tariff changes was of another kind, and it was left to the last; for here the opposition was very fierce, and the wisdom of his act was exceedingly questionable. By the abolishing of the Corn Laws Peel made one of the most vital changes in English history; and it is by this act that he will be finally judged.

This matter of the Corn Law was the climax of his career; but before reaching it there were two other conspicuous events which preceded the Corn Laws in the deeds of his premiership. These were the Factory Act of 1842 and the Maynooth grant. They both reveal the inner mind of the man in an instinctive way.

Lord Ashley (the evangelical Anglican who was saving his own soul by the admirable method of rescuing the working classes from some of the horrors of the Industrial Revolution) had in 1842, after long previous labours with the sullen apathy of Peel's Government, forced through Parliament a Mining Act which forbade the labour of women altogether and of children, in part, in mines. Then he carried an Address to the Crown, demanding that the working classes should have more opportunities for "moral" education. There was such strong approval of this proposal that Peel's Government was compelled to bring in a Bill to carry out the scheme; and as a commission had just reported that children were being forced to work as early as four years of age, Graham, Peel's Home Secretary, felt compelled to make a restriction of these inhumane acts a part of his measure. The Manchester professors of political economy — that is, the philosophers hired by the manufacturing magnates — rose in rebellion at such a tampering with personal freedom; and the Government was probably only too glad to withdraw the Bill. In 1844 it was reintroduced with the educational clauses gone, and the age of permitted child labour raised to nine.

Here Ashley stood firm: he insisted on ten years being the lowest limit of the working age. Peel's hard economic soul was horrified by such a reckless disregard of manufacturing profits; he thought the English trade would be wiped out by cheaper foreign goods made by younger and cheaper labour. He besought the members of the House of Commons to be sensible before they were kind. He said that the children in the smaller workshops were in a still worse condition, and yet they were beyond the reach of any possible legislation; with a sob of his best rhetorical sentimentality he asked: "And will you legislate for these?" To his added horror the House with almost one voice answered, "Yes! Yes!" and Ashley's speech — of a gentleman, and not of a manufacturer's millionaire son — swept the House with a wave of decency; the Tories, with Disraeli and most of his group, followed Ashley into the Opposition voting lobby; and Peel was defeated.

Now this was not a matter of mere religion, like the Emancipation Bill, or of political theory, like the Reform Act; it was a matter of trade, that might lower profits and interest and rent. So Peel now stood firm. There was something relentlessly hard about that sentimental heart of his. Ashley had recently sat next to him at dinner; and wrote to a friend: "What possesses the man! It was like the neigh-

bourhood of an iceberg with a slight thaw on the surface."
It was (we know from the official family biography) the same
Peel whose favourite hobby as a boy had been to kill birds
by throwing stones at them. So he came back and told the
revolted House that this humane decision must be reversed
or he would resign. In short, he bullied his followers into
withdrawing this ten-year clause. They gave way like
whipped dogs. A few days later, they again voted against
Peel when he refused to give a preference to sugar grown by
free labour over that grown by slaves. Then again he
threatened to resign; and again they gave way. Whereupon
the sharp tongue of Disraeli was heard hissing that in that
House at least, the Prime Minister believed in slavery:
"There the gang is still assembled, and there the thong of
the whip still sounds" — and the sore House shouted with
joy at the poisoned wit. Hobhouse said that Peel and
Graham sat "in most painful silence and submission. . . .
I never saw them look so wretched."

There was probably never a famous statesman who was
so often chastised in public as Peel was. It happened again
in the case of the Maynooth grant. In 1845 Peel proposed
to give £30,000 for buildings at Maynooth, the Roman
Catholic college in Ireland; and also to increase the annual
State grant from £8000 to £26,000 a year. Here was the
man who had spent so much of his political strength in opposing the rights of the Catholic majority in Ireland now turning around and taking credit for doing what his opponents
had wanted to do years earlier, before Ireland was embittered beyond hope of conciliation. It was on this occasion
that Macaulay made one of his great speeches, which was a
biting criticism of Peel's career, in the paradoxical form of a
warm support of the Bill. As Macaulay himself recorded in
after years: "How white poor Peel looked while I was
speaking." There is small wonder, for the words would have
chilled a braver heart than Peel's. They are worth quoting

at some length, for they are as much part of Peel's biography as of Macaulay's eloquence.

There is too much ground for the reproaches of those who, having, in spite of a bitter experience, a second time trusted the Right Honourable Baronet, now find themselves a second time deluded. It has been too much his practice, when in opposition, to make use of passions with which he has not the slightest sympathy and of prejudices which he regards with a profound contempt. As soon as he is in power a change takes place. . . . Can you wonder that the eager, honest, hot-headed Protestants, who raised you to power in the confident hope that you would curtail the privileges of the Roman Catholics, should stare and grumble when you propose to give public money to the Roman Catholics? . . . the very men who, when we were in office, voted against the old grant to Maynooth, now pushed and pulled into the House by your whippers-in to vote for an increased grant? . . . Did you think, when you went on, session after session, . . . that the day of reckoning would never come? It has come. There you sit, doing penance for the disingenuousness of years.

Poor Peel went white, for it was a charge that no wise man would trust that what he promised to-day he would fulfil to-morrow. And even at that moment he was getting ready to turn his most famous somersault of all. He, the leader of the Protectionist Party, was going to repeal the Corn Laws. Now there are two points in this matter which it is necessary to keep apart. He may be accused of merely breaking a pledge — a small crime in the world of politics; or it may be proved that, quite apart from his promises, it was a fundamentally bad thing to cease to give British farmers effective protection against cheaper competing foreign corn. When Peel took off the duties on manufacturers' raw materials, it might possibly have been a breaking of his political pledge as an opponent of free trade. But it was an act of sanity nevertheless. Can the same statement be made concerning his repeal of the Corn Laws?

Hitherto it had been the general conviction of Englishmen that agriculture should be a chief and flourishing part of the national economy. Of course, there is no doubt that the ruling classes were in a large degree responsible for this conviction; for they owned the greater part of the national fields, and lived out of their rents. The rulers have usually looked after their own interests first. But there were many other good reasons why farming should be encouraged, if necessary by protective laws. There was the big reason of national food, particularly in time of war. There was the equally big reason of national health; for farming is a healthy trade. There was the greatest and widest of reasons in the fact that the tilling of the soil is one of the chief natural occupations of mankind; and the nations that have allowed themselves to neglect that work have always decayed, as all forms of life decay when they allow a great organ in their body to atrophy.

But for the last few generations before Peel, England had discovered that it was possible — though not necessarily advisable — to live by manufacturing goods in yards and factories, instead of growing corn in fields. The corn could be bought abroad out of the greater profits of the cotton goods and iron wares. Was it therefore necessary to bother about agriculture any longer? That was the problem which faced Peel, as it had faced many statesmen before in human history. The wise men have decided that agriculture must be saved at all costs, and to-day the farmer is the backbone of almost every country in the civilised world — in France, in Italy, in Russia — even industrial Germany has remembered its farmers; and England is the only great State which has deliberately allowed its agricultural classes to remain a struggling and even a pauper group of the population. It was Sir Robert Peel, more than any·man, who made that very important decision. It was made because Peel had a small mind.

The story of the repeal of the Corn Laws is a matter for the general history books; but the essential facts are few and clear. Peel looked out on the national life from the point of view of his family. He thought the production of cotton and other goods, as cheaply as possible, was the essential fact in British economy. In the course of making those cheap goods his family (and their kind) had reduced Great Britain to something near economic anarchy. When Peel came into office the people were crying out for food and employment. During August of 1842, Peel and his wife were writing to each other as to the best way of saving their country house in the Midlands against the attacks of rioters. On the 18th he wrote: "In the Potteries and other parts of Staffordshire there have been shameful outrages on private property." On the 20th he wrote saying that he had ordered "new arms in perfect order and ammunition to be sent to Drayton"; and on the following day Lady Peel replied: "We were armed at all points! I have felt *furious* with the vile mob who contemplated an attack." A few days later she wrote: "Dearest, dearest, All is quite safe. . . . I do not move from this and you positively must *not* come." She was a soldier's daughter and clearly had better nerves than her husband.

It is obvious that in a very personal way Peel was faced with the problem of appeasing an angry people. We have seen more than one piece of evidence that he was not prepared to legislate in order that they might have shorter hours or better wages. On such terms the Peels could not have become millionaires. But there was something else he could do. He could by law enact that the workers should have cheap food. In other words he might maintain the profits of the manufacturing classes out of the pockets of the farming classes. Probably Peel did not see it in this way; he had a very limited mind — having read classics and mathematics at Oxford instead of being educated in the world — and could only see life from his own angle.

There is plenty of evidence that Peel had made up his mind to sweep away the protective Corn Laws long before he seized on the excuse of the Irish potato famine; at least as early as the spring of 1845. He was only waiting for the best excuse. If the harvest of that year failed, then he must be ready to act very soon. It is said that he spent the summer watching the barometer: Graham, who was in his secret, wrote: "I know not that the state of affairs is exactly sound when Ministers are driven to study the barometer with so much anxiety." The weather of the latter part of the summer was very bad indeed and the crisis Peel expected — and almost seemed to desire — was clearly approaching. Then, in the early autumn came the news that the potato disease had reached Ireland, where half the population depended almost solely on that food.

The crisis was exceedingly serious. Once more there is evidence that Peel's nerves went to pieces. The Duke of Wellington wrote to Croker: "I never witnessed in any case such agony." The Duke thought it was dread of the fate of the peasants in Ireland; but Croker was more sceptical. He said it was "nothing but the result of *fright* at the [Anti-Corn Law] League. . . . I have had the most decided and authentic evidence of the fact . . . and yet he still goes on persisting in the humbug of the potato famine." When Wellington tried to defend Peel's anxiety by the letter quoted above, Croker again wrote: "The agony was real and intense but it was the agony of a man who was deluding and betraying his conscience and his colleagues . . . a disturbed conscience, and the fear of being anticipated by the Whigs, was the real cause of the agony." But probably Croker, intimate friend of Peel though he was, did not see — which the whole evidence as we now have it suggests — that Peel's main anxiety was that if the people did not get cheap food there might be another and worse outbreak of rioting; and the chief end of ruling, as Peel saw it, was to make property safe. He had so much himself.

The manner in which he forced the repeal of the Corn Laws through Parliament does not much matter here. Once more he had to go down to the House of Commons and reverse his former principles and the brilliant Disraeli tossed the pompous Peel about in debate as star-spangled conjurers toss many balls on the music-hall stage. Peel put on his most pious airs of moral loftiness. As he wrote to his wife: "How can those who spend their time in hunting and shooting and eating and drinking know what are the motives of those who are responsible for the public security. . . . I am perfectly at ease in my own mind and conscience." But his dearest wife replied with more than a touch of anxiety: "Will you assure me that at least you are confident of triumphantly proving (of course I know you can do so) your own highmindedness and high principles." This perpetual necessity of proving his spotless innocency was one of the trials of Peel's life. Simpler men like Wellington never worried about such egotistical matters — but perhaps he had no need to do so.

The Corn Laws were repealed in the greatest haste, in order, so Peel said, that the starving Irish peasants should be fed. There is no evidence whatever that free trade in corn for England put an ounce of food into a single Irish mouth. The Irish themselves said that what they wanted was not a law to give free imports in England; but one that would stop free export of corn from Ireland — which was exactly what was happening! But Peel would not listen to such simple reason; and continued to offer cheap corn to a people who could not afford to pay for anything cheap or dear. But if the new free trade laws for corn did not feed any one in starving Ireland, they satisfied those cotton manufacturers, Messrs. Bright and Cobden;

who wanted cheap food for workers, who might then accept cheaper wages. So Sir Robert Peel ended as a loyal member of the class from which he sprang; and some simple-witted historians have persisted in believing that he was one of the best and most unselfish Prime Ministers that Britain has ever possessed. It is a judgment based on sentimental fancies, and not on the facts.

BENJAMIN DISRAELI,
EARL OF BEACONSFIELD
1804-1881

BENJAMIN DISRAELI,
EARL OF BEACONSFIELD
1804–1881

To pass from Robert Peel to Benjamin Disraeli is very like leaving a back street tenement and going to live in a grand mansion on a main avenue. It is also the difference between a view from a molehill and the vision from a mountain. In spite of his great wealth, with all its possibilities of expansion, his expensive education and his successful career, Peel had always the mind of a small man. One can furnish a small room with taste; one cannot make it a large room. He was not built on the grand scale. There was always something dull and rather drab about him; he was the product of the dull skies of the Northern lands from which his people sprang. But Benjamin Disraeli was the child of other climes. His mind was bronzed by the fierce sun of the South; for he was a Jew of the great stock that had travelled (through many centuries) from the desert to England; probably by way of Spain, and in its last steps, certainly from Italy, and directly from Venice. If nature's environment has any effect on human character, it was inevitable that his racial mind should be steeped in all the sun and colours of the East without the dull shadows that had cast an intellectual gloom over the Peels.

But it is the less necessary to seek a cause for Disraeli's mind, because the thing itself was such a palpable fact. From the beginning to the end of his career it was a blazing glow of gorgeous colouring and luxurious rhetoric; an Oriental rhetoric, however, that rarely lost itself in the wilderness of sentimentality, but continually led its audiences to the refreshing oases of a vivid realism and a pungent wit.

It is the keynote of Disraeli that, if his colouring was ever gorgeous — and sometimes, perhaps, even glaring — there was always the most solid substance beneath this raiment of dazzling hues. Because he was a youth of such audaciously embroidered waistcoats, of such violently dyed jackets, timid people with dull Northern eyes thought he was only a dandy. It was a complete error. Disraeli was first and foremost a man of supreme intellect. The decorated surface was only a camouflage — which spared him from the attack of many dull fools.

The great Disraeli's grandfather came from Italy to England, where from very little he rose to a modest success as an Italian merchant, who seems to have gradually — after the manner of his race — merged into the stock exchange and finance, assisted by the capital, and some distinction in blood, of his wife. But it was all very modest and he left his only child, Isaac, no very great fortune. But he had some from his mother's family; and being a gentleman in tastes, and therefore not exceedingly ambitious, he soon decided "to devote himself for the rest of his life to the acquisition of knowledge." The "Curiosities of Literature" was a great success; and his books on James I and Charles I led the way in the scientific revolt against the partisan, unscientific Whig tradition. He showed his scientific instincts, also, by attempting to write history from original manuscripts and not from prejudiced rumour. This is an interesting fact in a portrait of his son, who was one of the few English statesmen who had an accurate knowledge of the history of the land he ruled. Isaac married the daughter of another Italian Jew, and their son Benjamin was born in 1804.

One might have thought, at the first glance, that the young Benjamin was very unlike his secluded and modest father,

BENJAMIN DISRAELI, EARL OF BEACONSFIELD
From a portrait National Portrait Gallery

who preferred knowledge to success. For the son was full of ambition to open the oyster of the political world and win its pearl. But ambition is scarcely the descriptive word for the desire to do wiser and better deeds than the petty acts of the small political fry who governed England when Disraeli was first looking out on his world. There was Wellington who was a great man, with Castlereagh a long way behind, but most of the rest were poor fellows for a ruling class. Between them they had brought Great Britain near to the edge of an abyss. It was not all their fault, of course; Napoleon and the rest of the half-mad autocrats of Europe had done their share of the destruction. But giving them the benefit of every excuse, the rulers of England had made confusion worse confounded; they had heaped blunder on crime, and stirred the cauldron of anarchy instead of assisting it to settle into peace. To do better than such men — which was Disraeli's early resolve — was not ambition. It was a modest desire not to be unutterably foolish.

But if this was not ambition, it showed a stern determination. For in the world of English politics, this youth was an outcast — a Jew, and of small fortune. In his early days the Rothschilds were becoming a power behind the political stage scenery; but though they had won more from the battle of Waterloo than the victorious Allies ever did, yet they were still nothing but the keepers of a colossal pawn shop, where the Christians pledged their bankrupt states. The power of money has always been overrated; so it is not surprising that it was the poorer Disraeli who, by weight of brains, easily passed the overloaded financiers on the road to acknowledged national respect.

Disraeli did so much in his maturer years that this portrait cannot stop to look at his youth. One or two points are, however, necessary. His father was so indifferent about the Jewish faith that he ceased to be a Jew; but he was so careless of any religious dogma that he did not trouble to become a Christian. His son, at the submissive age of thirteen (apparently as an act of worldly wisdom) was baptised by an Anglican priest. But he was sent to a Unitarian school, and when he discovered that the length of the journey to the Anglican church made the disciples of that faith late for Sunday dinner, Benjamin proposed to his other baptised schoolmates that it might be better to become Unitarians for the duration of term. His realist mind had already appreciated the value of cynicism in a world of too earnest dogmatism.

Disraeli was to become the standard bearer of British Imperialism, but his share in the Empire was not won on the playing fields of Eton or in the quads of Oxford. He was sent neither to a public school nor to a University. At the age of seventeen he was articled to a firm of solicitors. But he escaped the danger of too much law, as he had avoided the sterility of too many classics. As he wrote of his first hero, Vivian Grey: "to be a great lawyer I must give up my chance of being a great man"; and that same hero also discovered that "there were classics in other languages besides Greek and Latin." When he was discovered in office hours reading Chaucer instead of Conveyancing it was decided that he should be allowed to pursue the former. So he went out into life without the usual disabilities of an orthodox classical education which hampered most of the men in English political life of that period. He had other advantages. At Mr. John Murray's he met some of the most distinguished authors of the day; and he travelled. People began to see that here was a very brilliant young man, though nobody, including himself, seemed to know what he ought to do. Murray gave a very remarkable estimate of him in a letter to Lockhart:

> I may frankly say that I never met with a young man of greater promise. . . . He is a good scholar, hard student and a deep thinker, of great energy, equal perseverance and indefatigable

application, and a complete man of business. His knowledge of human nature, and the practical tendency of all his ideas, have often surprised me in a young man who had hardly passed his twentieth year, and above all his mind and heart are as pure as when they were first formed; and most excellent temper too. . . . I have been acquainted with him from birth. . . . I can pledge my honour with the assurance that he is worthy of any degree of confidence that you may be induced to repose in him — discretion being another of his qualifications.

That is probably one of the most successful character studies that has ever been written of a youth of twenty; for it would have been equally appropriate (with trivial modifications) as an epitaph on his tombstone. It is so penetrating because it entirely ignores, and indeed contradicts, the unimportant surface features of this man, trivialities that have nevertheless so often obscured him from the eyes of the world; and puts his hidden — because deeper — characteristics into clear view. It declares that Disraeli was a deep thinker, when so many people — especially his crushed foes — thought he was a buffoon; a capable man of business, when he posed as a dandy and a fop; a heart as pure as a child, when it was thought he was a heartless cynic; a man of honour, when he was held up to contempt as merely an adventurer. Of course the purity was tarnished by forty years of political life, in the same inevitable way that a miner's hands become dirty when he digs coal; and Disraeli was not a good man of business in the usual sense, for his personal affairs were always in a hopeless muddle — but that was because he devoted his time to the affairs of the nation, wherein he was very competent indeed.

The paradoxical manner in which the most intellectual of British Prime Ministers first appealed to the audience of his fellow countrymen was by writing a very smart, society, anonymous novel, "Vivian Grey", the first part of which was published in 1826, when Disraeli was twenty-two. At that age high spirits are not unexpected or even blameworthy. What alarmed the dull people was that the author was audacious and brilliant; and they were therefore scared away from the deep wisdom of this youth's mind. But indeed the wisdom — had they understood it — would have shocked them more than the cynical frivolity. "Mr. Dallas was a clergyman, a profound Grecian, a poor man. He had edited the 'Alcestis' and married his laundress; lost money by his edition, and his fellowship by his match." They said that such remarks were merely a new author trying to be smart. But when he wrote of the Army and the Navy that they were "in war time fit only for desperadoes, but in peace are fit only for fools"; or of the "great world" that it was "society formed on anti-social principles"; then this young man was being smart about great affairs, which the prim people took very seriously indeed. It is amusing to hear that when his publishers tried to make the public believe that the unknown writer was a man of the most fashionable set, an alert critic soon detected that many of the smart phrases concerned matters of which really fashionable people knew nothing whatever. "Vivian Grey" made a great sensation in the reading world; and it is, with all its immaturity, a useful indication of the quality of its author's brain.

Now it is the more necessary to take note of Disraeli's books, for in spite of all the obvious signs to the contrary, they are, and will always remain, more important than the political side of his life. They certainly affected that political career in a very clear way. For example, largely because Disraeli put the old line about "the world's my oyster" as a motto on the title page of "Vivian Grey", half the people of England for the rest of the author's life had an almost certain suspicion that he was an adventurer; though, of course, the colour of his waistcoats and the shape of his ties had also a great deal to do with this stupid judgment.

Benjamin Disraeli, Earl of Beaconsfield

There has been much error in judging Disraeli aright, and it has mainly arisen because the more trivial things he did and said have been put in the foreground, while the very important things he wrote have been overlooked. Much attention has been called to the fact that he became Prime Minister of Great Britain and signed treaties and introduced legislation of a more or less temporary kind, while the really important and the really brilliant sentences and principles, that he wrote down in his second book, "The Voyage of Captain Popanilla", have been neglected. This was, again, like "Vivian Grey", a work of his immaturity, published in 1828, when he was twenty-four; but there are matters in it of more permanent importance than anything he did during his premiership.

"Popanilla" contains the roots of Benjamin Disraeli's political and social philosophy; whereas his premiership contained only the dregs of that youthful earnestness; somewhat wearily performed when he had already discovered that the world did not want his deeper wisdom, but only his lighter side of frivolous compromise. That is the tragedy of this man's life. In his youth and early manhood he was full of wise enthusiasms, and did all his best work, which was expressed by his pen. In his later years he became successful, as they judge it in official circles; but his deeds, although of superior quality according to political standards, were only the weary cynicisms of a disillusioned man. The irony of it all is that in his youth, when they said he was an insincere cynic, an adventurer and a thoughtless dandy, — then he was very much in earnest. When — by the deterioration of age and disillusionment — he had just a little of most of these poorer qualities of which they accused him in youth, why then they called him a great man, and praised him and decorated him with honours. When in youth he had been profoundly wise and very earnest, they had only laughed.

There are two parts in Disraeli's life. There was the earlier, when he had been a great thinker, who had, somewhat miraculously, drawn full buckets from the well of wisdom and had told of his discoveries in his books. There was the second part, when he tried to put his philosophy into political form — and the result was a caricature of the original. In those later days, the real man was still there, but retired below the surface, as a snail withdraws within its shell. The real Disraeli, all that really matters, was in the former part.

"The Voyage of Captain Popanilla" is one of the clues to this man. It is a story in obvious line of descent from the satirical tales of Voltaire; and the Frenchman was first only in time, but not far ahead in the quality of his wares. Like its author's life, this satire has two parts: it begins with the people of the Isle of Fantaisie:

. . . a happy though a voluptuous and ignorant race. They have no manufactures, no commerce, no agriculture, and no printing presses . . . for corn Nature gives them the bread fruit; and for intellectual amusements they have a pregnant fancy and a ready wit; tell inexhaustible stories, and always laugh at each others' jokes. A natural instinct gave them the art of making wine; and it was the same benevolent Nature that blessed them also with the knowledge of the art of making love. . . . What further bliss remains for man?

Such was the ideal.

In later life Disraeli was to become the Prime Minister of the second land of Vraibleusia (True Blue), and of his supreme contempt for this second land — which is England — the rest of this book is the revelation. The social and political and economic laws of England are presented with the rapid vivacity of a first-class revue. As an exhibition of penetrating intellect, expressed with glittering wit, it has not been often equalled in English literature. There is little of its author's later political philosophy — even when he was Prime Minister — which is not outlined in this book. By the time he was the ruling leader of his country he had discovered that it was useless to talk of fundamental truths to dull electors; so he had dropped out of his practical programme most of the vital problems which are so important in "Popanilla"; and only worried the electorate on the trivial smaller matters.

The rippling scene where the gorgeous banker is the centre of the stage is more lifelike to-day than it was almost exactly a hundred years ago, when it was first published. Popanilla mistakes this magnificent banker for the king of the land. To-day, his mistake has become a palpable economic truth. The farce continues when Popanilla asks his native guide what a banker is. The native has to confess he has never thought out the answer: "He is a banker; bankers are always rich; but why they are, or how they are, I really never had time to inquire. But I suppose, if the truth were known, they must have very great opportunities." Men have written heavy volumes on finance and have not got so near to the truth.

There is that other rollicking scene on the subject of national debt, where it is explained to the confused stranger that this vast financial burden is convincing proof of the overpowering wealth of Vraibleusia.

"But, my dear sir," exclaimed the perplexed Popanilla, "if this be really true, how then can you be said to be the richest nation in the world?" "It is very simple. The annual interest upon our debt exceeds the whole wealth of the rest of the world; therefore we must be the richest nation in the world."

There seemed to be a hitch somewhere in the logic of the answer; so Popanilla presses for a further solution; and is told: "In Vraibleusia, we have so much to do that we have no time to think; a habit which only becomes nations who are not employed." He is referred on the matter of this debt to the great Secretary of Finance. "He, no doubt, will set it right; and if, by chance, things are past even his management, why then I suppose, to use our national motto, *something will turn up*." And the confused Popanilla went to bed clearly convinced "that the nation who contrived to be the richest people in the world while they were over head and ears in debt, must be fast approaching to a state of perfection."

There was unending audacity about Benjamin Disraeli; and the high-water-mark of his intellectual insolence was when he began his attempt to make himself ruler of England by making her a figure of fun. It was the moment in English history when the materialists and the utilitarians of the Bentham school had entrenched themselves in the governing centre of the national life. It was the age of great machinery and small ideals; of much false sentiment and little sound reason. And Disraeli tilted at the whole crazy social and political structure, with the reckless joy of a free lance, who cared not two pins for the drab mob that stood in his way. It was, however, not the most discreet of election addresses with which to allure a nation to his ballot box.

There followed, in 1831, "The Young Duke", also of autobiographical value, if of slight literary importance. It showed Disraeli, only twenty-seven, with a mature wisdom which most men cannot equal at seventy. In this book he summed up George Canning, dead only four years, with a knowledge that very few of his longest biographers have discovered:

He was a consummate rhetorician; but there seemed to me a dash of commonplace in all that he said, and frequent indications of the absence of an original mind. To the last, he never got clear of "Good God, Sir!" and all the other hackneyed ejaculations of his youthful debating clubs.

The author was condescending to Peel, who, at the time was leader of the House of Commons: he wrote of him that he was:

. . . the model of a minister, and improves as a speaker; though, like most of the rest, he is fluent without the least style. He should not get so often in a passion either, or if he do, should not get out of one so easily. His sweet apologies are cloying. His candour — he will do well to get rid of that. He can make a present of it to Mr. Huskisson.

It is an amazingly truthful likeness, both in its praise and still more in its subtle irony: where it detected Peel's half-insincere passions, his half-meant regrets, his half-hypocritical straightforwardness. It got behind Peel's guard at every stroke, while his older critics were duped — or pretended they were. Disraeli was not yet a politician: he was clever enough to know the truth, and he was honest enough to speak it out frankly. Incidentally, there was hardly a man of his time whom Disraeli, at one time or another, did not draw in a brilliant character sketch. In a few lines of verse he once got nearer to the Duke of Wellington than any one else; nearer even than Greville, with all his closer and more minute detail. Disraeli had a mind very like the Duke's in its instinct to go straight to the essential fact — though the Duke would have been horrified by the gorgeous embroidery with which the Oriental mind decorated the simple truth.

It was in "The Young Duke" that the young author tried to put on paper where he stood in the political arena. The statement was embroidered with cynic humour; yet it was as true an answer as he ever gave to a question that really had no precise answer that would have satisfied any party whip. The novelist put it thus:

Am I a Whig or a Tory? I forget. As for the Tories I admire antiquity, particularly a ruin; even the relics of the Temple of

Intolerance have a charm. I think I am a Tory. But when the Whigs give such good dinners, and are the most amusing, I think I am a Whig. . . . And yet — I feel like Garrick between Tragedy and Comedy. I think I will be a Whig and Tory alternate nights, . . . or I have no objection according to the fashion of the day, to take a place under a Tory minister, providing I may vote against them.

Of course a lot of this is fooling and romance at that. But Disraeli, like so many great men, was never so wise as when he was full of jests.

The cynics will say that all this buffoonery was not surprising, for Disraeli had been suffering from some kind of brain trouble from the middle of 1827 for three years. As a last hope of cure, he travelled from Spain to Greece, Turkey and Egypt during 1830–1831. His letters home to his family are a revelation of his vivacious mind; and the whole journey, like his previous wanderings in Europe, was a large factor in his future political philosophy. Instead of learning to write Latin verse at Oxford, he had been let loose in Europe to live, intellectually, on his wits. The startling result was the difference between Benjamin Disraeli and Mr. Gladstone.

He came back to England in sound health again; and with two new books well on the way to completion. But neither "Contarini Fleming" nor "Alroy" added much to his reputation. He was turning from literature to action. He reached home in the midst of the Reform Bill tumult of 1832. His friend Bulwer took him into the society which led the way to a public career:

Yesterday I dined at Eliot's . . . I sat between Peel and Herries. . . . Peel was most gracious. He is a very great man, indeed, and they all seem afraid of him. By the bye, I observed that he attacked his turbot most entirely with his knife, so Walker's story is true. I can easily conceive that he could be very disagreeable, but yesterday he was in a most condescending mood and unbent with becoming haughtiness. I reminded him by my dignified familiarity both that he was ex-Minister and I a present Radical. A few months before when Lord John Russell had "fished as to whether I should support them" I answered, "They had one claim upon my support; they needed it" and no more.

At twenty-eight this young man was irrepressible. It may be called conceit; but it was more than that; it was also the sound judgment of an observant critic that Peel and Russell, and most of their colleagues of both parties, were not of the divine essence that deserves worship.

Then he took the plunge and stood as a candidate at the by-election at Wycombe, before the Reform Act became law. So the electors were few and very unreformed. He got twelve votes and his successful Whig opponent received twenty. In those days this was called the voice of England. A few months later he contested the same constituency after the "reform"; and again he was at the bottom of the poll, with one hundred and nineteen votes. The two Whigs polled one hundred and seventy-nine and one hundred and forty. The national voice was certainly growing louder, if not wiser. These were probably the only two elections of his career where Disraeli really said what he thought. In his addresses to the electors he defiantly announced that he came "wearing the badge of no party and the livery of no faction." He promised to vote for the ballot, triennial parliaments and the repeal of the taxes on knowledge:

> I shall withhold my support from every Ministry which will not originate some great measure to ameliorate the condition of the lower orders. . . . Rid yourselves of all that political jargon and factious slang of Whig and Tory — two names with one meaning, used only to delude you — and unite in forming a great national party which can alone save the country.

And at a political dinner he said: "I care not for party. I stand here without party. I plead the cause of the people, and I care not whose policy I arraign."

We shall find good evidence in Disraeli's life — in his literary life, that is, though not so much in his political career — that he sincerely meant what he said. He was always unique as a politician. But it must have been hard to believe that here was the people's candidate at last, when one met the surprising young dandy at the smartest houses in London. To his sister, Sarah, he wrote, in 1833: "My table is literally covered with invitations, and some from people I do not know." His diary of this time is full of his surging emotions and raging intellect — the two were never far apart in this man.

Nature has given me an awful ambition and fiery passions. My life has been a struggle, with moments of rapture — a storm with dashes of moonlight.... My disposition is now indolent. I wish to be idle and amuse myself.... Alas! I struggle from Pride. Yes, it is Pride that now prompts me, not Ambition. They shall not say I have failed.

A man who had all this perpetual struggle with his own soul was clearly of too delicate a mould to go into the coarser life of the political world. He had to give to his own conscience the ceaseless care which the politician should be giving to the management of his electors. No one in British politics ever paid so much attention to the soul as Disraeli — except Mr. Gladstone; and *his* soul was sectarian. From the beginning to the end he was at heart convinced that the life of contemplation, of leisured study, of the acquisition of knowledge, was the higher life; the life of action being a somewhat vulgar yielding to temptation. He had developed that argument in "Contarini Fleming." His own life was to be, in its latter part, a falling into the traps of the devil.

The self-revelation in the diary continued.

The world calls me conceited. The world is in error. I trace all the blunders of my life to sacrificing my own opinion to that of others.... I have an unerring instinct — I can read characters at a glance; few men can deceive me. My mind is a continental mind. It is a revolutionary mind. I am only truly great in action. . . . Poetry is the safety valve of my passions, but I wish to act what I write. My works are the embodiment of my feelings.

He said that the trilogy, "Vivian Grey", "Alroy" and "Contarini Fleming", were "the secret history of my feelings. I shall write no more about myself."

For the moment he rather paused in his progress. In 1834 he had reached the distinction of Lady Blessington's drawing-room; he asked the Duke of Wellington to accept the dedication of an epic poem — an honour which the Duke with great courtesy refused; the dangerous Mrs. Norton gave him her portrait. Lord Lyndhurst took him up; so did Count D'Orsay. The salvation of the people of England was overlooked for the moment in the brilliant throng. But he had his famous talk after dinner with Lord Melbourne, who, being a thinker and a poet himself, was attracted by another of like qualities. He asked what Disraeli wanted and the answer was, "I want to be Prime Minister." Melbourne was a gentleman and did not laugh; but said it was impossible — Lord Stanley stood in the way. The day was to come when Melbourne was to say, "By God! the fellow will do it yet."

The struggling Independent, trying to become a statesman without dressing himself in the colours of one or other of the two parties that had seized, between them, the two sides of the House of Commons, was gradually losing his courage. He gave way — as the true Independent should; he negotiated with both sides, with Lord Lyndhurst the High Tory and Lord Durham the low Radical. He finally joined the Tories, not because he loved them, but because he hated the Whigs more. On December 6, 1834, Greville wrote: "The Chancellor called on me yesterday about getting young Disraeli into Parliament (through the means of George Bentinck) for Lynn . . . he said that Durham was doing all he could to get him the offer of a seat." It was a transition time when compromises were the commonplaces of the day; and Greville goes on to tell how the honest Melbourne was at that moment "compelled . . . to eat his words." But compromise for the moment did not help the case; and Disraeli was again beaten at Wycombe in 1834; for George Bentinck would not look at this unorthodox candidate at Lynn. He was to change his mind in the future, when Disraeli had raised Bentinck from a racing man to a statesman — of a kind.

Political success came in 1837, when Disraeli, at the age of thirty-three, became the second member for Maidstone, in the first Parliament of Queen Victoria. He quickly found his feet in the House. His first speech was far from the failure it has become customary to call it; it was only the deliberate interruption of the Radicals who tried to punish the late Independent for choosing the wrong side at last. The side, in truth, was a trivial error in Disraeli's political career; it was a place on any side of the House that might more justly be said to have blighted his youthful promise. He can scarcely yet have lost hope that some of his early political programme was within the wit of the legislature and administrative machine; for during these first years in the House, being of no official importance within it, he continued his literary life by writing three political novels which between them gave — or attempted to give — England a new philosophy of public life. "Coningsby", 1844, "Sybil", 1845 and "Tancred, or the New Crusade", 1847, are the three books in which Disraeli did his chief work as an English statesman. His two premierships were of very minor importance; they were the disillusionment after the dream.

There are some who maintain that Disraeli was from the first the ambitious adventurer who was always prepared to compromise; so long as he himself went forward in office and power, the programme might lag behind as slowly as the necessity of political intrigue required. There is an almost insurmountable difficulty in this theory. For just when Disraeli had got into Parliament, and the compromising intrigues should have been the most obvious next steps, — at this critical moment the assumed adventurer spoke out on the matter of the political craft in a haughty, pugnacious manner which is not the usual tone of a man who wants to smooth his path and allure his opponents to terms. It was rather as if a wily diplomat had prayed for peace by throwing bombs at his enemy. But the books themselves are better proof than any theories about his designs.

"Coningsby" was the first of this famous trilogy of political philosophy. In the preface to the fifth edition, which was published in 1849, the author explained that it had not been his intention to use the form of fiction, but he had realised that the novel "offered the best chance of influencing opinion." He also explained why it was necessary to write such a book at that moment. He said that the Conservative triumph of 1841 had set the "youthful mind of England" searching for an answer to the question "what, after all, they had conquered to preserve." It was therefore necessary to assure the people that "Toryism was not a phrase, but a fact."

In his dedication to Henry Hope there was one most characteristic sentence; one of those quick, mental flashes which at once revealed Disraeli's method and matter. He wrote that his desire was that his book would raise the tone of public life and make men "distinguish between facts and phrases, realities and phantoms." For Disraeli's chief mark of distinction from the bulk of his fellows — his chief evidence of genius — was that (like Wellington) he had a realist mind that instinctively marched straight to the essential fact and ignored the unnecessary fancies which caught so many men's eyes.

"Coningsby" is a rash cavalry raid right into the strongly fortified lines of the orthodox political parties. It is the examination of our political system by the alien mind of a man of another race, as if a man from Japan analysed European society. It opens in the room of Mr. Rigby, the man who "manages" the parliamentary seats of the Duke of Monmouth. The patron was a good deal of a cynical fool and the man was not very much above the level of the crawling worm. They both seem, in Disraeli's eyes, to be fairly representative of their set; for we are told that the leaders were "naturally of inferior abilities, and unfortunately, in addition, of illiterate habits." Even the great Reform Act, which is the chief question when the book opens, does not improve matters — "since Mr. Rigby was a member of the House of Commons." But he was a natural product of such an age; for the Industrial Revolution had been at work for two or three generations and "in the hurry-skurry of money-making, men-making, and machine-making, we had altogether outgrown, not the spirit, but the organisation, of our institutions." England had been ruled from 1812 to 1827 by "the Arch Mediocrity" as Disraeli named Lord Liverpool; to add insult to injury he added: "His long occupation of the post proved, at any rate, that the qualification was not excessive."

The two years that followed the Reform Act of 1832 had not brought reform, but only more political intrigue, "which really should only be the resource of the second-rate." Rigby was therefore very powerful; for "He was a man who neither felt nor thought; but who possessed, in a very remarkable degree, a restless instinct for adroit baseness." The ruthless pen at last finds some social and moral hope in a few aristocrats; there is a Duke who was "bounteous to the poor" and had a kind heart and many other virtues and good tastes, in part due to his ancient blood — "an accident of lineage rather rare with the English nobility." For his wife, the Duchess, there is no jeer; she had "that perfect good breeding which is the result of nature and not of education: for it may be found in a cottage and may be missed in a palace. 'Tis a genial regard for the feelings of others that springs from an absence of selfishness."

The analysis of England, its society and politics, goes on; it is savage; it is very true. Disraeli's truth-telling is health-giving — but it stings like pouring a strong antiseptic on a raw wound. On all sides are men without principles in the governing posts; Parliament is the seat not of legislative reform, but of personal intrigue. Mr. Tadpole, one of Rigby's worms, wants a dissolution. "How are you and I to get into Parliament if there be not one?" His political programme is "Amelioration — nobody knows exactly what it means."

What Disraeli desired to preach as an ideal — after his stinging tongue had destroyed the practice that he saw around him — is of course less clear. It is always easier to destroy than to build. In the course of the story a Conservative member is returned for the city of Cambridge, and one of his triumphant supporters suddenly began to wonder what they have been fighting for: "If any fellow were to ask me what the Conservative Cause is, I am sure I should not know what to say." And in the ironical answer to his question can be discovered Disraeli's serious answer in negative form:

A Crown robbed of its prerogatives; a Church controlled by a commission; and an Aristocracy that does not lead . . . the order of the Peasantry has vanished . . . and is succeeded by a race of serfs, who are called labourers, and who burn ricks. . . . The Crown has become a cipher; the Church a sect; the Nobility drones; and the People drudges.

The lately ardent electioneers realise they have been very foolish; and there is talk of a remedy. "There is nothing so difficult as to organise an independent party in the House of Commons," says one; and the sentence gives us the reason for Disraeli's submission to the Tory machine. But Coningsby, the hero, goes on: "Let us think of principles and not of parties"; and we again begin to understand the task this critical Jew had set himself as his life work in politics: to teach his party essential national principles; to push out the selfish personal intrigue. This alien philosopher preferred that England should be governed by a national monarch and an aristocracy of blood, rather than by professional politicians seeking places and by plutocrats seeking wealth. What he visualised was (in his own words): "a free monarchy, itself the apex of a vast pile of municipal and local government, ruling an educated people, represented by a free and intellectual press." Then followed the inevitable gibe: "Even statesmen would be educated." He wanted, in short, the citizens to govern themselves in their local councils, and to be less harried by an unrepresentative central Parliament.

Where the people came into this proposed political system is the main theme of the second volume, "Sybil, or the Two Nations", 1845. It is the story of "the Condition of the People" as the author put it in his preface. It is written with his inevitable vivacity, but there is a deeper tone of fiercer sincerity. Disraeli's sympathy for an overworked and underpaid labour world is very serious; and he here mixes many of his epigrams with salt rather than with the honey of wit as had been his wont. He was too much of a gentleman to jest at the sick bed of the poor — in Rigby's rooms it had been different. But there is wit enough, for all that, to float a dozen of the novels of commerce: and the politicians continue to get their knock-out blows, which make both themselves and the readers see stars.

What astonishes the reader of this book is that this alien Jew was one of our few British statesmen who knew much about the past history of his country, or had studied, in the flesh, its present condition. It is in large part an economic survey of England in the middle of the nineteenth century. It is the kind of thing a Royal Commission might have collected in a report. Only a commission, being full of orthodox propriety and primness, could only have told half the truth; and would probably only have recommended platitudes as a remedy. Whereas Disraeli — after his instinctive habit of realism — spent his whole time on the essential facts.

"Behind that laughing landscape" of England, "penury and disease fed upon the vitals of a miserable population." The picture is of a rural town, whose revenue "swelled the vast rental which was drawn from this district by the fortunate earls that bore its name." It is a picture, in miniature, of the two nations, the Rich and the Poor. There is a portrait of one of the rich, in Disraeli's most brilliant colours; one "Warren, who had made money as a Nabob in India by forestalling rice during a famine"; and "at the same time had fed, and pocketed millions." He had ended as Lord Fitz-Warene in the peerage of Ireland. His English estate had developed, during the war — the beginning of so many fortunes of patriots — into a great manufacturing town; which his son had inherited with its vast rent roll and its surrounding estate; but "he was over-educated for his intellect; a common misfortune . . . he most fully, entirely, and absolutely believed in his pedigree." He became an English earl.

That is one side of the picture. On the other, in the earl's own words: "Every man at Marney may be sure of his seven shillings a week, for at least nine months in the year; and for the other three, they can go to the House, and a very proper place for them." The moral is not the usual "class war" claptrap of the class-conscious agitator; for the working man, when he rose in fortune, made the worst of masters.

The district of Wodgate — which was "land without an owner, without manorial rights, where cottages could be built without paying any one a rent" — was no better than the manors of lords. The working-class masters were "ruthless tyrants", and their slaves only "animals." Yet Disraeli quickly adds, with that instinct to recognise real merit, these rough master workmen locksmiths did know their job: "It is a real aristocracy, it is privileged, but it does something for its privileges"; and therefore its slaves had some kind of respect for it. But still it was all very evil — and the remedy was still to be sought. Even the once-earnest labour leaders, Dandy Dick and Devilschild, blossom out as the partners of the flourishing capitalist "firm of Radley, Mobray and Co. . . . and will probably furnish in time a crop of members of Parliament and peers of the realm."

What is the solution of the problem? Or is there any? Disraeli had no hope in Democracy, as it is painted by the flattering lips of the professional agitator or the amateur reformer. Sybil murmurs some vague phrase that "the People have learnt their strength." To whom the sympathetic, but better informed, Egremont replies: "Dismiss from your mind those fallacious fancies. The People are not strong; the People never can be strong." He may have been wrong in the sphere of the philosophers and the final judgment; but Disraeli was writing as a practical politician, as a member of Parliament who was trying to discover how to get something done. So it was not snobbishness, but common sense that made him preach that the Democracy of the middle of nineteenth-century England was a broken reed as a weapon of attack or defence. And yet, perhaps, he believed in the People more than any great English statesman. Beside his genial democracy, Mr. Gladstone had the thoughts of a very superior person. There are many proofs that although Disraeli was so bright and sparkling in fine

"Society", it was the mill girls in "Sybil", and even Clotilde and Ermengarde, those very questionable young French ladies in "Coningsby", with very kind hearts and very misty morals, whom he really respected and enjoyed.

Since the People, with a capital letter, were of little strength, Disraeli looked around for something more effective as a political weapon. His contemporaries were still hopeful of the parliamentary reformers. Disraeli would as soon have hoped for assistance from the Betting Ring — wherein, strange to say, he was afterwards to find it in the unexpected person of Lord George Bentinck. He raked the politicians with his continual fire of wit and sarcasm, as he had done in "Coningsby" and, indeed, in almost everything he wrote — surely a curiously dangerous card for an "adventurer" to play. He paints the picture of "the gentleman in Downing Street" giving lessons in the political trade; and every word is a revelation of hypocrisy and deceit. Here is one scrap of advice:

> If there be any dissenters on the deputation, who having freed the Negroes, have no subjects left for their foreign sympathies, hint at the tortures of the bull-fight and the immense consideration to humanity, that, instead of being speared at Seville, the Andalusian Toro will probably in future be cut up at Smithfield. This cheapness of provisions will permit them to compete with the foreigner in all neutral markets.

And so he goes on, pouring gravel into the political machine with savage bitterness. The "adventurer" was clearly burning all the boats in which he might escape in time of need.

His proposal of "a free Monarchy and a privileged and prosperous People" — to take the place of the privileged governing class — cannot be expounded now. For it would need great length, being based on the long story of historical growth. "It is the past alone that can explain the present," he wrote. The English had forgotten their history, and so had wandered far from any solid ground of stable principles in public life. It is one of the great paradoxes that it was a Jew who tried to teach them this forgotten national wisdom.

In "Tancred, or the New Crusade", 1847, the lesson was continued. In his preface, Disraeli announced that he had "recognised in the Church the most powerful agent in the previous development of England, and the most efficient means of that renovation of the national spirit at which he aimed." Like his great rival, Gladstone, Disraeli believed that a true religion was the basis of a true political life. In the heat of parliamentary rhetoric, they failed to observe that they were, in this most important matter, nearer to each other than any two men in the House of Commons. These misunderstandings so often arise in political life, when two men both want to be Prime Minister at the same time.

In "Tancred" the trilogy of satirical political economy comes to its end in a significant way. It is a symphony of religious passion. Disraeli, like all great men, cannot be fitted into any small definition; but above all else he was a creature who was continually allowing his imagination to sweep him into the open sea of the unknown and the mysterious. He was first and foremost a poet, and therefore he had a religion; although it was not of a kind that would necessarily have been always recognised by the professional priests. Indeed, there was much in this book which they must have profoundly disliked.

There is a portrait of an Anglican bishop which would have brought down the hierarchy in peals of laughter — if bishops had not been too serious to listen to wit. This particular victim "combined a great talent for action with very limited powers of thought. . . . He was one of those leaders who are not guides. . . . All his quandaries terminated in the same catastrophe; a compromise. Abstract principles with him ended in concrete expediency." He had raised materialism to a fine art; and had been rewarded by the endowments of an episcopal chair.

Tancred was seeking a more serious faith: "Nobody now thinks about heaven. They never dream of angels. All their existence is concentrated in steam-boats and railways." The fair lady of fashion, with whom he talked, murmurs that this is very true: "Jerusalem has been the dream of my life. I have always been endeavouring to reach it, but somehow or other I never got further than Paris." But Tancred set off for Palestine. "I go to a land that has never been blessed by that fatal drollery called a representative government."

The religion of Disraeli was not a matter of sentiment; it was always very closely connected with this material world. It is significant that this romance of faith opens with a brilliant chapter on French cooks in London; and Tancred ends — as Disraeli himself ended — "all mixed up with intrigue, and politics, and management and baffled schemes, and cunning arts of men." Against all his deeper intelligence, his wiser emotions, Disraeli was now in the thick of the parliamentary battle — or was it only a game? Tancred had said: "Parliament seems to me to be the very place which a man of action should avoid," yet Disraeli the poet, the dreamer, who had written these words, could not resist the allurement of the political stage.

It would have needed a saint to resist his parliamentary temptation; for he was an enormous success in the House. Within a year of his entering it, there was a rush to hear him whenever he rose to speak. He was invited to the grandest political dinners. When he resisted the repeal of the Corn Laws, as early as 1838, "in the lobby all the squires came up to shake hands with me. . . . They were so grateful, and well they might be, for certainly they had nothing to say for themselves." The witless, speechless gentlemen of sober England had found a spokesman at last. Is it surprising that the man with the witty tongue enjoyed using it before such an appreciative audience? It was the more delightful a sport, in as much as while so many members of the House were shouting with joy at his jests the rest were shrieking for his blood. Disraeli was in his element. "I think I have become very popular in the House; I ascribe it to the smoking room." The haters he enjoyed more than the friends.

At this period he announced that a legal counsel, in a parliamentary petition case, had libelled him; but he was not surprised he said, "because Mr. Austin is a member of an honourable profession, the first principle of whose practice appears to be that they may say anything provided they are paid for it. . . . It may be the custom of society to submit to it in practice; but for my part, it appears to me to be nothing better than a disgusting and intolerable tyranny, and I, for one, shall not bow to it in silence." The future Tory Prime Minister of Great Britain (as he became when he was tamed) was now a rebel against convention and tyranny in every drop of his blood; and he thus tried ineffectually to get the offending lawyer to meet him in a duel.

Peel took office in 1841, but disregarded Disraeli's appeal for a post in his Government. There is some evidence that Lord Stanley threatened that "if that scoundrel were taken in he would not remain a member of Peel's Ministry." His instinct was probably sound; it would be suicide for the nobles of England to allow common men of culture and wit to intrude into the British ruling circles. He had possibly heard of the domestic tragedy in the cuckoo's nest. So Disraeli's energies were turned into other directions; he brought down the Government that had rejected him. And Stanley had to eat humble pie later on.

There was a small group of aristocratic young men in the House of Commons who hated, in a vague sort of way, the new Industrialists, the new Free Traders and the new politicians who were legislating to suit the new man. "Coningsby" and "Sybil" gave this "Young England" set a policy and a tongue; and Disraeli became their leader. They were rather a poor lot, and most of them were ready to be bribed into silence by the first offer of office. But they were enough to give Disraeli a start as something more than a free lance; and as the Corn Law debates developed he gradually became the leader of the whole Protectionist Party.

It was much more, as far as he was concerned, than a squabble about tariffs. For two sessions Disraeli had supported Peel's Government with consistent energy; but he began to hesitate when he saw, or at least suspected, that Peel meant sooner or later to repeal the Corn Laws, which protected British farmers against foreign competition. This was a direct challenge to Disraeli's political philosophy. If "Coningsby" and "Sybil" had any clear meaning, it was that England should get back to its healthier agricultural past rather than go forward to a still dirtier and smokier industrial future.

By the beginning of 1844, Peel (who was one of the smoky future party) had shown his resentment at Disraeli's independent speech by withholding the invitations sent out to other members of the party; nevertheless, Disraeli still voted with the Government in the next important division, on Ireland. But it was at this moment that he published "Coningsby"; and, as we have seen, that book was a challenge to the whole orthodox political system. He was also at work on "Sybil" and was putting its subject matter into his speeches: "I had seen that while immense fortunes were accumulating . . . the working classes, the creators of wealth, were steeped in the most abject poverty and gradually sinking into the deepest degradation." This he said in a speech during 1844. In the same year he voted with Lord Ashley in forcing a Factory Bill on the Government, while the two chief Free Traders, Bright and Cobden, supported the manufacturers' demand for long hours. Then Disraeli voted (against the Government) for an amendment to the sugar duties; an amendment which would have given a preference to sugar grown by free labour over sugar grown by slave labour; and Cobden and Bright, the Free Traders, voted in favour of black slavery, as they had been in favour of white slavery in their English mills when the Factory Bill was discussed. Peel, in the case of both the Factory Bill and the sugar duties, by threats made the House reverse its decisions. It was a humiliation for which the spirit of Disraeli had no liking; and — as we have seen — he hit at Peel with one of his most famous gibes.

Everything was thus working for the final crash which was to put Disraeli in the front rank of the House of Commons. It was now open war between Peel and his rebellious follower. "Sybil" had just appeared with its savage anger at the new industrialists who were ruining England and turning it from a place of beautiful fields into a factory yard. At this psychological moment in Disraeli's mind, Sir Robert Peel made it clear that he had at last decided to abolish the Corn Laws, with their protection for English farmers. The Prime Minister was gathering together in his own person all that Disraeli detested in social and political and economic life. Peel was blocking the factory reforms. But was it unexpected? For was he not a millionaire, living on a vast fortune which had been made out of sweated children? The Peel family summed up all that Disraeli has scourged with his wit and wisdom in "Sybil." When Peel declared for Free Trade in corn, the cup of Disraeli's anger was overflowing. This dull-thinking product of an industrialised, machine-driven England was about to hammer one more, perhaps the final, nail into the coffin of the older England whose history Disraeli knew so well and loved so fondly. So the man of imagination and knowledge vowed vengeance on this machine-made, official, dummy Premier who had climbed by his wealth (and every safe and prim belief) into the chief governing seat of his nation — while Disraeli had remained an impatient outcast.

After Peel was dead, Disraeli drew his picture with his pen. It had the dignified, courteous reserve of a funeral oration; but there were phrases of vitriolic irony — which were truer than the eulogy:

He was without imagination. . . . His judgment was faultless, provided that he had not to deal with the future. . . . He embalmed no great political truth in immortal words. His flights were ponderous; he soared with the wing of the vulture rather than the plume of the eagle. . . . What he really was, and what posterity will acknowledge him to have been, is the greatest Member of Parliament that ever lived.

Disraeli had just told all who cared to read just what he thought of Parliament and its politicians; so this last phrase was like the hissing of a caressing viper.

It was this figure of official propriety and philosophical impropriety and dullness that stood up before Disraeli in the House of Commons as the embodiment of all that he scorned and hated. Never were passionate hatred, sound intellect, injured pride and thwarted ambition so completely gathered together in a political opponent. So Disraeli hit at Peel with the weight of a thunderbolt and the brilliancy of a lightning flash. There has been nothing in the history of the House like this political duel in 1845 and 1846. But it was scarcely a duel; it was more like a war dance on the body of a speechless foe, in an arena that was shouting with laughter at every flash of the victor's sword.

By one of those inexplicable freaks of illogical fortune, Disraeli, late wanderer in the wilderness of political life, found himself no longer the leader of merely a little group of "Young England" aristocrats, who were of as little account as freaks usually are. For the main battle had gathered round the Corn Laws; and on this question it was no longer a few freaks who agreed with Disraeli, but almost all the country gentlemen of England. It was the last great rally of Old England and its fields against New England and its factories.

The gentlemen of England were a slow-speaking race and not very bright in their wits; so when they saw Disraeli tearing their enemy Peel into fine shreds of mutilated flesh before their eyes they shouted with joy. It reminded them of fox hunting, which was more in their line than political oratory. They knew little about political economy and finance; so they clung to this amazing Oriental stranger as drowning men at sea cling to an unexploded mine — hoping desperately that it will not go off. Besides, so many of them did not even guess it was a dangerous mine at all — they were so dull! They probably never guessed all that their leader intended, if he succeeded. They did not understand that a protected agriculture was to him only part of a political philosophy of economic liberty for the people, and not merely high rents for their landlords. They had every reason to know what Disraeli wanted, for his democratic earnestness had been repeated a hundred times on his many pages. But probably they did not understand his wit. It would have been asking too much of human nature to have expected Disraeli to examine the passports of every man who rushed to enroll in his raiding party into Peel's ministerial fortress in the House of Commons.

So Disraeli, the Jew, whom they had so often called an adventurer, and whom Stanley had called a scoundrel, became the leader of the English country gentlemen. That might not seem a conclusive proof of his democratic convictions. But when he turned to face his opponents there was proof enough. Who were the leaders of the Free Trade Party? They were the wealthy manufacturers; who financed the Anti-Corn Law League with such plutocratic generosity because they hoped that cheap food would mean cheap labour in their mills. They were the men, like Bright and Cobden, who were vigorous opponents of factory reform, because they wanted to be allowed to sweat their labourers at their pleasure. Of course they wrapped up their intentions in rhetorical phrases about liberty and freedom of contract, which they had found in the political economy lectures of the university professors. For the professors had posts for life and fixed salaries, and therefore believed in free competition for others. So if Disraeli led the gentlemen's party who wanted high rents, his enemies were the pick of plutocracy who wanted low wages. It was undiluted joy to the writer of "Sybil" to face such foes; and when they were led by a pompous Peel his joy became a poetic ecstasy.

Peel had gone into office pledged to a Tory programme, of which protection for English corn was one of the chief vows. And now he was outbidding Lord John Russell in his offer of Free Trade. Peel spent his life in proving the sincerity of his conversions by the blackness of his treacheries. He was always showing his good faith by betraying his friends. Disraeli had an enemy whose battlements were exposed on every side; and he raked them from every quarter. So many of the phrases in his speeches have become historic. "The right honourable gentleman caught the Whigs bathing and walked away with their clothes. He has left them in the full enjoyment of their liberal position, and he is himself a strict conservative of their garments." And so on, and so on. But it was the exquisite skill of the delivery that made the words so effective. He baited Peel as they bait bulls in a ring. The night he reminded the Prime Minister of his Protectionist speeches before his conversion, after making him ridiculous by his humour, he ended: "Dissolve, if you please, the Parliament you have betrayed, and appeal to the people who, I believe, mistrust you. For me there remains this at least — the opportunity of expressing thus publicly my belief that a Conservative Government is an organised hypocrisy"; and the fox hunters behind, who loved hard-riding and had plenty of courage, if they had no tongues, made a scene which was described in a contemporary journal as "perfectly unparalleled. No man within our recollection has wielded a similar power over the sympathies and passions of his hearers."

Gladstone recalled many years later that Peel only dared to answer once — and then "failed utterly." Disraeli was like a bull standing in the ring with his victim between his horns, and no one dared to go to the rescue. His greatest triumph had been on the first night of the great session of 1846, when Peel had retaken his office with the final determination to repeal the Corn Laws. The Protectionists had lost hope; and Peel's speech seemed as if it would be unchallenged. Then Disraeli rose, and when he sat down the agricultural party had the heart of a lion instead of the faces of sheep.

Disraeli had made himself famous; and it was only a matter of time until he should become Prime Minister. But the essential point to note is that he became famous in politics by being defeated as a great constructive statesman. For wit and logic and historical proofs were nothing against Peel with a majority of votes. The manufacturers won; they got their free corn; and English agriculture has been allowed to decay. Cotton and wool and iron and silk stockings can perhaps earn dividends more easily if they are not hampered by the competing labour market of a prosperous countryside. But the balance of English life has been lost. Alone in Europe, Peel and the social system which he founded decided that England can do without an agricultural heart. It is the basic trade of humanity, but Englishmen have been persuaded that they can live safely and soundly by making silk stockings and motor cars, and fittings for wireless sets.

Disraeli was the last great statesman to protest against such an amazing fallacy.

The day that Peel swept away the Corn Laws, Disraeli and his angry friends defeated him on an Irish question. The Irish have rarely received reforms from the English governments; but they have taken many revenges; and this was one of them.

Disraeli thus began his successful career as a famous English politician. But all that mattered — which nobody heeded — he had already done. His contribution to statesmanship was in his books and not in the Houses of Parliament. His political career was the measure of his failure and not of his success. For all that he did was so trivial beside the measure he had himself set before statesmen.

It must not be imagined that he failed as the politicians estimate success. He even did far better than the rest, and several times played with the fringe of his own ideals. He forced the hand of his followers and gave England its first franchise worthy of the name of democratic, in 1867. As Premier, in 1875, he gave the Trade Unionists an act which saved them, in part, from the clumsy Liberal Act of 1870; it had been, in great measure, the revolt of Labour against this last which put Disraeli in power in 1874. During the same ministry there were several useful Acts of social reform, which must have revived in the Prime Minister some memories of "Sybil" and its ideals. There were memories in his foreign affairs of those romantic visions of an Eastern policy which was in the blood of his race. He made his beloved Queen the Empress of India; and be it noted that his imperialism was always nearer the ideal of the poet than the trade of the commercial traveller — which is the rather mercenary imperialism of most of the men who now spin fine rhetoric round his name.

All that he did as a political leader can be read in the historical textbooks; and all together it was but a fragment of the ideals of "Coningsby" and "Sybil" and "Tancred"; while "Popanilla" would scarcely know that the island of Vraibleusia had been touched by its creator's hand. Yet in spite of failure, and temptations to be as others were in the political game, he kept his ideals before his eyes and his honour unsoiled. In 1855 when Lord John Russell was behaving like a self-seeking adventurer, Disraeli offered to resign the leadership of the Tory Party he had just so hardly won, if Palmerston cared to enter a Coalition Government and lead the House of Commons. It was not the only lesson in political morality that this Jew taught the aristocrats of England. When the Indian Mutiny came and vulgar crowds were shrieking for another conquest, with the blood of retaliation, Disraeli remained a gentleman and a statesman, and asked a Liberal Government to remember that mercy was the greatest victory.

He had been lured into political life by the temptations of his brilliant tongue. But it was not his natural place in life. He began his career as a dreamer of dreams — and so he ended. As the old man was slowly dying, an earl of the nation he had conquered, worldly men might have said that he had succeeded in life. But he himself knew better. A visitor to his country home tells how his host sat before the fire in half-conscious musing. He had been one of the greatest speakers of his time, but now the only words the guest could hear were "Dreams, dreams, dreams." They were the keynotes of Benjamin Disraeli's life.

WILLIAM EWART GLADSTONE
1809–1898

WILLIAM EWART GLADSTONE
1809-1898

If the English people had wearied of the dazzling Benjamin Disraeli and turned to seek a new Premier who was entirely different, then they must have been altogether satisfied when they discovered Mr. Gladstone. For it was as if they had left the company of the wittiest of audacious philosophers in order to spend their days with the primmest of orthodox saints. It was as if they had put Lucian's dialogues on the shelf and taken down a volume of St. Augustine; or thrown aside Heine and Anatole France, and picked up the odd remnants of a theological library. It was the difference between the sun of Venice and the damp mists of Scotland, which were the respective immediate sources whence these two men came.

To pass from the ever alluring variety of the great six-volume biography of Disraeli by Mr. Monypenny and Mr. Buckle to the three-volume life of Gladstone by Lord Morley, is like passing from a gorgeously decorated romance to the story of the stern struggles of a great man in narrow circumstances. One's first impression is that Disraeli was a philosopher and Gladstone a fanatic. In the one case there is the breezy open air of free thought — which was only restrained by the limits of a superb common sense; while the other has all the dull oppression of a mental cell, shut in by the limits of every irrational convention that has tricked the mind of man. But in spite of essential differences, these two men had also equally essential resemblances. For they were both mystics and dreamers, though Disraeli was dreaming of the seen beauties of the earth, while Gladstone was musing on the unseen glories of heaven. They were, also, both great speakers in the Houses of Parliament; but while the Jew sharpened his words until they had the cutting edge of the razor, the Scotsman wove his sentences until they had the intricate texture of ancient tapestry, where the colouring is very beautiful but the design is not always understandable. There is no doubt that they both had great masses of brain tissue which they used with terrific energy in two very opposite directions; and by the time they had reached their two goals — which of course they never did — they were as the two poles apart. For the one had pursued the mystery of hard facts — and became a realist; the other was swept away by the intricate variety of abstract thoughts — and lived in a (sometimes very beautiful) cloudland that can only be reached by those lofty souls who are too good for this ignoble earth.

The early life of Gladstone was sufficient reason for the rest of his career, even if his more distant heredity be forgotten. His whole education must have confirmed his instinctive impression that it was better to learn life from books in libraries than from facts outside them. He always persisted, in later reminiscences, that he had no particular inclination towards acquiring knowledge. Whereas the young Disraeli had a restless mind that was searching everywhere into everything; but then, the Jew spent very little of his youth in schools and none at all in colleges, but out in the world, largely in Continental travel. He was the product of that open world. Whereas Gladstone was the product of Eton and Christ Church, as George Canning had been; and the result in both cases was essentially the same; both men made their political reputations by their gift for words, rather than their judgment of facts. Of course, there was the distinction that Canning was very deficient in the higher morality, while Gladstone was more conscientious than anything else.

The hereditary origin of Gladstone was strangely like that of his political master, Sir Robert Peel. They both came of trading stock with strong evidence of feudal nobility farther back. The wealthy Gladstone merchant father dedicated his son to a political career as the elder Peel had done. Both fathers sought the orthodoxies by a public school education followed by Oxford University — in order to crush out all possibility of "unsound" thought in their sons. But there was a fine strain of Celtic imagination in Mr. Gladstone's mother that often made her son an uncertain element in the political circles — as we shall see. He would often insist on doing what he thought was right — which is always an unexpected complication in political life.

During Gladstone's time at Eton there was practically no education in any scientific sense of that term. The only fraction of life to which any attention was drawn was the literature of Greece and Rome; and there was a persistent and morbid desire to turn English thought into Latin verses. As Lord Morley put it: "Science even in its rudiments fared as ill as its eternal rival, theology. There was a mathematical master, but nobody learned anything from him, or took any notice of him." Gladstone himself said that one master incited him to work, but "even then as I had really no instructor, my efforts at Eton, down to 1827 (the year he left), were perhaps of the purest plodding ever known." He also wrote in later days: "the actual teaching of Christianity was all but dead, though happily none of its forms had been surrendered" — which was (with his persistent obliviousness to the facts) scarcely true. For, after Latin verses, the chief education at Eton was to blacken each other's person by fighting. The headmaster of this time, Doctor Keate, has lived in history as the man who flogged eighty boys on one day. The only admirable thing which Gladstone learned at Eton was a great horror of physical violence. His mind always lived in the realms of thought; and he could see no fit reasons for adopting the manners of a prize fighter. But this was probably not what Doctor Keate and his system had intended. Indeed, the famous playing fields of Eton had in this case one of their most conspicuous failures; for, instead of sending out Mr. Gladstone to enlarge the empire, they made him a very conscientious gentleman; and even a "little Englander", as some of his opponents crudely said.

So Gladstone was not educated at Eton. He may rather be said to have survived it and passed on to Christ Church, Oxford. There he continued to mix with the same raw mental set that had endeavoured to teach him the rules of the "best" society at school. In Lord Morley's words: "Christ Church in those days was infested with some rowdyism, and in one bear-fight an undergraduate was actually killed." Gladstone was elected to a scholarship, having written a theme and "passed a nominal, or even farcical examination in Homer and Virgil." After two years of the system he wrote to his father: "I am wretchedly deficient in the knowledge of modern languages, literature and history; and the classical knowledge acquired here, though sound, accurate, and useful, yet is not such as to *complete* an education." Nevertheless, amid these somewhat tarnished scenes of scholarship and high society, Gladstone took a double first in classics and mathematics. So he was clearly the superior of most of the youths around him. He finished his university career with a mind solidly set — as in concrete — with every convention of orthodox thought which Christ Church considered safe for the young men who were going out to govern England. For it was the holy shrine of the governing set; and young Gladstone, as young Peel before him, had been sent there by a wise and wealthy father who was determined that his son should learn the orthodoxies which were the passport to political power. No two fathers ever had more piously correct sons, who swallowed down

William Ewart Gladstone 245

their intellectual pap with the automatic energy of sea-lions at the Zoölogical Gardens. Their Oxford classics and mathematics had very marked effects on both men; they alike developed brains that were very efficient for their parliamentary careers. They could both do an enormous amount of mental work; could talk for hours at a time, and persuade other people that black was white. No one stopped to ask what particular reason there was why a man who knew so much about Greek and Latin verbs and conic sections should be best fitted for governing England in the nineteenth century.

Gladstone was almost — not quite — a typical product of the Oxford idea. He spent a large part of his life believing every statement which was made by the very select (and somewhat limited) group of philosophical and literary persons who were considered "safe" by the Christ Church staff. He came down from Oxford with scarcely an original idea left in his double first brain. He did not believe in anything except what the "authorities" said he ought to believe. And above all else he believed with his whole heart that everything he was told at church was true. In short, everything that mattered or was true in the world was written in Greek or Latin or Hebrew. He had — in his early life — the most carefully trimmed mind — like an old box hedge in an ancient garden.

Mr. Gladstone went farther than his masters intended. He not only said he believed all he was told — he really *did* believe it. He was the most serious believer who ever made politics his profession. He had a very great brain, and he gave almost all of it to believing whatever he was told at Oxford. He was the greatest success of that ancient institution. It had spent the many centuries of its career in teaching the world two subjects; to believe in the Latin — and later the Greek — classics, and in the Christian Church. Mr. Gladstone swallowed the whole curriculum. His world revolved round these two points. But as, strictly speaking, there can only be one centre to a circle, he had to decide whether Christ or Homer was the real centre.

There is a characteristic entry in his diary on August 4, 1820:

> Began Thucydides. Also worked up Herodotus. . . . Uncomfortable again and much distracted with doubts as to my future line of conduct. God direct me. I am utterly blind. Wrote a very long letter to my dear father on the subject of my future profession.

The matter had come to this early issue. Was Gladstone to spend his life in saving the souls of men, according to the Christian manner? The letter he wrote to his father was of the most primitive fanaticism — more usually found in the local lay preacher.

> The conviction flashes on my soul with a moral force I cannot resist, and would not if I could, that the vineyard still wants labourers . . . there can be no claim so solemn and imperative . . . why will you not bring to fellow-creatures sitting in darkness and the shadow of death the tidings of this universal and incomprehensible love.

He goes on with the frantic terror of the revivalist, with hell fire hissing behind him:

> Of my duties to *men* as a social being, can any be so important as to tell them of the danger under which I believe them to be, of the precipice to which I fear many are approaching, while thousands have already fallen headlong, and others again, even as I write are continuing to fall in a succession of appalling rapidity?

Christ Church had reached the climax of its career as the teacher of the orthodoxies. It had turned a youth with all the latent signs of genius — let there be no disputing that fact — into the unbalanced figure of a preacher in a village tin chapel. The result may have been unexpected by the college authorities, for we are told that "the service [in the chapel] was scarcely performed with common decency."

The father had no such intentions when he sent his son to Eton and Oxford; and counselled a delay in such an important decision. He recommended a Continental tour; and gradually the son gave way — to the temptations of the world, as he clearly regarded it. For he went on protesting that he had strength to crush the lower earthly desires for the honour of "being permitted to be the humblest of those who may be commissioned to set before the eyes of man, still great even in his ruins, the magnificence and the glory of Christian faith." Then he went on to confess how the devil was tugging at his heart to tempt him to a political or legal career: for he added: "I feel that my temperament is so excitable, that I should fear giving up my mind to other subjects which have ever proved sufficiently alluring to me, and which I fear would make my life a fever of unsatisfied longings and expectations."

It was a remarkable declaration. Here was a man who believed that a political career was a falling into sin. To the youthful fanatic the future premiership loomed ahead as the triumph of Satan. But he was giving way! In 1831 he wrote in his diary: "Politics are fascinating to me; perhaps too fascinating." However, his nimble mind was already finding a satisfactory excuse; he will do the work of heaven in whatever department of life he may find himself: "May God use me as a vessel for his own purpose." He had "a fervent and buoyant hope that I might work an energetic work in this world, and by that work (whereof the worker is God) I might grow into the image of the Redeemer."

So Mr. Gladstone, like Oliver Cromwell, went into public life with the sure and certain hope that he was the personally conducted agent of God. When in 1832 he received the offer of a parliamentary seat — in a rotten borough which was the property of the Duke of Newcastle, whose most famous political utterance was that he had "the right to do as he liked with his own" — he received it almost as the call to set out on a pilgrimage. But he had always a convenient skill in making this world fit in with the next. On the way to Newark, his constituency, he travelled on Sunday with a fellow passenger who agreed with him that it was wrong to use the Lord's day in this manner — as they were both using it — and the diary records: "gave him some tracts. Excellent mail. Dined at Yeovil; read a little of the *Christian Year*." His political career had begun with a convenient blending of his faith and the world. But this interest in his religion was always his consuming fire. In 1834 he wrote: "conversation of an interesting kind, with Brandreth and Pearson on eternal punishment; with Williams on baptism; with Churton on faith and religion in the university; with Harrison on prophecy and the papacy." This man had that intense interest in religion that most of his class had for horse racing and pheasant shooting.

From the very first he regarded his power of speech as a direct gift from God. In 1834 he was trying to screw up his courage to speak on a university question; and his diary runs: "What a world it is, and how does it require the Divine power and aid to clothe in words the profound and mysterious thought." A few months later he wrote: "Spoke 30 to 35 minutes on University bill, with more ease than I had hoped, having been more mindful, or less unmindful, of Divine aid." The time had soon come when this assistance was urgently necessary; for his maiden speech in the House of Commons was to defend his father from a serious charge of ill-treating his slaves on his West Indian sugar estates. The son, presumably under the certainty of divine instructions, said that the slaves ought to be freed at some future time, but only after compensation to the owners. As he said himself, in 1838, when he had again to speak on the same subject: "Prayer, earnest prayer for the moment was wrung from me in my necessity; I hope it was not a blasphemous prayer, for support in pleading the cause of justice" — and the family income.

Soon after his maiden speech he had to rise again; this second time in order to defend his father's fellow citizens of Liverpool, who had been caught selling their parliamentary votes. Providence was indeed testing its youthful prophet by peculiar tasks. Then the divine inspiration told him to oppose Hume's attempt to admit Dissenters to the universities; and he told his electors at Newark that as it was a righteous thing for Englishmen to maintain an Anglican Church, so, also, it must be right to make Irish Roman Catholics do the same — an assertion of mental tyranny which the speaker was to reverse with great honour to himself in later years. As his life developed there is an extraordinary fascination in watching the greater and deeper instinctive genius of the man, which had been buried under the clumsy mass of the Eton and Oxford orthodoxy, gradually pushing its way to the surface. At the end he was to reverse a great part of the decisions that he made in the earlier portion of his life.

At the age of twenty-five, in 1834, he became Assistant Lord of the Treasury under Peel, who had discovered that this man of ardent faith had also a more worldly capacity for figures and finance. In 1835 he was promoted to be Under Secretary for the Colonies. His father had been right. It was much easier to make a rapid career in the State than in the Church. But this Tory Ministry was a very passing event, and Gladstone was soon out of office until 1841. He continued to protest against even the timid changes that Lord Melbourne and his colleagues put before Parliament. Thus, the Dissenters were not to have reform of church rates, which they naturally resented paying; again, he would have nothing to do with giving national money for education,

if the same heretics were to share in the benefits; and he
would not yet allow the Jews to be admitted to Parliament.
All of which opinions he was to reverse sooner or later, of
course.

But as yet, he was too full of religious dogmas to listen to
reason. It was in 1838 that he wrote his famous book on
"The State in Its Relation with the Church." He was
gradually throwing off his crude evangelicanism of the village
preacher type and putting in its place a more scholarly and
very magnificent conception of a stately Church which was
to be the official soul of the human race. As was almost
inevitable, this dream first came to him when he was in Rome
in 1832. Being a Scotsman, he could not venture too near
the incensed shrines of an Italian faith, for the wild terror
of John Knox was still in the blood of his superstitious race.
But he took the next safest step; he became a High Anglican.
It was an obvious courtesy he owed to Oxford. Gladstone
wanted to make his Church the supreme factor in the State,
which was to spend its money on the preaching of the truth and
only on the truth as it was recognised by the Anglican dogmas.
He wanted a State Church in every sense of the term.

He said all this in his book; and the High Churchmen
were, of course, delighted to be told that they were of such
immense importance. But the politicians were, as naturally,
annoyed when they were told that they ought to take as
their master a Church which, so far, they had usually found
a most obedient servant. They had enough trouble on their
hands; and had no desire to add the labours of the apostles
to their secular work. Sir Robert Peel simply could not
understand such a want of political propriety; he said
of Gladstone: "With such a career before him, why should
he write books?" Newman wrote with tender sympathy:
"The *Times* is again at poor Gladstone. . . . Poor fellow!
it is so noble a thing." He was entirely right in his judgment. It was indeed a noble — even a stupid — act to

lose the good will of the *Times* and Peel, for the sake of the dreams of a restless conscience.

Deep in the roots of Gladstone's emotional nature there was a foundation of worldly judgment which even Oxford had never been able to undermine. He soon saw that he was writing for a heedless governing class. "Scarcely had my work issued from the press when I became aware that there was no party, no section of a party, no individual person probably, in the House of Commons, who was prepared to act upon it." By the year 1843, at latest, he had resigned himself to a purely political career: "Of public life, I certainly must say, every year shows me more and more that the idea of Christian politics cannot be realised in the state according to its present conditions of existence. For purposes sufficient, I believe, but partial and finite, I am more than content to be where I am." It was, perhaps, his half apology for having fallen from grace, for he had hoped to be a direct servant of the Lord preaching to sinners — and, instead, he was merely the president of the Board of Trade in Sir Robert Peel's Cabinet. But he still refused to surrender all hope; he had just before written: "I contemplate secular affairs chiefly as a means of being useful in church affairs, though I likewise think it right and prudent not to meddle in church matters for any small reasons." "Prudent" is not a word that was ever in the mouth of the martyrs; and when he wrote it Mr. Gladstone had crossed the Rubicon which separates the defiant saints from the weaker men.

But among the sinners he was of the noble sort. His finely made conscience, his instinctive grasp of what was right and his rejection of what was wrong always kept him near the true line of human morality. And as he grew in years, this deeper righteousness was to push farther and farther from his path the petty quibbles with which the sectarian and classical dogmas (of his Liverpool and Oxford days) had hampered his progress. In 1840 his passionate indignation was roused by the Chinese War — that cynical attempt to force opium on a people that had a superior culture, which a nation of factory owners could not understand. Gladstone, at his lowest, never sank to the level of the Cannings, the Peels and their kind, who — with all their rhetoric — were only the agents of a nation of shopkeepers, to whom the world was little more than a possible market, and foreign policy only a manual for commercial travellers. In this matter of China, Gladstone told the House of Commons: "I have not scrupled to denounce the traffic in opium in the strongest terms. I have not scrupled to denounce the war with equal indignation." The cynic might observe that the indignant orator had now a freer scope for his righteousness — for his father was, fortunately, not in the opium trade, as he had been a sharer in the slave trade on an earlier occasion. But it may be an unfair sneer; for Gladstone would not allow the China War to rest unchallenged; and when he became a member of Peel's Government in 1841, he was continually worrying his chief by threats of resignation if the opium question crossed his conscience again.

All through his political life Gladstone was much in the position of a teetotaller who had to serve as a barman in a beer shop. It was a continually appalling problem of serving God and Mammon. It was one long struggle to resist temptation. The most famous occasion, when his conscience got entirely out of hand and almost ruined his worldly career, was in 1845. He was then holding his first Cabinet post and earning great praise for his skill in administration as the president of the Board of Trade. He was taking a prominent part in Peel's work of sweeping away useless (and sometimes useful) tariff duties; and he had made himself a man of distinction in parliamentary life. At this pleasant moment, Peel suddenly resolved to offer a convinc-

WILLIAM EWART GLADSTONE
From a portrait by G. F. Watts, R. A., in the National Portrait Gallery, London

ing apology to the Roman Catholics of Ireland for having done them so much harm in his earlier career. He said he intended to make the State grant to Maynooth College three times as large as before, and a permanent subsidy, instead of being voted from year to year. Now Gladstone had said in his Church and State book that the State could only give money to the true Church — which was the Anglican and not the Roman. In these circumstances it was natural that he should feel compelled to resign when the new policy of his Government went dead against his previously avowed convictions. But as a matter of fact, Gladstone had already changed his rigid opinion on this matter. He said he not only would not oppose the Maynooth grant, but would even vote for it. Nevertheless, being a man who was always more interested in the abstract than the concrete (and more particularly anxious about the internal abstractions of his own mind than anything else in the world), he argued to himself — and to his long-suffering chief who regarded the arrival of Gladstone's conscience at his office door as ordinary men watch the arrival of the income tax collector — that he must demonstrate to the world that his Maynooth vote was not given, as a slave, in order to retain his post. So he resigned his office; and then spoke and voted for the grant as a free and spotless man. The men of the world shrugged their shoulders and thought he was a little mad. He made an hour's speech in the House, explaining why he had resigned; and that only made matters worse. After it was over Richard Cobden turned to another member of the Commons: "What a marvellous talent is this; here have I been sitting listening with pleasure for an hour to his explanation, and yet I know no more why he left the Government than before he began." Cobden had not the calibre of mind that could have appreciated any subtle argument; but everybody else appears to have agreed with him on this occasion. Greville said that "Gladstone's explanation was ridiculous"; and Disraeli thought it "involved and ineffective."

One is tempted to wonder whether the speaker himself knew what he meant; whether his explanation had satisfied that inner mind which was throughout his life the chief object of Gladstone's care. This intense interest in himself; this continual persistence in explaining at great length what he meant and why he thought so, in a lesser mind would have been intolerable conceit. But in this case the mind was so amazingly interesting as a psychological study that one can even forgive its owner for taking a part in the examination. In later years, when he could look back on himself almost as a historical event, and with the impartial mind that one can apply to a tombstone, he wrote a sentence of self-analysis which may surely be regarded as one of the keys — if not the master key — to his whole career. He said that he shrank from giving "a history of the inner life, which I think has been with me extraordinary dubious, vacillating, and above all complex."

Those words were a confession that this autobiographer had been baffled by his own mind; and there is every reason to believe that it was a sincerely true statement. There is certainly every possible excuse for this victim of his own complexity. From his earliest days of boyhood until the end of his life he seems to have been totally incapable of writing a simple sentence of unqualified prose. Let it be admitted that there are times when obscurity is the politician's greatest skill; for half political life is the concealment of the truth, and not its revelation. It is possible, for example, that when Gladstone rose to explain to the House of Commons why he resigned from the Government on the Maynooth question, his whole object may have been to conceal that he had no good reason. The obvious reason — that he did not want to be accused of changing his opinion in order to save his office — could have been put clearly in half a dozen sentences. But Gladstone was so baffled by the maze of his mind that he pursued all possible — or impossible — explanations through an hour's oration; and then they certainly eluded his hearers — and perhaps himself.

Whatever excuse there may be for obscurity in public oratory, there is surely none in intercourse with private friends. But there are in existence despairing letters which passed between Gladstone's intimate colleagues, wondering and wondering what some important statement by him can possibly mean. Thus, on August 8, 1885, Lord Hartington wrote to Lord Granville: "I never can understand Mr. Gladstone in conversation, but I thought him unusually unintelligible yesterday. . . . On other questions he seemed to be tolerably reasonable, though vague." But it is perhaps unnecessary to quote the statements of third parties when we have discovered above a far more convincing confession by the accused himself. A man who found himself "dubious", "vacillating" and "complex" must obviously have been a mystery to the outer world.

The matter is important, for it may be in some considerable degree the secret of Gladstone's power. For a longer period than any other English statesman of his century he held a great position in the national life. A man who accepted with such passive submission the orders of the leaders of old Greece and Rome, and the dogmas of the Christian religion as they might excusably have seemed reasonable in an entirely uncritical age, long before his time, cannot be accepted as a man of great intellect, in the strict sense of the term. The man who believed in the Bible in very much the same way that the uneducated mediæval serf believed in it, was not a man who depended on intellectual knowledge, as a Darwin or a Lyell would have understood that phrase. There must therefore be some other explanation of Gladstone's power.

It is quite arguable that intellect, in this rigid sense, is not the most desirable or greatest of human qualities. It is probable that the artist knows more about the world, and is therefore a greater part of it, than the learned man who accumulates what he hopes are "facts." The more one examines Gladstone, the less one finds in his intellect and the more one finds in his art. The fewer "facts" one discovers in his mind, the more passions one finds in his soul. For in this man there does seem to have been a distinction between mind and emotion; his intellect was small, but his "soul" was very great. He was a magnificent artist; but he built his gorgeous tapestry of words on a very slight structure of intellectual thought. Of course the mere suggestion of this mental lack will drive his admirers mad with indignation; but then the kind of people who are hypnotised by a great artist in words are often themselves of the more emotional sort.

The "Liberal" mind, which supplied Mr. Gladstone with the chief strength of the rank and file of his political army, is distinguished from most other political schools of thought by always giving more value to an abstract phrase than to a concrete fact. It has, for example, always attached such priceless importance to that very beautiful thought termed "liberty", that it has continually forgotten that it has often ended in the freedom of a few and the enslavement of the many. Thus it was that the Tory Lord Ashley demanded a Factory Act that would prevent the ardent Liberal Mr. Bright overworking his labourers. It also needed the Conservative Government of Disraeli, in 1874, to correct some of the serious assaults on labour made by Mr. Gladstone's ministry after it came into power in 1868. The Liberal always prefers a principle to a fact.

Mr. Gladstone was full of the principles dear to his Liberal mind; and they were very noble ones, indeed. But his chief strength was that, whether they were right or wrong — and they were usually right — he believed in them with such intense conviction that he was able to sweep men off their feet and carry them along with him in the terrific rush of his political passions. Analysing this great power still more precisely, it will be discovered that if passionate conviction of great principles was his chief substance, a magnificent technique in the craft of rhetoric, the manipulation of words, was his chief method. The secret of Gladstone's power was that he was able to express great emotional ideas as the most superb actors of the dramatic stage would alone have put them to an audience. In a single phrase, the final key to Gladstone's colossal power over men is that he was a great preacher who had the genius of a superb artist in the spoken word. His intellectual gifts — which were, in mere brain weight, naturally very great — had been almost extinguished by an education at Eton and Christ Church, and what survived were swamped by the flood of his magnificent oratory. Mr. Gladstone always felt before he thought; and he usually felt so strongly that he had no time or energy for thought.

Whether this theory of Gladstone's greatness be true or erroneous can only be tested by the facts of his career. So far we have seen him resigning his office in Peel's ministry in 1845 because he had changed his mind about a grant to Roman Catholics. It may be called the turning point of his political life. Gladstone had just discovered that it was not a want of reverence to his Deity to allow Roman Catholics to worship him in a manner that did not precisely coincide with the rules of the Anglican Church. It was but the first step to a still greater advance in toleration, which was finally to go so far that he found the whole Tory Party intolerable.

If he had possessed the Duke of Wellington's realist intellect he would have known that the trouble in Ireland was high rents and bad farming. But Gladstone, being a man of ecclesiastical principles and passions, was still worrying about the Church; though he had already realised that the Anglicans in Ireland were not perfect. In August, 1845, he wrote to Bishop Wilberforce: "I am sorry to express my apprehension that the Irish Church is not in a large sense efficient"; and then he went on to worry about the apostolic succession, or some other visionary matter which would not bother the intellectual mind. A month or two later he was writing to Hope:

> Let me rebuke myself and say, no levity about great and solemn things. There are degrees of pressure from within which it is impossible to resist. . . . The Church in which our lot has been cast has come to the birth, and the question is, will she have strength to bring forth? I am persuaded it is written in God's decrees she shall; and that after deep repentance and deep suffering, a high and peculiar part remains for her in healing the wounds of Christendom.

He was again arguing with himself whether he was right in having chosen a secular political career; but there is also, surely, a note of doubt in the "will she have strength to bring forth?"

Whatever Gladstone's inner voice may have told him, the outer world could only see, a few months later (in December, 1845) that the mystic had evidently decided that some of the wounds of Christendom could be healed by repealing the Corn Laws; and he accepted office in the new ministry that Sir Robert Peel formed for that specific worldly purpose. Mr. Gladstone was Secretary of State for the Colonies, which seemed an inappropriate occupation for a man who was worrying about apostolic succession. There was a further difficulty. Gladstone had so far sat in Parliament, not because the inhabitants of Newark wanted him, but because the Duke of Newcastle, the owner of Newark, chose him as a safe representative of the ducal mind. But since the Duke believed in protected corn, the free-trading Gladstone had to go. So during the great Free Trade debates of 1846 he was not a member of the House of Commons; and he went out of office, also, when the Protectionists had their revenge on Peel in June, 1846.

He remained out of Parliament until the General Election of 1847, when Oxford University, with its persistent lack of political sense — which is one of its sweetest virtues — chose Gladstone for its second member. As Lord Morley said: "The prime claim advanced for him by his proposer, was his zeal for the English church in word and deed, above all his energy in securing that wherever the English church went, thither bishoprics should go too." Now, in so far as one of the chief ends of Oxford University was to produce bishops — as factories produce calico — it must be admitted that this was an admirable reason. Yet it was lack of sound sense on the part of the electors, because, as we have seen in the Maynooth case, there were already signs that Gladstone's still, small inner voice was beginning to order him to remember that the principles of liberty and truth were not limited by the bounds of the Church of England. The day was not so far away when he was even to disestablish the Church in Ireland, and was to give votes concerning Jews (and even atheists) which would seriously trouble the Oxford official mind. Oxford, "the home of lost causes", had thus indiscreetly chosen the wrong man. But they think slowly in that seat of knowledge; and it took its learned voters almost another twenty years to discover their mistake.

No sooner had he returned to the House than he voted for the admission of the Jews to the rights of citizenship. Pusey, who had been one of his Oxford supporters, was shocked and angry; and Gladstone was astonished at himself; for he wrote in his diary: "It is a painful decision to come to, but the only substantial doubt it raises is about remaining in Parliament, and it is truly and only the church that holds me there." He had to give another of those involved speeches in the House, explaining why his vote did not coincide with his theories. One friend gave him sensible advice before he rose: "Be as little as possible like Maurice [the theologian] and more like the Duke of Wellington"—who had become almost a proverb for honest frankness. Nevertheless, when Gladstone went down to Oxford soon after, to receive an honorary degree, "there was great tumult, about me, the hisses being very obstinate." And so the inner "dubious", "vacillating", "complex" mind continued to lure its owner away from the orthodoxies.

It was, nevertheless, a stiff fight. For the Gorham case came on in 1849; and Gladstone plunged into the theological turmoil with the enthusiasm of an Irishman searching down the street for a head to crack. He wrote to Manning: "I should wish to converse with you from sunrise to sunset on the Gorham case. It is a stupendous issue." Of course it was nothing of the sort, being only a squabble about regeneration by baptism which might have been settled either way, or no way at all, without ninety-nine per cent of England knowing that anything had happened. But to Mr. Gladstone's emotional mind, which had not been trained to consider facts, the world seemed at stake. In one way he was justified in his excitement. For the court of law which had finally decided the Gorham case was the secular Privy Council; and Gladstone who had mixed with enough men of State to know that their religion was of uncertain stability, protested, very justly, that a point of ecclesiastical law ought not to be decided by heretics; just as he might have asked why a point of medical practice should be decided by lawyers. It was now (and partly because of the Gorham judgment) that his dear friends Manning and Hope joined the Church of Rome. But Gladstone had the blood of the race of stubborn John Knox in his veins and said, as he grieved over their departure: "One blessing I have; total freedom from doubts. These dismal events have smitten but not shaken."

It was gradually becoming clearer to the onlooker, though not perhaps to Gladstone himself — who was an amazingly blind creature in the affairs of this worldly life — that in his nature there was a far more deeply rooted belief and veneration than his worship of the Anglican Church and its dogmas. When we look back on his life and its actions as a whole, we see that the chief polestar which shone as the guide in his mental sky was the conviction that "freedom" or "liberty" was the most priceless possession of the human race. When it came to the crisis, he always decided that it was more important that a man should be free to act in accordance with his own conscience than that he should be compelled to do what was right. It is a creed which would generally be described as extreme individualism of an anarchical, rebellious and irreligious type. But this was beyond the understanding of Gladstone's emotional and artistic mind.

It was this conception of the beauty and desirability of a free mind, as the rightful possession of man, that made Gladstone write very subtly stinging words to Manning when he went over to the Roman Church: "I would earnestly pray that you might not be as others who have gone before you, but might carry with you a larger heart and mind, able to raise and keep you above that slavery to a system, that exaggeration of its forms, that disposition to rivet every shackle tighter and to stretch every breach wider."

He went to Italy about this time, and in Naples had seen, with his own eyes, such a mass of festering political corruption and unrestrained tyranny of a most revolting sort — the physical horrors of the foulest dungeons was its method — that when he came back to England, he threw himself at the Foreign Office door with an imperative demand that something should be done to make the half-witted knave who sat on the throne of Naples do justice to his subjects.

Of course the diplomats were more careful of their prim propriety than of justice, so they showed no sign of action; and Gladstone, in an open letter to his friend Lord Aberdeen, startled England and Europe with the scathing indignation of his cry for reform.

It was one more proof that the member for Oxford University who had been taught to believe rigidly in authority, both secular and divine, had now decided that the authority of the State must be defied when it dared to restrain the free liberty of the body and soul of man. Madame de Lieven said that Gladstone had been fooled by intriguing men — and it was not indeed a very difficult task to dupe his credulous mind — but in this case he had the facts on his side. However, that is immaterial for the moment, the point at stake being that when Gladstone believed that righteous liberty was in danger, then the authority of the State must be sacrificed. The authority of religion was here involved also. For the Pope of Rome was the supporter of the King of Naples, and the Roman clergy and their press were the open friends of tyranny. Gladstone wrote to Manning from Naples (Jan. 26, 1851): "The temporal power of the pope, that great, wonderful and ancient erection, is gone. . . . God grant it may be for good. I desire it, because I see plainly that justice requires it." Then he continued with words of the gravest importance in his mental history: "Not out of malice to the popedom; for I cannot at this moment dare to answer with a confident affirmative, the question, a very solemn one — ten, twenty, fifty years hence, will there be any other body in western Christendom witnessing for fixed dogmatic truth?"

If that sentence has any meaning, it is that because he saw that "justice required it" Gladstone was prepared to sacrifice what might prove to be the only bulwark between a dogmatic faith and heretical anarchy. *Fiat justitia, ruat cælum!* It is a motto of great value and, used with reasonable discretion, of considerable utility. But, as the life principle of the member for the University of Oxford, in 1851, it must have been exceedingly alarming to his nervous constituents, and even to the honourable member himself.

But if the Pope and the King of Naples, and the Church and States of Italy, were to be made to do justice and love freedom, the same measure should be granted to them in return. Gladstone's respect for freedom was not partisan — it was completely cosmopolitan. It even included liberty for tyrants themselves. When the Pope, in 1850, published one of those stately documents (with which small men love to swell themselves to a fictitious size) which declared that Roman bishops were to take territorial titles in England, Lord John Russell, then the Prime Minister, lost what fragment of an intelligent mind he ever possessed and declared all kinds of blatant opposition to the aggression of Rome. He ought merely to have shrugged his shoulders and said that it was not of the slightest importance. But he went into political hysteria and brought in a Bill making the Roman bishoprics illegal.

In opposition to this Bill, Gladstone made one of the greatest speeches of his career. It was full of scholastic learning and ecclesiastical law, which fascinated the House of Commons probably in much the same way that a superbly clever conjuror would also have caught the fancy of the members. But all that was trivial beside the gorgeous colours of his oratory, when he begged his fellow members to remember that in their hands lay the honour of maintaining that tradition of religious freedom which their ancestors had committed to their keeping. Of course it was only partly true in fact, but it was very noble in ideals — and Gladstone was always more conscious of ideals than of facts. He besought them, in words of limpid eloquence, to remember that they did not adopt the principle of religious freedom in haste; but all the world acknowledged that our minds, when once made, were very stable:

> You are not a monarchy to-day, a republic to-morrow, and a military despotism the day after. . . . Your fathers and yourselves have earned this brilliant character for England. Do not forget it. . . . Show, I beseech you — have the courage to show the pope of Rome, and his cardinals, and his church, that England too, as well as Rome, has her "*semper eadem.*" . . . The character of England is in your hands. . . . We cannot change the profound and resistless tendencies of the age towards religious liberty. . . . We are, I trust, well determined to follow that bright star of justice, beaming from the heavens, whithersoever it may lead.

If one desires to distinguish this man from his rival Disraeli, this debate is an illuminating test. While Gladstone was swept away by his fierce indignation that religious liberty should be tarnished for one instant by the breath of coercion, the cynical Jew was moved only to a contemptuous irony that Russell and his Whigs should blunder like hysterical schoolgirls. To Disraeli, liberty of thought was a most desirable convenience: to Gladstone, it was a grand passion, almost the greatest passion of his political life.

In 1851, Gladstone was again faced by one of his ever-recurring problems of political conscience. The purely Tory administration of Lord Derby and Disraeli held office from February to December of that year; Gladstone was officially still a Tory, and, with any desire on his side, he would have been offered a post. But was he a Tory? But again, was he a Whig? Or did he fit into any creed of any party? In fact, he was in the embarrassing position of having to answer all these questions in the negative. But, on the other hand, a man who does not belong to any party has a possibility of joining any of them when it suits his convenience; and Gladstone had one of those subtle "vacillating" minds which are sometimes convinced that a course is right when it is convenient; where a simpler brain might not have detected the loophole of escape. His conscience, of course, had to be carefully examined before he would move. Thus, he could not join the Tory Government, because it was Protectionist and uncertain on matters of religious freedom. But then Lord John Russell had upset him still more on the latter point; while the great *Civis Romanus sum* speech of the Whig Palmerston, in 1850, had shown no hope of a resting place with that British Jingo. However, the peculiarly delicate nature of political ethics was to end in making all these worldly statesmen into his close colleagues. The Prime Minister who took Gladstone for a friend must have really considered him of material value, for he could rarely have agreed with the opinions of a man who was unlike everybody else in political life — being nearer a mediæval saint, who knew very little about worldly affairs.

Gladstone's answer to Palmerston's great patriotic speech in 1850 was another landmark in the history of his mind. The bouncing jingoism of Palmerston was only distinguished from the public-house variety by the trivial differences of the Latin tags, which the saloon bar would have translated into equally robust English. They would have put it: "no b—dy foreigners", which was just what Palmerston said in Latin. To all this Gladstone replied in language which was very much like reading Plato's Republic to the audience at a boxing match.

It would be a contravention of the law of nature and of God, if it were possible for any single nation of Christendom to emancipate itself from the obligations which bind all other nations, and to arrogate, in the face of mankind, a position of peculiar privilege.

He then asked Palmerston who was this Roman citizen whom he was so anxious to imitate?

He was the member of a privileged caste; he belonged to a conquering race, to a nation that held all others bound down by the strong arm of power. . . . Is such, then, the view of the noble lord as to the relation which is to subsist between England and other countries? . . . Certainly, if the business of a Foreign Secretary properly were to carry on diplomatic wars, all must admit that the noble lord is a master in the discharge of his functions. What sir, ought a Foreign Secretary to be? . . . I understand it to be his duty to conciliate peace with dignity . . . to exalt in honour among mankind that great code of principles which is termed the law of nations. . . . Sir, I say that the policy of the noble lord tends to encourage and confirm in us that which is our besetting fault and weakness.

He ended by appealing to the judgment of the civilised world; he put on one side the vulgar assertion of force. "Let us recognise, and recognise with frankness, the equality of the weak with the strong." He was, in short, like a missionary endeavouring to persuade a party of cannibals to become vegetarians.

Gladstone must have found all the political parties uncongenial company and a mere *pied à terre* at the best. But he did manage to quiet that overboisterous conscience of his — his critics said this could always be done if he were given time to search for the convincing excuse — and he joined the Aberdeen-Russell-Palmerston ministry that took office at the end of 1852. It was just as well that this was a coalition government, for by this time it would have been rash to assert that Gladstone was still a Tory. Only the year before he had written a letter to the Bishop of Aberdeen, in which he announced:

I am deeply convinced that among us all systems, whether religious or political, which rest on a principle of absolution, must of necessity be, not indeed tyrannical, but feeble and ineffective systems; and that methodically to enlist the members of a community, with due regard to their several capacities, in the performance of its public duties, is the way to make that community powerful and healthful, to give a firm seal to its rulers. . . .

The awful rumour of this letter spread round Oxford: it was almost as terrible as if the Vice Chancellor had joined the Communist Party. When the news was broken to the Dean of Christ Church he said: "You have proved to my satisfaction that this gentleman is unfit to represent the University." However, at the election of 1852 he was again chosen as the second representative of Oxford; for he was too distinguished a man to toss on one side; and above all, when it came to arguments, he had a scholastic mind that could split hairs — which Oxford loved, as small boys love conjuring tricks.

Lord Derby had tried to get Gladstone to join the Tory Government in 1852; but Peel's most ardent follower could scarcely — with decency — prove that protection was a good thing; so the negotiations broke down. Indeed, it was Gladstone's terrific attack on Disraeli's budget that drove the Tories out of office within a few months and put Lord Aberdeen in power; and, naturally, he made Gladstone Chancellor of the Exchequer. In 1853 came the first of the "Budget" speeches, which have got into history books as almost the most famous events of Gladstone's career. But this is a very hasty error of judgment, probably because the ordinary man is more interested in taxes than in the other more subtle departments of government. It was so much easier to have an opinion whether Gladstone had done well or ill in reducing the tax on tea, than it was to analyse his theories of the morality in international affairs. It was not so difficult to follow Gladstone's columns of figures as to pursue his ethics through the clouds of the higher philosophy.

The Gladstonian budgets have been overrated. They were not original in substance, for on the main they were only the national development of the Free Trade theories of Peel, who had, in turn, got them from his predecessors.

Gladstone imposed legacy duties on landed estates; but that was not exactly a stroke of genius. Neither was the abolition of the duty on soap final proof of the master mind. What won the national gratitude was his promise to reduce the income tax gradually to extinction. But for the moment he made more people pay than before, since he lowered the taxable limit to £100 — which scarcely seems a good reason for all the popular praise he has ever since received for his democratic finance.

The real secret of Gladstone's budgets was not their figures, but their art. They were undoubtedly masterpieces of rhetoric. They were more; for they were manifestations of the titanic imagination and volcanic mental energy of this man. That subtle mind could make figures romantic; and that golden tongue could make romance into dramatic art. Even the sinful man glows with delight when he is convinced, by unanswerable eloquence — not by logic — that the payment of income tax is a function of the higher morality. If he must be taxed, it is nice to feel how noble it is to suffer for the general good. It was satisfactory to know that cheap soap was pleasing in the sight of heaven. Of course, a large part of this glowing financial poem turned out, later on, to have been pure imagination. As even Lord Morley had to admit: "The succession duty brought in no more than a fraction of the estimated sum . . . the proposal for conversion proved . . . to have no attraction for the fund holder. The operation on the South Sea stock was worse than a failure. . . ." But when men said these things in the House of Commons, Gladstone made another amazingly dramatic speech, and his hearers were as convinced as they would have been by a great actor in a melodrama. One of the greatest strokes of Gladstone's first budget was his exceedingly attractive idea of thinking ahead for seven years. It sounded very splendid, and prophetic, and wide-visioned. But it all came down with a terrible crash; before two years were over the Government had allowed itself to be dragged into a war with Russia which swept away all Gladstone's plans of economy as a cork is swept away by a torrent. The man who budgetted for seven years ahead may have had a great imagination; but he certainly had not much worldly sense. The student who desires to discover why Gladstone was such a great man need not trouble much about his finance; but his budget rhetoric is of vital importance.

Gladstone had not very much to do with the blunders of the Crimean War which began in 1854. Lord Aberdeen, the Premier, hated war; but not having a subtle mind that could twist the facts, he could not find any sound excuse for his blunder. Whereas, his Chancellor of the Exchequer, much though he also (and very sincerely) hated war, could find all sorts of reasons why he was right in defending his Government for this war in defence of heathen Turkey against Russian Christians. But the nation did not worry about the morality of it; it merely insisted that it should be fought in a businesslike manner; and on the mismanagement of the war the Aberdeen Government fell, in spite of Gladstone's valiant defence.

It was a question whether Lord Derby, the protectionist Tory, or Lord Palmerston, the militarist Whig, should succeed the gentle Lord Aberdeen. Gladstone could not join either with any conviction; but he convinced his "dubious" mind that he could work with Palmerston, though in principle he hated almost everything that light-hearted, materialist nobleman did and thought. However, he changed his mind and resigned within three weeks, and became a private member of the Commons, not only without an office, but without a party — which is not unnaturally the position of a great man. There were many negotiations with Lord Derby, trying to come to terms for a return to the Tory fold. But he had gone too far for that ever to happen again.

For the present he had plenty to do. While the Crimean War continued to rage he retired to the Welsh mountains, and wrote to Lord Aberdeen: "I am busy reading Homer about the Sebastopol of old times"; just as when he was preparing his budget he had read Dante's "Paradiso." Now he gave up a lot of his time to a book on Homer, who had more effect on his politics than Derby or Palmerston. He helped Disraeli — who was one of his chief obstructions in the Tory party — to attack the budget; and both these rivals also fought against Palmerston's blatant barbarian militarism in forcing a war on the civilised Chinese. Disraeli's weapon was the sharp edge of the sword of worldly sarcasm. But Gladstone's speech was a sermon by a scholar-preacher of the Middle Ages. He said we ought not to fight China because it was against the law of "natural justice which binds men to men; which is older than Christianity . . . which is broader than Christianity . . . and which underlies Christianity." The House did not really understand all this scholarship, and its ethical content was beyond its reach; nevertheless, as usual, it was "enthralled", as a listener said; adding that this speech was "the finest delivered in the memory of man." The evidence was thus continually accumulating that his gift of tongue was perhaps the greatest asset of Gladstone's public career. With such a rhetoric he would have convinced his audience if he had talked poor sense; and he would have been still more understandable to the common man if he had left out all the higher morality. But then he would not have been the great man he undoubtedly was. The speech did not really affect the issue and Palmerston swept the country at the general election of 1857, for the English morality had been swamped by the materialism of the Industrial Revolution. It had become the national hobby to get rich — a process which could not afford to waste time on international ethics.

Then Gladstone for a period lost all measure of reason (as it is estimated in this world) and opposed the Divorce Bill of 1857 as though the future of the human race was at stake. According to the laws of his Church, marriage was a sacrament and divorce an immoral relaxation. So he fought with an almost mad energy, as a savage would fight to defend the idols of his tribe. In one sitting he made twenty-nine speeches and questions, and over seventy speeches in the whole passage of the Bill. He was full of theoretical principles, and sometimes rather empty of concrete facts. As Lord Aberdeen said: "When he has convinced himself, perhaps by abstract reasoning, of some view, he thinks everybody else ought at once to see it as he does, and can make no allowance for difference of opinions." While Greville wrote: "His religious opinions, in which he is zealous and sincere, enter so largely into his political conduct as to form a very serious obstacle to his success."

Lord Aberdeen, in the letter just quoted, added: "Gladstone intends to be Prime Minister. . . . He is supreme in the House of Commons." It was perhaps on account of this intention that this subtle mind was able to swallow so many principles in 1859 and join Palmerston and Russell in the government of which the former was Prime Minister. A simple, honest mind could not have done this acrobatic feat; but Gladstone was only honest — and not simple. So he again became Chancellor of the Exchequer under a premier whom he had practically called a low fellow. Oxford quite reasonably said that their member had now gone over to the enemy. But Gladstone proved that there was nothing inconsistent in opposing a motion of censure of the late Tory Government and then accepting office from the new Liberal Ministers who had pressed that censure. At Oxford, where quibbles are often respected more than logic, they reëlected the acrobat.

Of course, he soon had friction with his new chief. Both

as a Christian and as a Chancellor of the Exchequer Gladstone objected to spending money on building forts to defend our naval bases. He threatened to resign; whereupon Palmerston calmly wrote to the Queen that "It would be better to lose Mr. Gladstone than to run the risk of losing Portsmouth or Plymouth." The premier's next letter to his sovereign is a delightful and brilliant miniature portrait of both men:

Mr. Gladstone told Viscount Palmerston this evening that he wished it to be understood that, though acquiescing in the step now taken about the fortifications, he kept himself free to take such course as he may think fit upon that subject next year; to which Viscount Palmerston entirely assented. That course will probably be the same which Mr. Gladstone has taken this year — namely, ineffectual opposition and ultimate acquiescence.

The cynic was correct: Mr. Gladstone was still Chancellor six years afterwards when Palmerston died! He had doubtless convinced himself that it was the duty of a Christian saint to bear with sinners.

The repeated triumphs of his budgets do not reveal anything new about their author. They were fresh marvels of rhetorical art. As the cool Greville wrote: "Everybody I have heard from admits it was a magnificent display, not to be surpassed in ability and execution." It was a great art, but the finance was only of modest, if admirable, ability. The chief feature was the repeal of the duty on paper, the beginning of a cheap popular press. To-day, when we have got rather more cheap newspapers than we can consume with utility, one might not be so enthusiastic as the Liberals were in 1860, but the lords were undoubtedly dull-witted when they rejected this measure. Palmerston was quite pleased at their action; and Gladstone scarcely knew whether he disliked his own Prime Minister more than the Tory peers. But he put the same repealed paper duty into the next year's budget, and the lords gave way in 1861. Gladstone had now tasted blood in the war against the aristocrats; he had burnt his Tory boats behind him. In 1865 Lord Palmerston died; and the other chief obstacle in his way, Lord John Russell, soon retired. So at last the Christian ambition of Mr. Gladstone to serve his country as Premier was attained; and he became First Minister in 1868. But he had ceased to be the member for Oxford University at the election of 1865. There was a limit to the reasonable patience of its learned electors; for it needed a more subtle knowledge of logic than most of them possessed to understand that their versatile member was carrying out the policy of the Tory Party, for which he had been elected. One had to read a lot of classics before one could be certain that black was white. In March, 1865, Gladstone had spoken in the House of Commons on the Irish Church; and had practically declared for disestablishment. It was worse than that; for, as Stafford Northcote wrote next day, he "denounced the Irish Church in a way which shows how, by and bye, he will deal not only with it, but with the Church of England too.... He laid down the doctrine that the tithe was national property, and ought to be dealt with by the State in the manner most advantageous to the people.... It is sad to see what he is coming to." To expect Oxford University to accept any such dangerous doctrine was as unreasonable as if he had asked the brewers to vote for temperance reform. For the Church was very nearly the private estate of the graduates of the Oxford colleges.

So they drove Gladstone out of his spiritual home; and he was elected, instead, as a member for Lancashire, the chief manufacturing county of England. It was a revolution in his life. The man who represented (he thought) the views of Homer and Horace, St. Augustine and Archbishop Laud, now spoke for the audiences of the Free Trade Hall, Manchester; where they were more concerned about the price

of cotton than the philosophy of the Greeks. But their new
member had drawn up so many budgets that he was getting
accustomed to the grosser side of life. After all, when he
had gone into politics instead of the Church, had he not
decided to serve Mammon as well as God — and the Free
Trade Hall of Manchester was Mammon's chief shrine.
When Gladstone went down to Lancashire he was risking
his soul, as a missionary risked his life when he landed on a
cannibal island. But the money-makers of Lancashire
were as fascinated by his glowing rhetoric as the Oxford
dons had been in earlier days. It was that rushing torrent
of eloquence which carried him along everywhere. As an
observer had said after his great budget speech of 1861:

> He is, in his ministerial capacity, probably the best abused or
> best hated man in the House; nevertheless the House is honestly
> proud of him, and even the country party feels a glow of pride in
> exhibiting to the diplomatic gallery such a transcendental mouth-
> piece of a nation of shopkeepers. The audacious shrewdness of
> Lancashire married to the polished grace of Oxford. . . . The
> man who can talk "shop" like a tenth Muse is, after all, a true
> representative man of the market of the world.

In short, Lancashire believed it had found as true a representative of itself as Oxford had once hoped was her own
possession. All which was one more proof that the skill
of the tongue was Gladstone's greatest asset — for Oxford
and Lancashire could surely have nothing in common in his
subject matter.

When Palmerston died a few months later, Gladstone
had become the leader of the House of Commons, under
Russell, now in the House of Lords. In 1866 the Tories
took office again; and Gladstone and Disraeli faced each
other as the two leaders in the House of Commons. It
was one of the great political duels of history. It is interesting to note that Disraeli could not apply against Gladstone

the methods he had used against the dull Peel. For Gladstone, like himself, was a man with the imagination of the great artist, who could meet his opponent on equal terms. It was a struggle between the Oriental Democrat, and the mediæval mystical Tory, by a similar erratic destiny made leader of the political group which called itself the people's party. Disraeli was the cool realist — and also a poet — who continually faced facts; while Gladstone was the man of fierce emotions, who would cling to a principle in defiance of all the facts under the sun. But when one gets down to the deeper foundations of both men, they were not nearly as far apart as they seemed on the surface. They were both very honest and unselfish, thinking first of the State, and always more anxious to make the many happy than to make the few rich. Their heroic combats were often about small differences, and perhaps they as often as not were merely enjoying the excitement and triumphs of the political game. Though it would have horrified Mr. Gladstone beyond measure if he had even thought of such a sinful lapse.

How else are we to explain why Disraeli protested against the franchise measure which Gladstone introduced into the Commons in 1866; and then himself carried a more drastic Bill in 1867? Of the two men, Disraeli probably feared the people (and indeed loved them) more than the mystical scholar of Oxford ever did. For if Gladstone loved the people, it was because he thought it was a principle of his religion; whereas one fancies that the romantic Jew cared for his fellow men with a sympathy that was entirely human. The fact remains that it was the Tory who first gave the working people of England a political place in their nation. Nevertheless, it was Gladstone who had suggested a large part of it and had given his help to the Tory Government in forcing it upon its reluctant followers. The Franchise Act of 1867 was honourable to both men; and those who have read the letter which Queen Victoria wrote to Lord

Derby on October 28, 1866, will add that it was the better-balanced monarch who insisted on the squabbling politicians coming to terms.

The longer Gladstone lived the more energetic he became; and energy has an inevitable habit of ending in what timid (and sometimes wise) people contemptuously call "radicalism." One by one the authorities that he had obeyed in his more nervous youth were tossed on one side. The double first of Oxford had rubbed his mental edges against the great world on every side; and the great brain — or was it the still greater emotional heart — was being polished into a maturity of surface that was undoubtedly a very beautiful specimen of the human race. His tumultuous mind was unbound. At this time Lord Houghton met him at a private dinner table. "He was very much excited, not about politics, but the cattle plague, china, and everything else. It is indeed a contrast to Palmerston's Ha! Ha! and *laissez faire*." He was swept away by the intensity of his thoughts. There was a lack of proportion about his values. As a friend told Mr. Lionel Tollemache: "He will talk about a piece of old china as if he was standing before the judgment of God"; and that same authority tells how one night Lady de Tabley "hurried me across the room just in time to see Mr. Gladstone holding up a piece of old china, and to take note of the flashing eye and the Rhadamanthine solemnity with which the great enthusiast was winding up his discourse."

It needed all his energy to stand up to Disraeli after the latter had got this franchise Bill through Parliament. For the moment the Jew was supreme. Bishop Wilberforce wrote: "The most wonderful thing is the rise of Disraeli. . . . He has been able to teach the House of Commons almost to ignore Gladstone, and at present lords it over him"; and Houghton said: "I met Gladstone at breakfast. He seemed quite awed by the diabolical cleverness of Dizzy, who, he says, is gradually driving all ideas of political honour out of the House, and accustoming it to the most revolting cynicism." It is an amazing picture. After all these years of political life, Gladstone has still the mind of the good boy from the village Sunday School, when faced by his first week of metropolitan worldliness. Of course, Gladstone was utterly wrong in this judgment. Disraeli's ethics were as sound — or better — than his opponent's; and the village youth began to sob about "revolting cynicism" because the other fellow was winning.

But the mind of the people is full of sentiment and Disraeli was far too intellectual to get a firm hold on the popular heart. Smart parliamentary tactics are a joy to the political groups, but they do not appeal to the man in the street. For the common person, Gladstone, in spite of all his religious fancies — or perhaps because of them — was a much more attractive person. For the common man loves rhetoric and fine phrases. So when Gladstone appealed for aid in disestablishing the Anglican Church of Ireland, the electors promptly turned out Disraeli, who had given them a parliamentary vote. Gladstone became Prime Minister in 1868 for the first time; and his first great measure, when at last he was in control of a government of his own, was to disestablish one branch of that Anglican Church which he had always declared to be his chief delight in life. The cynics may say that he was indeed a faithful pupil of Sir Robert Peel; for like him he had used his power to overthrow the promises of a lifetime. But it would be shortsighted to say any such thing. Gladstone was only unburying his own mind from under the surface of all the accumulated authorities which had so long covered it. He was now prepared to maintain that the principles of liberty and justice were more fundamental things than the principles which the Oxford dons had read into their Anglican Church. *Amicus Plato, sed magis amica veritas.*

The rest of Gladstone's life — his political career was to

last more than twenty years and to contain three more premierships — is rather a matter of detail than of any new principles in his character; and the story is more appropriate for the textbooks. The main line of his policy — which was his inner mind — was now clear. It was an almost passionate respect for liberty of conscience and, as far as reasonably possible, for liberty of action. In practice it led to a somewhat callous disregard for the constructive side of social organisation — for that would have meant a certain restriction on individual liberty; and an almost exaggerated concern for the negative virtues of personal and national freedom from the intolerant dictation of anybody else. This fanatical hatred of the "authority" to which he had once bowed with such reverential respect can be traced in all the great measures of his later premierships. The peoples must be free — whether Irish or Bulgarians. The conscience must be free, even if it was that of the atheist Bradlaugh. Mr. Gladstone came to disaster in Egypt and allowed General Gordon to perish. But then he could not take any real interest in conquering other countries, in order that the British Empire might the more easily dictate to the Universe. He entirely disbelieved in force as a method of governing the world; it was, at the best, only a disagreeable necessity.

Of course, in everyday life, this sometimes made him as helpless as a saint in a cavalry charge. The imperialists and the military and naval officers went out of their minds with fright when they thought that by the grant of Home Rule Ireland might become an enemy country in their rear and beyond their control. The materialists simply lost their heads when they were addressed in the terms of mind instead of matter. Whereupon all the empty-brained and loud-voiced people began shrieking and foaming, and said that Mr. Gladstone was a traitor to his country — because he had been a loyal guardian of the dignity of the human race. This outcry was all beyond the comprehension of the mystical mind of the accused statesman, who probably was never on intimate terms with a completely normal human being in his whole life. His real friends were of the freakish kind; and all the others he (unconsciously) ignored. He could never understand the common man's world. He did not even see it. He lived in a world of the abstract. When he went to Rome in 1866, Lord Morley, on the authority of a fellow traveller, has recorded that "Mr. Gladstone seemed to care little or not at all about the wonders of archaeology alike in Christian and pagan Rome, but never wearied of hearing Italian sermons from priests and preaching friars." Any educated man who could ignore the physical sights of Rome had clearly no use for that world of matter which is so interesting to the normal mind.

The British military disasters at Majuba Hill, 1881, against the Boers, and at Khartoum, where Gordon was killed by the Mahdi's army in 1885, were not unlikely events under a Prime Minister who knew nothing about soldiering, except that it was a crude contradiction of his fervent belief that a man's soul was infinitely more important than his body. The trouble at Khartoum paradoxically happened because the besieged General Gordon was in entire agreement with the Prime Minister on this point. With a mystic at each end of the problem, disaster was inevitable. Gordon was reading the Bible in Khartoum and Mr. Gladstone was reading it — and all the other classics — in England; and, between the two, the most obvious material precautions were overlooked. But what annoyed the materialists was that, after Majuba and Khartoum, this mystical Premier, instead of avenging himself on his enemies and saving the honour of his nation, insisted on practically withdrawing from both the Transvaal and the Sudan. A man who could derive no satisfaction from extracting an eye for an eye and a tooth for a tooth was clearly not of the bulldog breed which

his old University of Oxford so dearly loved, and still loves.
In the matter of war and imperialism, Gladstone's whole
life was a continual going from bad to worse, as it is estimated
by the barbaric mind. At the time of the Crimean War he
had not yet shaken off the gospel of the sword, which he had
been so earnestly taught by the Christian teachers of his
youth; but the rest of his life, in the affairs of China, South
Africa, and Egypt, was a gradual supplanting of emotional
materialism by a rational idealism.

His most famous moments were devoted to the subject of
Ireland; and they were most typical of his whole character,
to its deepest foundations. He began, as a mystic naturally
would, by believing that all the restless Irish wanted was a
religion of the Anglican kind. Then his irresistible sense of
free conscience led him to see that it was the Roman Catholic
Church they wanted, not having yet appreciated the Protestant Reformation at its true value. So, to the amazement of
his old friends, this enthusiastic churchman disestablished the
Anglican Church in Ireland, in 1869. It was so like his
simple, unworldly soul to be certain that all that was the
matter with chaotic, miserable Ireland was that they had
the wrong religion. Those who looked at facts, instead of
fancies, knew that the trouble was high rents and absentee
landlords and all the economic ills that cling round a country
governed by a conquering race. But Gladstone's head was
in the clouds and did not see the creeping men on the earth.
He certainly did attempt to deal with the economics of rent
by the Acts of 1870 and 1881; but they were not truly beloved children of his visionary mind, and anyhow, Ireland
was as discontented as before.

Gladstone was looking round for a more abstract solution
than the control of rents and landlords and the improvement
of potatoes. So having found that a new Church was no
remedy, he next conceived of a new political constitution.
In 1885, at the age of seventy-seven he suddenly thought of

the policy of Home Rule, with an independent Parliament in Dublin. It was almost the same idea which had been suggested to him by the humble person who made his bed while he was a student at Oxford. It was another proof that his mind was of that rare quality which grows more susceptible to the truth every day it lives. Having found that neither a new Church nor a new Constitution would make Irishmen rationally contented, it is almost certain that if Mr. Gladstone had lived to be a hundred he would have discovered still more profound truths and thrown as much energy into the economics of Ireland as he had wasted on its religious and political abstractions. He might have done as much for Ireland as a worldly government of Tories did by the Wyndham Land Purchase Act of 1903; and if he had only lived to be two hundred years old, that wonderfully elastic mind might have reached the wisdom of his bed-maker at Oxford, and offered Ireland its own king — or its own republic. For by that time he would have grown so wise that a political constitution would have seemed too small a thing to waste time in debating.

His conception of the Irish problem was the classical example of Mr. Gladstone's mind. It was one magnificent and stately progression from the narrow to the broad, from the blindness to facts to their enthusiastic acknowledgment. But had he lived to one thousand years, it would never have been as most other men's minds; for, from beginning to end, it lived within itself, forever rotating round its own thoughts and very serenely indifferent to the world outside. He always defiantly refused to admit that matter had any equality with mind. The material world was on a lower plane. Gladstone lived in an immaterial world.

Of course — after the inevitable habit of the introspective — in practice it was necessarily his own mind in which he dwelt; and the abstract man is more conceited than the modest fellow who listens to the evidence of external facts.

The man who revolves round his own ideas is a figure of vanity beside the humble explorer of the world outside himself. But there was a boyish zest in Gladstone's pursuit of his own complex mind which disarms criticism and even adds to his charm. He listened to the most trivial opponents with the gravest seriousness; he was always ready to re-explore his own "dubious" thoughts with any traveller who chanced to be passing by.

He was therefore the easiest of victims for the enemies who wanted to torment him in the House of Commons. The smallest bait in the trap would catch that ravenous mind; and a flood of intellectual emotion would pour out to overwhelm opponents who could have been easily drowned in a teacup. The sympathetic and intimate observer, Mr. Tollemache, admitted that Disraeli was not altogether wrong when he said that his great rival was "inebriated with the exuberance of his own verbosity"; for, added Tollemache, "Mr. Gladstone was sometimes not the master but the servant of his emotions, and even of his metaphors." Walter Bagehot, a still greater critic, wrote: "He is interested in everything he has to do with, and often interested too much. He proposes to put a stamp on contract notes with an eager earnestness as if the destiny of Europe here and hereafter depended upon its enactment. . . . The higher faculties of the mind require a certain calm, and the excitement of oratory is unfavourable to that calm." Jowett was also very critical: "An orator of genius," he said, "utters many words and phrases which linger in men's memory, and hardly any word or phrase so lingering has been uttered by Mr. Gladstone." Beside Disraeli's crisp epigrams, the Liberal statesman's rolling passages may seem diffuse and dull; but yet there was in the Gladstonian oratory, at its best, a deep murmuring of the mighty ocean of thought — which Disraeli preferred to express by a lightning flash. It is noteworthy that scarcely anything Gladstone wrote —

whether in theology or classics, or anything else — is now reprinted, as Disraeli's works are continually reappearing in new editions.

But they both dealt with the greater elements of existence: though they put their thoughts and acted their deeds in such very different ways. Gladstone knew so little of men; whereas to Disraeli they were the study of his life. While Gladstone was designing great principles and dreaming of great ideals, Disraeli was criticising and analysing his fellows and endeavouring to make of their small facts and low thoughts a better society. He was just as passionate and lofty in his political intentions as Gladstone; but he had the mental reserve of the man who is too modest to tell all that he knows and feels — or even to be quite certain that it must all be true. Whereas Gladstone had the unconscious conceit of the man who is so sure that he is right that he has no hesitation. Being convinced that he was, like Oliver Cromwell, in close touch with the Almighty, it would have been cowardice not to declare a message that was really the voice of God. He was so intently listening to the inner voice — which he thought was divine — that he forgot to listen or look to the world outside him.

Britain had never before had a man of his kind to govern her. Beside him, Becket and Laud were rather small-minded persons. He stands alone in our political history. One does not know how to label him. He was not a democrat, for he had more respect for the voice of God than the votes of the electors; though he was such a clever man that he could sometimes convince himself that the voices were the same. In the matter of the Parnell divorce he even proved quite conclusively that (in his later days, at least) he was ready to allow his religious theories to be dominated by his political necessities. He used Parnell's liaison as long as it was useful; and did not turn against him at the end because he was an immoral man in the eyes of the Christian

Church but because the electors showed clear signs of leaving Mr. Gladstone if he would not leave Mr. Parnell. The whole incident throws grave suspicions on his sincerity — but then the genius is always throwing suspicions on himself. To continue, Mr. Gladstone was not an autocrat; for he was always passing laws, or making speeches, which would allow people to do or think what they pleased. He was certainly not an imperialist; but he raised Britain higher in the opinion of foreigners — which is the greatest contribution to national strength — than Palmerston ever did. But since he stands alone in our parliamentary records, perhaps it is not strange that none of the partisan names fit him.

He was a genius — which is a convenient word to express admiration for some one whom we cannot explain or understand. There were only two other statesmen of that high rank in nineteenth-century Britain — Wellington and Disraeli — and the three were as unlike as one human creature could be from another. But the Duke and the Jew had this in common that they had both the realist mind that estimates a fact as more important than a fancy. With such gross materialism Gladstone had no patience. He was a genius; and his peculiar quality was this: a great organ of brain by its early training was handed over to the unlicensed control of a great imagination. The great intellect was continually struggling to regain its freedom. But fortunately it never quite succeeded — and English history was given the honour of having produced one of the few statesmen who have put high principles before low expediency. He was not a great intellectual and constructive thinker; but he was that rarer human phenomenon — a great moralist with the tongue of a great artist. The world would be a duller and more evil place if some of its great men did not — like Mr. Gladstone — allow their emotions to overwhelm their intellects.

QUEEN VICTORIA
1819-1901

QUEEN VICTORIA
1819–1901

THERE was one almost priceless advantage which Queen Victoria had over the statesmen who were her Prime Ministers. She came of a race that had been for hundreds of years professionally trained in the science and art of governing. It had been the occupation of her family since a time where history faded away into romantic myth. The records of Britain, and of much of Europe, were there to examine as advice and warning of what her ancestors had done or left undone. If heredity has any meaning and effect, the Queen was eminently fitted for her task.

Whereas her Prime Ministers were the chance collection of innumerable occupations, some of which were even serious disabilities for the difficult and exacting work of ruling a nation. They came from families of fox hunters, landlords, cotton lords, financial and legal adventurers, and what not, who came into political life, often by mere chance, and sometimes with ideas which were prejudiced by their class selfishnesses; or perhaps without ideas of any kind worth mentioning. Thus Peel found himself faced by the insistent demands of his own middle-class manufacturers that he should make laws for Free Trade. One of Gladstone's first obligations in the House of Commons had been to defend the slave system, which was a great part of his father's fortunes. Even the honest and charmingly unprejudiced Melbourne had gone into politics because he could think of nothing else to do; while Canning had spent his whole life in winning the premiership at all costs, with his country as rather a poor second in his thoughts. So likewise was it with the scores of smaller men who were the leaders and Cabinet ministers of the nation. They were, for better or worse, in the main only amateurs in their political careers.

Whereas Queen Victoria came of an ancient race of craftsmen to whom the work of governing a nation was as natural as for a fish to breathe in water. They were specialists in their occupation. They knew all the laws — and perhaps the tricks — of their trade, from the lips of fathers who had learned them (by practice, not theory) in the unbroken sequence of centuries of kingship. For it is not necessary to believe in the transmission of germ cells, and the subtleties of the science of heredity, in order to prove that a royal race has peculiar knowledge of the art of governing. It is sufficient to realise the simpler laws of learning at one's parents' knees. The business of ruling was as inevitably the chief topic of Queen Victoria's family circle as the technique of the circus is the common knowledge of the family of the travelling clown. One does not suggest that it was always safe rules that they learned in royal homes. But their blunders are as instructive as their successes. Her immediate Hanoverian ancestors had made enough blunders to teach the young Victoria more about government than all the soundest philosophy, from Plato to Hegel, could have taught her. The great successes and the disastrous experiments of the royal Houses of Brunswick and Saxe-Coburg Gotha, of King Alfred of England and his heirs, and the Wettin race, from mythology itself, had taught them more than the misty ideal of amateur philosophers. The ancestors of Queen Victoria were among the most experienced craftsmen in the art of governing.

The record of the early years of Victoria's own life might be circulated as a lesson in the science of technical education. The Pitts and the Peels, and Cannings and Gladstones, and all that sort of amateurs, had been allowed to waste their time, at school and college, on every kind of remote subject which had no more to do with the profession of ruling a nation than conic sections had to do with cheese making. Government had become a complicated science and art. It was no longer a matter of leading an army into battle; but the much more difficult problem of controlling the affairs of peace. For a hundred years and more there had been some ridiculous notion that to become the ruling statesman of Britain it was enough to have composed Latin verses at college and to have hunted foxes or shot pheasants during the vacations. The education of an English country gentleman was once considered sufficient qualification for ruling his nation. It became the proud tradition of the premiership to open their game-keepers' reports before they looked at their official despatches. There were a few men who survived their system: Robert Walpole and Wellington, and Gladstone also, in great part; and above all Disraeli, who escaped it altogether. They had enough genius — which is often only common sense — to overcome their low intellectual origin; but the history of England in the eighteenth and nineteenth centuries is disagreeably conclusive proof that most of its leading statesmen were mere amateurs at their job. They had many virtues and charms and bright wit, but of the technique of their craft they were alarmingly ignorant. They usually had the gift of persuasive speech; which is an admirable quality for an auctioneer. But the business of a statesman is not to sell his country; but to keep and preserve it by careful attention to the multitude of complicated laws by which societies are guided.

Men were made foreign ministers who could speak no language but their own, who knew little of the world beyond their own fields and their neighbours' woods and streams. There were chancellors of the exchequer who knew a great deal of Horace and Catullus — most admirable knowledge — but only a mere fragment about trade and finance. There is, in short, the trail of the amateur through the whole of our political history. With all their faults, the Hanoverian monarchs knew more about the laws of government than almost all of their Ministers put together.

For the moment, we are concerned with the qualification of Queen Victoria. From her earliest childhood she was sternly trained in the rules of her future profession. At the age of nine she began to receive those letters from her uncle Leopold, who was soon to be the King of the Belgians. They were models of skilful advice and high morality. If Pitt could have read them, instead of wasting his time over classical orators, they might even have made him competent enough to fill an undersecretaryship; had the brighter intellect of Charles Fox seen them, he might have given up gambling and Virgil and led a useful public life before he was too old for anything else.

When she was only fourteen her uncle was telling his serious niece that "the delightful pastimes of childhood must be mixed with thought appertaining already to a matured part of your life." The elder Fox about that age was sending his son to Paris, to teach him to be a rake! Leopold's letter goes on: "I know that you have been very studious, but now comes the time when the judgment must form itself." Had any Prime Ministers of England ever been advised to worry about their judgment at fourteen? The letter continues:

"Self-examination is the most important part of the business . . . every evening to recapitulate the events of the day, and the motives which made one act. . . . Amiable dispositions like yours will easily perceive if your own motives *were good*. Persons in high situations must particularly guard themselves against selfishness and vanity. . . . To judge oneself with truth and impartiality must be the great objects of one's exertions."

Then comes the closing advice to put on one side the small things of life: "Nothing is so great and clear a proof of unfitness for greater and nobler actions than a mind which is seriously occupied with trifles." It is an axiom which would disqualify most of the amateur statesmen from ever entering the pages of history.

A year later, October 18, 1834, the little niece has been sent for a holiday to Tunbridge Wells, but she is sternly pursued even there: "I feel convinced that care and exercise are most useful to you. In your leisure moments I hope you will study a little; history is what I think the most important study for you. . . . Unfortunately history is rarely written by those who really were the chief movers of events, nor free from a party colouring." Then he gives an exceedingly pungent sketch of French history and strongly presses his pupil to study the period of Henry IV until the minority of Louis XIV: after which "*Intrigues* and *favouritism* were the chief features . . . and Madame de Maintenon's immense influence was very nearly the destruction of France." He then particularly asks her to study the "Memoirs of the great and good Sully." The young Victoria replies, begging for a copy of Sully, for "reading history is one of my greatest delights." She then gives a long list of the books she is already reading, including Clarendon's "History of the Rebellion", "Histoire Ancienne" by Rollin and "La Rivalité de la France et de l'Espagne" by Gaillard.

It will be observed that her reading was of a kind peculiarly appropriate to the business of a ruling monarch. She was reading history which directly bore on her subject; while her Prime Ministers, at least most of them, had been kept to a couple of dead languages, which they were taught in a manner that seemed more likely to bury the dead than to revive them. We have found diaries of Mr. Gladstone which suggest that at an equally early age he could not be made to take any great interest in any books; there is one passage which says that even Froissart only attracted him in the battle scenes. Whereas this young lady of the professional governing class was discussing with kings, with shrewd intelligence, the intricate matters of European diplomacy.

At the age of seventeen she wrote:

The state of Spain is most alarming and unfortunate. .... The Christinos have gained a victory over the Carlists. I take a great interest in the whole of this unfortunate affair. I hope and trust Portugal may not suffer by all the affairs of Spain, but much is to be feared. . . . You did not send me the King of Naples' letter. You do not mention France, so I hope all is quiet.

And a few months later:

I cannot tell you how distressed I was by the late unfortunate *contra-revolution manquée* at Lisbon. . . . Mamma received a letter from Lord Palmerston. . . . I thank you much for the *Constitution de la Belgique.* . . . *En revanche* I enclose a paragraph from a speech of O'Connell's I think worth your reading.

She was, in short, plunged deeply into European politics at an age when her Prime Ministers had been chiefly interested in cricket or dogs or Latin verbs. The results of her technical training were already obvious. She had a maturity of judgment which is almost uncanny — and sometimes even quaintly comical in one who was still a child in years. In November, 1836, she wrote: "I am reading away famously. I like Mrs. Hutchinson's Life of her husband only *comme cela;* she is so dreadfully violent. She and Clarendon are so totally opposed, that it is quite absurd, and I only believe in the *juste milieu.*" The young lady was criticising and comparing historical sources which her amateur politicians — except perhaps Mr. Gladstone — had rarely even heard of at that age. There is a strange comment at the same date on Malcolm's "Life of Lord Clive", "which is very interesting, as it gives much insight over the affairs of India, over parts of which, I fear, it would be well to throw a *veil.* I am reading it by myself, *et je vous le recommande.* . . ." She already possessed a mind of her own; reading books which were not, apparently, recommended to her by her tutors — and criticising the wisdom of her country's rulers. The common child is usually nothing but a violent patriot.

Before she became Queen she was balancing the party politics with the seasoned mind of a patriarch. In January, 1837, she told her uncle:

Our friend, Mr. Hume made a most violent speech. . . . He called Sir R. Peel and some other Tories "the cloven foot", which I think, pretty strong. I think that *great* violence and striving such a pity, on both sides, don't you, dear Uncle? They irritate one another so uselessly by calling one another fools, blockheads, liars, and so forth for no purpose. I think violence is bad in everything.

If her Prime Ministers ever talked politics at such an age, it was generally to make their reputations by some violently partisan speech at the Eton debating club — while their future mistress had already formed the judgment of a philosopher. By March of 1837 she had completely passed the vague sentimentalists who were gushing about Greek liberty, based on some vague memory of Marathon in their school classes. Victoria got her information from a more recent and more direct source: "I have heard from various people who have been staying in Greece that they very soon get to like the Turks much better than the Greeks, who are very untrue, and are quite banditti-like." At the age of sixty-seven Mr. Gladstone was to risk a European war, by rhetoric concerning the Balkans; he had even then none of the balanced wisdom which his sovereign had displayed at eighteen.

There was, of course, a danger that the continual lectures by her devoted and learned uncle, and the innumerable solemn persons by whom she was surrounded, might have ruined their whole endeavour by making their pupil a prig.

With all her weight of knowledge she might easily have become as pompous a person as the two Pitts became without any learning whatever. Being filled with so many exhortations to be good and true and faithful in the service of her people — which was her hard-working uncle's constant refrain — she might have grown as insufferably self-conscious of her virtue as Sir Robert Peel became when he was busily engaged in making England into a safe paradise for his own middle class.

But the much preached at, much instructed young lady kept her head and remained a very delightful girl. Here, again, she was saved by the long inheritance of her family. She was not of the *nouveaux riches* in politics and therefore unlikely to go to pieces by a sudden rise to power and responsibility. It was the customary habit of her race to be faced by the problems of government. She was inured to them by the traditions of centuries. So she took them as a matter of course and maintained her balance as a normal being. Whereas, within a few years of her own birth, the strain of ruling had already sent two amateur statesman — Castlereagh and Romilly — to suicides' graves; and only a few years later Canning died before his prime, because the attaining of such great political power was beyond the tension point of his family temperament.

But it all came in the day's work with this member of a professional ruling house, who lived healthy in mind and body until over eighty. In the same letter which discussed with such discernment the affairs of Greece, she appears as a very lively human being with the most generous tastes:

> We had a dinner on Saturday which amused me, as I am very fond of *pleasant* society . . . and I longed sadly for some gaiety. . . . We had the Archbishop of Dublin, a clever, but singular man and his lady; Lord Palmerston with whom I had much pleasant and amusing conversation after dinner — you know how agreeable he is. . . .

Then she goes on with a long list of notable persons who were also guests, including Sir John Hobhouse, the Radical, and the Solicitor General for Ireland, Woulfe, whom she describes as "a Roman Catholic and a very clever man." She was already learning that the best people in the world were of all sorts and manners; for Palmerston was very far from an archbishop in his habits, while Hobhouse was a suitable balance to Stanley, another guest, who was later to become Earl of Derby and her only die-hard Tory Premier. Young Gladstone and young Peel had no such advantages in life; they were, on the contrary, being reared in the belief that there was only one right opinion on anything — and that was the rigid judgment of the paternal mind. "Amusing conversation" with Lord Palmerston was far more bracing than the prim gossip of Lancashire, which was too much the tone of the Peel and Gladstone households.

Her girlish head was already full of excitement concerning her future husband, for she had been informed by her uncle that Prince Albert should be her wise choice; by 1836 she wrote of him and his brother with the kindly condescension of an elderly aunt: "They are both very amiable, very kind and good, and extremely merry, just as young people should be; with all that, they are extremely sensible, and very fond of occupation." She added that "Albert is extremely handsome." A few months later: "Tell both young gentlemen, with my kindest love, that I *often* think of that night and of many other pleasant evenings we passed together." She had all the sentiments of the "sweet young thing" of the common drawing-room, combined with an amazing sense of responsibility and anxiety for public affairs. In this last letter she even had the grandmotherly touch: "I trust, notwithstanding what you say, I may yet live to see Spain and Portugal settled. But I greatly fear that the time is far distant." A little later — not quite two months before she ascended the throne — she was deeply concerned about the health of the ministers of state:

Lord Melbourne looks remarkably well, Lord Palmerston not very well, and as for poor little Lord John Russell, he is only a shadow of himself. [He was to survive over another forty years!] It must be dreadfully fagging work for them; they sit so very late too, for when the Spanish question came on, the division only took place at four o'clock in the morning, and I saw them at the Drawing Room the same day afterwards.

The day of her succession to the throne grew obviously very near and her devoted uncle was pouring forth wise advice and useful information until the little head — had it not been a very sound and well-balanced one — must have buzzed. Above all she must be truthful and sincere, "cultivate always a genuine feeling of right and wrong, and be very true and honourable in your dealings." Be considerate to all. "I know you are adverse to persecution, and you are right." The great day came and she wrote in her diary: "I shall do my utmost to fulfil my duty toward my country; I am very young and perhaps in many, though not in all things, inexperienced, but I am sure that very few have more real good will and more real desire to do what is fit and right than I have." It was only the family training of a thousand years that could give such a firm touch — without affectation — to a girl of eighteen. The greatest of ministers of State would have died of fright at such an offer of power at such an age — except the younger Pitt — but he was so ignorant of the world that he had the innocency of the half-witted.

The wise uncle still went on whispering the sanest of advice — even when it was sometimes very cynical and worldly:

You never can say too much in praise of your country and its inhabitants. Two nations in Europe are really ridiculous in their own exaggerated praises of themselves; these are the English and the French. ... The Established Church I also recommend strongly; you cannot, without *pledging* yourself to anything *in particular, say too much on the subject.*

That is the supreme advantage of these ancient ruling families: they have seen too many changes of national frontiers and national religions to worry over narrow quibbles about races and sects. They have acquired something of the mellow wisdom of the ages.

It was almost miraculous how quickly the young Queen grasped the sceptre. She wrote to her uncle of her good fortune in having Lord Melbourne by her side: "He is not only a clever statesman and an honest man, but a good and a kind-hearted man, whose aim is to do his duty to his country and not for a *party*. I have seen almost all my other Ministers, and do regular, hard, but to me *delightful*, work with them"; and the wise uncle replied: "Remember that *cleverness* and *talent, without an honest heart and character, will never do for your* Minister."

Then began that very pleasing romance of the young Queen and the very polished elderly statesman. It was on the grand scale, after the manner of a stately and graceful dance in an eighteenth-century Court, and doubtless it was all very correct; for both parties were full of dignity and with a fine sense of the responsibilities of their respective positions. It had an enormous effect on the Queen's future life. For he set an early direction to her policy which she never afterwards radically changed. She was already the soul of conscientious straightness and common sense, and Melbourne did much to make her nature a habit. He aroused her enthusiasm: "I was sure you would be of my opinion relative to Lord Melbourne. Indeed, dearest Uncle, nothing is to be done without" — the grandmotherly touch again — "a good heart and an honest mind; I have, alas, seen so much of bad hearts and dishonest and *double* minds."

That woman of the world, Madame de Lieven, wrote to Lord Aberdeen of the whole matter as if it were a picture — as indeed it was, and one of great charm:

> *J'ai vu la Reine deux fois, je l'ai vue seule, et j'ai vue dans la société du soir, et avec son Premier Ministre. Elle a un aplomb, un air de commandement, de dignité, que avec son visage enfantin, sa petite taille, et son joli sourire, forment certainement le spectacle le plus extraordinaire qu'il soit possible de se figurer. Elle est d'une extrême reserve dans son discours. On croit que la prudence est une de ses premières qualités.* Lord Melbourne *a auprès d'elle un air d'amour, de contentement, de vanité même, et tout cela mêle avec beaucoup de respect, des attitudes très à son aise, une habitude de première place dans son salon, de la reverie, de la gaieté, vous voyez tout cela. La Reine est pleine d'aimables sourires pour lui.*

This skilful picture after the style of Meissonier — with a touch of Watteau — is a valuable document among the historical sources of its period.

There was another important factor in the education of this royal stateswoman. On October 12, 1839, she wrote to her uncle: "The dear cousins have arrived.... Albert's beauty is *most striking*, and he is so amiable and unaffected — in short, very *fascinating*." On the 15th she wrote: "My mind is quite made up — and I told Albert this morning of it.... He seems perfection.... I love him more than I can say.... Lord Melbourne, whom I have of course consulted about the whole affair, quite approves my choice and expresses great satisfaction." She then says that she and Lord Melbourne — Albert is mentioned as merely a consenting party! — considered that the marriage should be in four months: "My feelings are a *little* changed, I must say, since last Spring, when I said I couldn't *think* of marrying for *three or four years;* but seeing Albert has changed all this." It seems difficult to find any explanation for these impossible "three or four years" except the stately royal minuet which had been danced for two years, with such exquisite propriety, by the fascinating Lord Melbourne.

The more passionate appearance of the young Prince introduced an element of human sentiment which is of too commonplace a character — even when it happens in royal palaces — to need analysis. She put it all down on paper — without the slightest attempt to cover its popular and democratic origin in any regal trappings — in a letter of October 29th: "Oh! dear Uncle, I do feel so happy! I do so adore Albert! he is quite an angel, and so very, very kind to me, and seems so fond of me, which touches me much." She goes on to mention that she even extends this loving affection to Prince Ernest, her beloved's brother, who was unfortunately suffering from jaundice at the moment, she adds. Then inevitably and apparently with irresistible attraction, she goes back to Lord Melbourne, the silent figure now in the background: "There are not many *such* honest kind friends to be found in this world." But with gradually increasing force Prince Albert became the chief formative factor in his royal wife's life, and therefore a masterful factor in English political history.

There is no doubt that the Prince Consort had a mind of very admirable substance in a member of the ruling class. It was too well-balanced to have the qualities called genius; it was methodical, infinitely patient, honest and entirely unselfish when the welfare of the nation was concerned. But except for his honesty and tact, he was in almost everything else the precise negative of Lord Melbourne. If that polished nobleman and cynic had lived longer, and the Prince Consort had not arrived, it is probable that the adjective "Victorian" would have borne another meaning. It happened by the turn of fate that it denotes a condition of society in which the whirl of machinery and the prim propriety of young ladies are, in some unexpected manner, strangely blended; while the Anglican figure of Mr. Gladstone and Mr. John Bright, the Quaker, triumphantly imposed their will on the audacious and brilliant Mr. Disraeli. There were hundreds of complicated factors in the picture, all of which would doubtless have happened in some more or less obvious manner, even if there had been no Prince Consort at all. Yet, somehow, they all seem to fit in with the rather pedantic outlines of Albert the Good — and certainly they are not in harmony with that mental and physical temperament which is so admirably symbolised by the second Viscount Melbourne. The age of the early railway engine and the Blue Danube *valse* would perhaps have come in spite of all personalities; but one feels that it would not have been named after the wife of the Prince Consort unless he had been her very serious husband.

A proper judgment of Queen Victoria's place in our political history has been obscured for a rather trivial reason. There has been a tendency to discredit her because she has been deemed peculiarly responsible for this unnatural primness which is considered a hall mark of the Victorian Age; and this character has prejudiced the estimate of her part in the greater political events of her reign. The prejudice is without good reason. It might have seemed unlikely that the masterful young Queen, who astonished every one of her Ministers by her self-possession when she received their first homage, would ever be a submissive wife. Yet so it was. In February, 1852, when she was thirty-three years old she wrote: "Albert becomes really a terrible man of business; I think it takes a little off from the gentleness of his character, and makes him so preoccupied. I grieve over all this . . . but I am every day more convinced that *we women*, if we are to be *good* women, *feminine* and *amiable* and *domestic*, are *not fitted* to *reign*. . . ." When we remember the young self-reliant sovereign, who smiled on Lord Melbourne before the quick eyes of Madame de Lieven, we begin to suspect that this new influence must have unex-

QUEEN VICTORIA, THE PRINCE CONSORT AND FAMILY
From painting by *Winterhalter in the Collection of His Majesty King George V at Buckingham Palace*

pectedly dominated her life; and that the "Victorian" Age should really have borne the triumphant name of the Prince Consort.

The new Greville diary, which has only lately supplied the suppressed passages, gives some fresh light on this matter. There are new passages that suggest almost conclusive proof that it was the Prince Consort who insisted on the "Victorian" propriety. In February, 1843, Greville was writing impatiently of "the prudery of Albert"; he had been already told by Melbourne, in September, 1841, that, whereas the Prince Consort was "extremely strait-laced and a great stickler for morality," the Queen was "rather the other way and did not much care about such niceties of moral choice." The next day the Duke of Wellington told Greville that this was also his opinion: "it was the Prince who insisted on a spotless character, the Queen not caring a straw about it." All the evidence goes to show that the young sovereign was a very healthy-minded woman, while her husband had already lost that nice balance of life, between intellect and emotion, which is necessary for the greatest accomplishment.

The Prince Consort was a man who took his responsibilities as a ruler very seriously indeed. He had the kind of conscience which is considered the standard of excellent virtue in every Sunday School class. It was certain that he would never do anything dishonest and improper. As far as he could see into the laws of life he was an eminently just man; and he would have always sacrificed his ease in order to do his duty. He was very near in type to Sir Robert Peel. They were, alike, very clever men, full of good resolutions, and even of good deeds; yet without a spark of genius or farseeing imagination. They were both type-specimens of the "Victorian" Age of prosperous wealth making and dull imagination. As far as any two men of the ruling class could be responsible for a vast economic and social revolution, Prince Albert and Sir Robert Peel might be charged with the moral and artistic catastrophe of the middle part of the nineteenth century in English history. It is not a sweet place in the story of the higher civilisations; but the Prince and the plutocratic baronet were just the kind of men who were so lacking in the deeper wisdom that they mistook its vices for virtues.

If the healthy honest Queen and the cultured Melbourne, with all their many intellectual frailties and carelessnesses, had been left in supreme possession of the destiny of England, there is no indication that they would have built a Great Exhibition of 1850, wherein the arts and sciences and the commercial travellers would have met in that dangerous intimacy of which the Victorian Age, at its worst, was the illegitimate child. But the prim minds of the Prince and Peel were never conscious of their own misconduct. They did not know that a too strict propriety of emotion and intellect was the mother of most of the vices.

There is no doubt that after Melbourne had left the stage of public affairs, the young Queen was gradually dominated by the rigid mind of her husband. It was certainly only a gradual surrender; for eighteen months after the marriage there was a letter from Melbourne to his Queen, advising her that her husband was "well worthy of her confidence"; an approval which could scarcely have been necessary if the confidence had been beyond dispute. But the confidence grew into something near obedience, and until his death, in 1861, he had a very large part of the royal power in his hands. There is something very natural in this partial surrender of a self-willed queen to her masterful husband. It is corroboration of the important fact that she was a very normal, and therefore very sound, woman. She gave way not so much to the intellectual assertion of the Prince Consort as to the material and maternal fact that she became the mother of a large family. That this family should claim her energies before her kingdom may have been a misfortune for her country, though it was certainly a testimony to her unaffected naturalness. But the choice was not made without a struggle. When her first child was born, within ten months of her marriage, her uncle offered the hasty wish that she might become "*Maman, au milieu d'une belle et nombreuse famille*"; and the young mother promptly protested: "I think you will see with me the great inconvenience a *large* family would be to us all, and particularly to the country, independent of the hardship and inconvenience to myself; men never think, at least seldom, I think, what a hard task it is for us women to go through this *very* often." This had certainly not the true "Victorian" touch; and it required some years of that rather crude, masterful "Consortian" mind before submission came. But come it did; and even after his death the memory of him controlled his widow's opinions and deeds.

At the beginning of her widowhood there was an almost morbid condition which is not very easily fitted into the rest of her common-sense life. There is a letter which she wrote to Lord Derby on February 17, 1862, two months after her husband's death, which is not the kind of letter which often gets among State documents. The following extracts are enough to prove that Queen Victoria was first a woman, and only a queen by hereditary chance.

To express what the Queen's desolation and utter misery is, is almost impossible . . . she feels as though her life had ended on that dreadful day when she lost that bright Angel who was her idol, the life of her life; and time seems to have passed like one long dark day. She sees trees budding, the days lengthen, the primroses coming out, but *she thinks* herself *still* in the month of December . . . with but one consolation — to *rejoin* him again — never to part . . . and is gratified to see justice done to *him* whom she was *allowed* to call *husband;* a privilege she *ever felt* to be the greatest which ever fell to the lot of woman.

It is just because that letter might have been written by a few millions of her people — if they had possessed as much affection for their husbands — that it is further proof that the Queen was nearer her subjects than were her great ministers and diplomats, who sternly ignore budding trees and flowering primroses when they write official letters to each other. Still, the twenty years' retirement from public life, after the Prince Consort's death, was an excessive display of grief which must remain an unexplained exception to the Queen's sense of duty and practical mind. But when one reads so much of the unpopularity of the Queen during these years, it must be observed that it was her absence which her subjects resented. A monarch has been too often disliked for his presence.

Soon after her marriage Lord Melbourne told Mr. Anson, the Prince Consort's secretary, that his master was bored and wanted clever society at Court, more literature and more science; but the Queen opposed this substitute for the domestic chess after dinner, because she did not feel her education would bear the strain; and "she is far too open and candid in her nature to pretend to one atom more knowledge than she really possesses." Yet, as he added, she was "accomplished" as the world would understand that term; for she spoke and wrote French and German with elegance, understood Italian, and was even so unVictorian as to know some Latin. But his chief point was in the closing judgment: "The rest of her education she owes to her own natural shrewdness and quickness, and this perhaps has not been the proper education for one who was to wear the Crown of England."

For once the clever Melbourne was entirely wrong. It was just because Queen Victoria escaped from the pedants' schools — which had made "the double first" Peel into a dull fellow and almost condemned Mr. Gladstone to a (narrowly escaped) lifelong imprisonment of fanaticism —

that the freer Queen was almost always wiser than her over-educated ministers. They had been made her ministers because they were supposed to be able to give an expert opinion on national affairs. It was most of it mere theory and, indeed, even pure bluff — but such was the conventional pretence. Whereas, the Queen was the embodiment of unaffected common sense; the domestic, motherly person, who never talked rhetoric but only discussed practical details. The advantage in statesmanship of an absence of rhetoric would be hard to overestimate. Fluent language is so often useful as a method of concealing a defective intellect. If one can talk brilliantly it is not so necessary to think. One can guess at the sort of affairs that would have interested the Prince's scientific friends. For example, they would have told with joy of the possibility of finding more coal — to make the fields of England blacker than ever. Just as to-day they would discuss the advantage of one poison gas over another. If the Queen had no morbid passion for such useless — even dangerous — conversation, it was not such a reflection on her intellect as Melbourne imagined.

Another chief advantage that Queen Victoria possessed over the statesmen was that she had scarcely any trace of "class" feeling. Those who take the trouble to read the State documents of 1866 will see that it was the Queen who insisted on the Reform Bill of 1867 being a fair and substantial settlement. If she had any prejudices, it was against the powerful and the rich and in favour of the poor. She probably thought it necessary to maintain the hereditary monarchical system because it seemed more likely to produce good results than an untrained unorganised democracy. But it was certainly not from any conviction of peculiar sanctity. In 1851 she wrote to her uncle concerning the coming education of his son, and suggested that he should be sent to Bonn University as an ordinary student. For, she said: "It is the common contact with his fellow-creatures, the being put on a par with him, the being brought to feel that he is as much *one* of them as any other, in spite of his birth, which I think of such great importance for him." She had the instincts of the simple person. Only a few days after the last mentioned letter, she was writing from "our little bothy" in the Scotch hill: "it is very cold . . . our little Shiel is very snug and comfortable and we have a good little piano in it." The simple life of the Highlands became one of the passions of her life. The present writer had it from the lips of a visitor near Balmoral (the Queen's home) how one day he was having tea in a peasant's cottage. The Queen's carriage drove up to the door, and the stranger hastily offered to leave the parlour for her use. He was told to remain where he was, as her Majesty always preferred to sit in the kitchen.

If Victoria had been an autocrat, instead of an exceedingly punctilious constitutional — and very limited — monarch, it is probable that the poor would have been considered with more sympathetic attention than they received from ministers who protested their democracy on every election platform. There was one occasion when she gave a severe lesson in practical democracy to Mr. Gladstone, who had so often discussed it with enthusiasm as a theory. He had drawn up one of his famous budgets which have been the cause of such praise in certain democratic circles. His royal mistress, who had a matter-of-fact mind that was not often confused by sentiment — except in the matter of her much beloved husband — sent her democratic minister the following crisp comment:

The tax on beer she also regrets, as the poor never drink wine, and the loss of beer will be deeply felt by them. The rich classes who drink wine, and who are not in any way restrained in their indulgences, can well afford to pay for wine. But the poor can ill afford any additional tax on what is in many parts their only beverage.

The Radical politicians have probably been wise in objecting to the interference of the Crown in public affairs. If this letter had been printed on an election poster, it might have done serious injury to the rhetorical effect of many a brilliant Radical speech on the high philosophy of Liberalism.

It is a great advantage for a nation to have a sovereign who has a simple mind that remembers that poor people drink beer. It is one of those significant facts that sometimes get lost in the mists of a fine oration. It was just one of the points which would occur to Queen Victoria.

The high thinkers — in revenge — have circulated the opinion that the Queen did not care for their conversation because she could not understand what they were talking about. It is just possible that she did not think it worth while to try.

There is much valuable information on this matter of the Queen's mind, in a diary that Mr. Gladstone kept when he was Minister in residence at Balmoral, in 1863. "She talked very pleasantly and well upon many matters public and other. As to politics she talked most of America and Germany; also some Lancashire distress. . . ." Of course his earnest soul (at the age of fifty-four) was still astonished that a Court was not as bad as was commonly believed in the evangelical circles of his youth. "Last evening I was summoned to dine. . . . It was extremely interesting. We were but seven in all, and anything more beautifully domestic than the Queen and her family it was hard to conceive. . . . She talked about many things and persons." On this first evening the conversation was frankly of the homely kind: ". . . among others the Lyttelton family, and asked me about the boys *seriatim*, but pulled me up at once when, in a fit of momentary oblivion, I said the New Zealander was the third." The oblivion was probably not so "momentary" as Mr. Gladstone believed. It was a small matter, but not without psychological and political interest that the great statesman was so full of philosophy and classics and rhetoric that he confused even his own relations; whereas his Queen, with a mind less hampered by the abstract, could correct him at once. She did not ignore the world around her in a continual pursuit of the ideal. For that simple reason she often insisted on discussing facts, when her ministers were prepared to go to war for a theory.

There was another dinner a few nights later: "Everything quite as pleasing. The Queen talked Shakespeare, Scott, the use of the German language in England. . . . Guizot's translation of the Prince's speeches. . . ." and so on: "The household life is really very agreeable when one comes to know them. One way and another they have a great deal in them." Another evening the Queen discussed

Guizot's comparison of the Prince and King William, about Macaulay, America and the ironclads, where she was very natural and high-spirited [the scientific friend of Prince Albert must have got past the barrier one night!]; and Schleswig-Holstein, in which she is intensely interested, because the Prince thought it a great case of justice on the side rather opposite to that of Lord Palmerston and the government policy. She spoke about this with intense earnestness, and said she considered it a legacy from him.

Not long after he recorded a Cabinet meeting on this matter of Denmark; and says that "the Queen wrote a letter, which I think did her great credit. Her love of truth and wish to do right prevents all prejudices from effectually warping her." What she wanted was "a more staid and quiet foreign policy." One cannot conceive of anything more admirable in the way of international affairs than to adhere to the truth and to peace. It was one more proof of the advantage of possessing the domestic and simple mind — that could even remember the correct order of the Lyttelton boys.

Later on in the same year he was again at Balmoral: "She has not said a syllable about public affairs to me since I came, but talked pleasantly of all manners of things." A day or two later there was an interview: "She was as good and as gracious as possible. I can hardly tell you all the things talked about." Then follows ten lines of print; giving some of the subjects which interested this lady, who had been rumoured to be narrow in her tastes. With the exception of "Lucy and the Hagley boys", "the Prince Consort on dress and fashions, Prince of Wales on ditto" — and, possibly, "young married women" — they were just the sort of questions which ought to be set in an examination for young *attachés* in the diplomatic service; and the conversation must have been exceedingly useful in tearing Mr. Gladstone's mind away from Homer. It must have been always peculiarly bracing for her Cabinet ministers to spend a few days in a palace where they were always discussing and examining the ways of the normal world, instead of the purely freakish ways of foreign office chiefs and their senior clerks.

There were several occasions when Queen Victoria came into collision with her advisers in the matter of foreign affairs. Her most famous duels were with Lord Palmerston and with Mr. Gladstone. Strangely enough they arose, apparently, for precisely contrary reasons. She was annoyed with Palmerston for being too militant and with Gladstone for being too peaceful. She was, on the whole, right against Palmerston; and she had a good few excuses for being annoyed with the Liberal mystic who allowed his nation to get into scrapes which even a visionary should have avoided. There was some excuse for being impatient with a man who would insist on spending so much time on Dante and the Early Fathers when his country was in the midst of a war with the Madhi round Khartoum.

The Queen's case against Palmerston was, in substance,

that he did not know the technique of his craft of diplomacy. Or, if one likes to put it another way, he had not the manners and tact of a gentleman. The chief business of the Secretary for Foreign Affairs is to be so clever with the pen and the tongue, in persuasiveness and intrigue, that there will be no danger of war. A foreign minister who — like Palmerston — was always rubbing everybody the wrong way, causing friction and fear and anxiety all over Europe, simply did not know how to do his office work. The diplomatist who tries to get what he wants by threats and violent language knows no more of his trade than an ironmaster who tries to collect iron out of chalk.

The Queen objected to her minister diplomatically careering over Europe like an ill-bred boy who amuses himself by cracking a whip round everybody's legs. It, undoubtedly, must have been great fun to write brilliant and audacious despatches to other foreign secretaries, saying quite frankly what Lord Palmerston thought of their acts and opinions, and how contemptible they all looked in noble, pure, and fearless British eyes. However, that is not the work of diplomats, but of rather cheap journalists hoping for an increased circulation. Queen Victoria was almost always anxious to keep the peace, and she therefore objected to Lord Palmerston writing despatches which might easily lead to war.

It was not merely a question of whether Palmerston was right or wrong in protesting against what he considered tyranny on the part of some foreign government. The Queen insisted on considering also whether one ought to right the wrong at the risk of a war. When the rebel Hungarian, Kossuth, arrived in this country Palmerston said he was going to invite him as a guest to his house. The Queen promptly wrote to Lord John Russell, the Prime Minister, saying that this would be a serious offence to the Austrian Government with whom we were at peace. Russell replied, saying he entirely agreed with her, but Palmerston had defied him. Would her Majesty please stop him! Then he reconsidered the matter and said he had better get the Cabinet as a whole to act; but the Queen, who was extremely prompt and businesslike, had already written to Palmerston. She told Russell that he was quite right in referring the matter to the Cabinet; but "she has the right and the duty to demand that one of her Ministers should not by his private acts compromise her and the country."

For the moment Palmerston gave way. However, he almost immediately drafted another of his smart despatches; and the Queen had again to protest: "the tone in which it is written is so very ironical, and not altogether becoming for a public despatch from the English Secretary for Foreign Affairs to be given to the Ministry of another State." Then followed the sound professional reason for her objection: "The substance is quite right, and a dignified explanation of the absurdity of the conduct of the Parma officials would very likely produce its effect, but some expressions in this draft could only tend to irritate, and therefore prevent, that readiness to comply with our demand which is to be produced." In other words, the Queen who knew her business as a diplomatist was annoyed with Palmerston because he did not know the elementary rules of his profession. He was not going the right way to get the desired results. He was behaving like a clumsy, egotistical ignoramus. She was in earnest in getting an evil reformed; not in being smart.

But Palmerston preferred to behave like a spoilt child instead of a responsible foreign minister. After Kossuth left England, the Foreign Minister received a deputation of his admirers who presented an address in which the Emperors of Austria were called "odious and detestable tyrants." The Queen again protested that "the best interests of her people, as well as her own personal obligations to the sovereigns with whom she professes to be on terms of peace and amity, were seriously compromised." She added that she would at once give way to the Cabinet's decision, but they must take the responsibility. Again, surely, by all the rules of international affairs she was right. If England objected to the acts of Russia and Austria the Government should say so officially, and not try to get out of its responsibilities by allowing the Foreign Minister to pretend to be acting on his own. It was cowardly, not courageous. Russell, being mortally afraid of Palmerston, tried to make excuses and said the English people supported Palmerston; and the good will of the people was "a great security in these times." Whereupon the Queen sent a reply that proved that at diplomacy she could beat the Foreign Minister at his own game. She ironically hoped that the Cabinet would make "that careful inquiry into the justice of her complaint that she was sorry to miss altogether in Lord John Russell's answer." Then she added a defiant sentence which showed how little she had been swayed by the "class" prejudices of the royal caste in all these negotiations: "It is no question with the Queen whether she pleases the Emperor of Austria or not, but whether she gives him a just cause of complaint or not. And if she does so, she can never believe that this will add to her popularity with her own people." Little did Palmerston care if British soldiers had to die in battle as the climax of his brilliant despatches. The Queen cared very much indeed, and was determined that not a single unjustifiable risk should be taken. She was not a politician hunting for votes at the next election; but a stateswoman, who tried to give the soundest advice and was prepared to take the risks of her opinion.

Having seen the fierce struggle that Palmerston made in order that he might show his respect to Kossuth, the judicial student may consider it necessary to inquire whether he was worthy of such a battle royal. A passage in the shrewd Greville's diary (November 22, 1851) will enlighten him:

Kossuth is at last gone ... openly announcing that he does so for the purpose of stirring up war against Austria ... in which he expects England to take a conspicuous part. ... That he is very able, and especially a great speaker cannot be denied; but I take it that a more hypocritical, unscrupulous, mischievous adventurer never existed.

The Queen was more careful in the choice of her nation's friends than Palmerston ever was.

Almost immediately after this struggle with Palmerston concerning Kossuth there followed the still more famous affair of Napoleon's *coup d'etat*. The Frenchman suddenly followed the family tradition, of which he was so proud, and made himself autocrat of France by force of arms. The wife of the English Ambassador in Paris wrote of his method in horrified words: "The bloodshed has been dreadful and indiscriminate, no quarter was shown, and when an insurgent took refuge in a house, the soldiers killed everyone in the house whether engaged in the *émeute* or not." As the indignant lady said, these proceedings were "so contrary to and devoid of law and justice and security that even the most violent Tory would be staggered by them." Lord Normanby, her husband, never for one moment imagined that Napoleon could be stopped — and in any case it was not England's place to impose an opinion on the French nation — indeed he even hoped the *coup* would succeed quickly, so as to get the slaughter over as soon as possible; "but that is another thing to approving the way it was begun, or the way it has been carried out."

The Queen, being a clear-headed and humane woman who knew that disorder and bloodshed — for any cause — were anti-social, immediately wrote to Lord John Russell, the Premier, that she was much surprised and concerned by the news and thought it was of "great importance that Lord Normanby should be instructed to remain entirely passive." She also took steps to prevent her own relations, the Orleanist princes, from making matters worse by joining in the civil war. It was peace and order she wanted, not the victory of princes. But Palmerston was not so particular; he had an instinct for brute force, and not the slightest objection to being the avowed friend of people who shot their opponents. His colleagues in the Cabinet had told him to be strictly neutral, but he had no sense of discipline — he ought to have been a pirate instead of a diplomat — and cared for nobody's opinion except his own. So he told the French Ambassador in England that he was quite pleased with what Napoleon had done. It was a paradoxical situation. Here was the diplomatic friend of liberty saying how pleased he was with the methods of military adventurers. As Lady Normanby again wrote from Paris: "One would have supposed that Palmerston would have been the last person to approve of this *coup d'état.*" She says he had written to her husband, and "the curious thing is that it is a letter, or rather letters that would completely ruin Palmerston with his Party. He treats all the acts of the wholesale cruelties of the troops as a joke — in short, it is the letter of a man half mad."

It was against this "half mad" Foreign Minister that the sane Queen had the sense and courage to stand firm. She insisted on his dismissal from his office; which his weak-kneed colleagues would never have had the pluck to do. The conclusive proof of the soundness of her judgment was to come years later, when Napoleon had become a dangerous nuisance to the peace of Europe. Palmerston's views were always the short-sighted glances of a hasty, violent man; whereas Queen Victoria looked farther ahead than the next general election. It is one of the advantages of a monarchy that it is not always thinking of votes. Her wise uncle wrote to his niece immediately Napoleon struck his blow: "A military Government in France, if it really gets established, must become dangerous for Europe." The

history of the next ten years was a conclusive proof of his
and his niece's sagacity. Napoleon's reign was a period of
unrest and wars — in Italy and finally in France, where his
insane folly brought the German armies over the Rhine.
In the still farther future, it is perhaps not very far from the
truth to say that if there had not been a second French
Empire there would not have been the catastrophe of the
war of 1914-1918. This freebooter Palmerston had no
conception of all this; he was not a calm statesman, like his
royal mistress.

There was something detached and international about
the mind of Queen Victoria when she came to consider foreign affairs. It was near akin to the minds of Castlereagh
and Wellington. All three of them were good patriots up
to a point, but one always feels conscious of the bigger touch.
They saw Britain as merely one unit in a greater whole. The
smaller men, like Palmerston and Canning, were content if
they could pull off a success that would look well in to-morrow morning's newspaper, or sound effective as a debating
point in their next parliamentary speech. They thought in
days and months, not in generations and centuries.

The internationalism of Queen Victoria's mind, the big
outlook, was very marked during the Danish War with
Prussia and Austria in 1864. She had at first seen the faults
on the Danish side more clearly than their just grievances;
but was firmly against war as the way out of the quarrel.
Her ministers were not so balanced; and Russell (who had
the mind of a schoolgirl, at times) threw down the glove of
challenge, saying that whoever dared to touch Denmark
would have to fight England as well. Then, when the war
came — encouraged by this loose language — all the bluster
ended in nothing, and Denmark was left to its fate. The
Queen, of course, was a considerable factor in this refusal to
fight; though her ministers admitted that it was their decision which decided the matter. But then the Queen had not

helped on the catastrophe by promising assistance; and she showed how entirely impartial she was — in spite of all her German family relations — by turning on Prussia with fury when that power made unscrupulous use of its victory. She wrote to her daughter, the Crown Princess of Prussia, that now they had got what they professed to be fighting for (the severance of the duchies from the dominion of Denmark) "let Prussia also show that she does not mean to keep them for herself, and all will be well." By August of 1864 her language was stronger. Her private secretary wrote to Lord Granville: "Her Majesty thinks Prussia should at least be made aware of what she and her Government and every honest man in Europe must think of the gross and unblushing violation of every assurance and pledge that she has given, which Prussia has been guilty of." She had no national prejudices that would bear the strain of dishonest conduct. She now considered that Prussia, of which her daughter would one day be Queen, had behaved dishonourably; and she said so in very pointed language which Palmerston himself might have used — without such a good excuse.

Her sense of the urgent importance of being true to one's pledged word came out in the matter of the Italian wars. She objected to an alliance with France in order to attack the Austrians in Italy; because those Austrian possessions had been guaranteed by the Treaty of 1815, which England had signed. Now, it is arguable that there must be an end to the validity of treaties, else Europe would be still enforcing the decrees of the Roman emperors. Italy, sooner or later, was justified in getting rid of her conquerors. But the Queen looked far ahead; she did not see any particular advantage in lowering England's peculiar boast "to stand by treaties", as she put it, in order to make Napoleon strong instead of Austria. Her family had been troubled by a strong France for centuries, and Austria had often been very useful as an ally. Palmerston seems never to have heard of the history of Europe. In any case, being a diplomatist, the Queen did not consider a European war the best way of giving the Italians their freedom; besides, it was a very sound rule in international affairs to keep one's pledges and insist on the same favour in return. A world run on that principle would have many imperfections, but it would probably be saved many more disadvantages. The avoidance of war was, with a few exceptions, always a chief object in Queen Victoria's diplomacy; and that was why she showed such courtesy to Napoleon III's rule in France, much though she distrusted his aims. She could not be blind to the fact that it was largely his own folly that had led him into the disaster of the Franco-Prussian War in 1870; or, at least, given Bismarck such an admirable chance of forcing the contest. But Victoria had no love for Prussia; and her European mind looked at the question as a whole, and decided very quickly that Prussia had no right to inflict such crushing terms. The English Court was pro-French during the war; and as early as September, 1870, the Queen wrote to the King of Prussia asking him "to shape your conditions of peace for the vanquished that they may be able to accept them." The siege of Paris and its horrors set her anti-militarist nerves on edge. By July 31, 1871, she "Talked with good Fritz about the war. He is so fair and kind and good and has the intensest horror of Bismarck . . . bad and unprincipled." When there was a persistent rumour that the vanquished French had recovered too quickly, the Queen of England wrote (May 6, 1875): "Saw Mr. Disraeli and talked about the very alarming rumours from Germany as to war. . . . I said this was intolerable, that France could not for years make war, and that I thought we ought, in concert with the other Powers, to hold the strongest language to both"; and to the Crown Princess of Prussia she wrote: "You know that the Prussians are not popular unfortunately, and *no one* will tolerate any Power wishing to dictate to all Europe. . . . This country, with all the greatest wish to go hand in hand with Germany, *cannot and will not stand* it."

In short, compared with such unruly ministers as Palmerston and Russell, Queen Victoria was a diplomatist of long vision, who was always ready to stretch the virtue of international courtesy to its full limit, because she was so well-instructed in her family profession that she knew that only by such methods of tact could one get the best results. She also assumed, as a fundamental axiom, that war is not a rational method of negotiation, except as a last resource in a most urgent situation. Her broad sanity was typically expressed in her comments on Bismarck's proposal of a treaty between Germany and Austria:

The value of such an alliance, however, would be greatly diminished in my eyes, and I am certain in that of this country, if it were misconceived and were supposed to be of such a character as would give umbrage to France . . . I am certain that any league against France would never be tolerated in this country.

Such was her position as against men of the Palmerston type. But her struggles with Mr. Gladstone were of a very different kind. She usually opposed Palmerston because he could not act like a gentleman; her objection to Gladstone was generally that he acted like a saint. In the matter of the Gordon disaster at Khartoum, her persistent cry was that the honour of Britain was at stake; and ever afterwards she complained that Mr. Gladstone had dragged his country in the dust. Now in one way she was entirely right. She was a shrewd woman of sounder business habits than any minister she ever had; and she was naturally angry when she was compelled to look on (almost helplessly), while the Nile Expedition was delayed and mismanaged by the bungling Cabinet in London. If Mr. Gladstone had possessed the full courage of his peaceful convictions and had refused to send Gordon to Khartoum, well and good. But Gordon was sent there; and, even though he behaved in a very disobedient and fanatical manner — refusing to come back when he could have done so — having made themselves responsible for his presence in the Sudan, the Liberal Ministry in England should have brought him back in safety. So far Queen Victoria had every reason to be annoyed that her Government had behaved in an exceedingly inefficient manner.

But there was something deeper in the Gladstonian failure than a want of business tact. Against the very natural annoyance of his Queen, there was a greater answer which could never be offered, for the great principles are rarely permissible in public debate. Against Palmerston, Victoria could always score; for in the matter of the world she was usually more businesslike, more just, and wiser than he was. Her family training was in the ruling of men on earth, and she had become by tradition exceedingly skilled in her profession.

But Mr. Gladstone raised other problems of thought and practice. He was a mystic, who knew little of the ways of men and cared even less. When he withdrew the British armies from the Sudan, after the fall of Khartoum, as he had withdrawn them from the Transvaal after the defect of Majuba Hill, he was obeying laws which his worldly-wise and well-balanced sovereign could not altogether understand. She lived in a world of material things, and the British Empire seemed a very big part of it to her energetic, faithful mind. It was her public duty to protect the interests that had been committed to her hands by hereditary fate; and she was not going to be thwarted by ministers who could not manage military expeditions against a few savages or a tiny State.

But this Empire of lands and seas was a clumsy material

structure, which did not really interest Mr. Gladstone — who was only entertained by the world of ideas — and sometimes of words. He was therefore the only one of her ministers this clever woman of the world could never completely understand. The Queen and Mr. Gladstone were really trying to govern different worlds. Had she but known it, her adored and adoring Mr. Disraeli was also a dreamer in other spheres of thought, where the British Empire was of small account. But he was so exceedingly clever that she never discovered his mysticism. For he made her Empress of India, and she forgot that long before he had written in *Tancred:* "One should conquer the world not to enthrone a man, but an idea, for ideas exist for ever." It was the kind of thought Mr. Gladstone ought to have understood; and he would certainly have agreed with it, if he could have accepted anything from such a source. But he was such an innocent, unobservant fellow, and knew so little of the world and his ways; and he could never manage his royal mistress, as his rival could do so well. The Queen was naturally annoyed with Mr. Gladstone; for she could have governed her worldly empire so much more efficiently than this straggler from another world could ever do. However, that is no particular discredit to Mr. Gladstone.

On considering Victoria of England, one is inclined to believe that if she had been her own Prime Minister and Cabinet also, from her succession to her death, her nation would have been a freer, happier, more peaceful and more prosperous country. There were very few occasions of dispute with her ministers when she was wrong and they were right; when they were not tyrannical while she was democratic; when they were not warlike and she was peaceful. She was so often an expert, professional ruler, while they were so persistently amateur politicians, with all sorts of fads and fancies — theological, economic and social — that had little to do with the national welfare.

INDEX

INDEX

BEACONSFIELD, BENJAMIN DISRAELI, EARL OF, 205–38; compared with Peel, 205; his family history, 206; his father, 206; his ambition, 207; his education, 207–8; friendship with Mr. John Murray, 208; "Vivian Grey", 1826, 209–11; "Voyage of Captain Popanilla", 1828, 211–14; "The Young Duke", 1831, 214–16; criticises Canning and Peel, 214–15; discusses his political position, 215–16; his illness, 1827–1830, and his travels abroad, 216; "Contarini Fleming" and "Alroy", 216; goes into society, 216; candidate at Wycombe election, 217; struggles with his own nature, 218–20; his success in society, 219; conversation with Lord Melbourne, 219; negotiates with political leaders, 219–20; enters House of Commons, 1837, 220; "Coningsby", 1844, 221–24; "Sybil", 1845, 224–28; "Tancred", 1847, 228–9; success in House of Commons, 229; attacks lawyers, 230; the "Young England" Party, 231; begins to suspect Peel, 231; opposes Peel in Factory and Sugar legislation, 231–2; general opposition to Peel's political policy, 232–3; character sketch of Peel, 233; becomes leader of country gentlemen, 234–5; attacks Corn Law proposals, 235–6; Reform Act of 1867, 237; Prime Minister, 1874, 237; social reforms, 237; Trade Union Act, 1875, 237; his political career, 237–8; attitude toward Indian Mutiny, 238; dies a dreamer of dreams, 1881, 238; attitude towards Roman Catholic claims, 264; protests against China War, 270; supremacy in House of Commons, 276; his mystical Imperialism, 320.

CANNING, GEORGE, 53–100; contrasted with Wellington, 53; family history, 54–5; father and mother, 56–7; early life, 57; his mother's struggles and marriages, 58; Stratford Canning, his uncle, 58; at Eton and Oxford, 58; early literary work and verses, 59–60; early ambitions, 61; leaves Oxford and goes to London, 62; joins Tory Party, 62–65; Sir Walter Scott's story of his change of party, 63; opinion of French Revolution, 63–4; Lady Hester Stanhope's opinion of, 65; influence of his light verses, 66; first speech in House of Commons, 66; nature of his oratory, 66–7, 99–100; supports Pitt's policy by intrigues, 67–8; correspondence with Ellis, 68–70; his ethics and his verses, 70–1; Wilberforce's opinion of, 71; publishes *The Oracle*, 71; suspects "reformers", 72–3; work at Foreign Office, 1796, 73; Commissioner for India, 1799, 73; Joint Pay-

Canning, George (*Continued*) master of Forces, 1800, 73; marries Miss Joan Scott and fortune, 1800, 73–4; resigns office with Pitt, 1801, 74; writes more verses, and attacks Addington, 74–6; advocates return of Pitt to office, 77; Malmesbury's opinion of, 78, 81; Treasurer of Navy under Pitt, 1804, 78; letter to Lady Hester Stanhope, 79; defends Lord Melville, 79; poem on battle of Trafalgar, 1805, 80; Secretary of State for Foreign Affairs, 1807, 81; orders seizure of Danish fleet, 82; policy in Spain, and Sir John Moore, 82; Convention of Cintra, 83; intrigues against Castlereagh, and has duel, 1809, 83–4; offered Foreign Office by Castlereagh, but refuses it, 84–5; two famous speeches in 1813, 85–6; to Lisbon as ambassador, 1814, 86; returns to England, 1816, 86; President of Board of Control of India, 1816, 87; Queen Caroline's divorce, 87–8; offered Governorship of India, 1821, 88; succeeds to Foreign Office on Castlereagh's suicide, 1821, 89–90; his handling of King George IV, 90–91; the "Falmouth coast" speech, 1824, 91; his foreign policy, 92; policy concerning South America, and Monroe Doctrine, 93–5; policy in Eastern Europe; Greece, 95–6; succeeds Lord Liverpool as Premier, 1827, 96–7; dies Aug., 1827, 97; Greville's opinion of, 98–9; Wellington's opinion of, 98; William Hazlitt on, 99–100; Lord Melbourne's opinion of, 120–1; criticised by Benjamin Disraeli, 214.

GLADSTONE, WILLIAM EWART, 241–84; contrasted with Disraeli, 241–2; education at Eton, 242–4; family history, 243; at Oxford, 244–7; hesitates concerning his profession, 246–7; adopts political career and enters House of Commons, 1832, 247–8; early speeches on slavery and electoral corruption, 248–9; Assistant Lord of the Treasury, 1834, under Peel, 249; Under Secretary for Colonies, 1835, 249; opposes Whig reforms, 249; "The State in Its Relation to the Church", 1838, 250–1; becomes Vice-President of the Board of Trade under Peel, 1841, 251; protests against Opium War in China, 252; Magnooth grant, 1845, 253–5; analyses his own mind, 254; his obscurity of speech and writing, and his art, 255–6; principles and emotions, versus facts, 256–7; criticises Irish Church, 257–8; assists repeal of Corn Law, 258; loses seat at Newark, 1845, 258–9; elected by Oxford University, 1847, 259; supports admission of Jews into Parliament, 259; the Gorham case, 260; his passion for "liberty", 261; stinging words to Manning, 261; goes to Italy, 1850; tyranny in Naples, 261–2; speech on Roman Catholic bishoprics bill, 263–4; difficulties in choice of political party, 264–5; attacks Palmerston's *Civis Romanus sum* speech, 1850, 265–6; letter to Bishop of Aberdeen, 266–7; Chancellor of Exchequer, 1852, 267; his budgets, 267–9; Crimean War, 1854, 269–70; resigns office Feb.,

1855, 269; studies Homer and Dante, 270; again attacks policy of war against Chinese, 270; opposes Divorce Bill of 1857, 271; joins Palmerston's Ministry in 1859, 271; reëlected the member for Oxford University, 271; opposes military expenditure, 272; his budgets; the paper duty, 272; rejected by Oxford University and elected by Lancashire, 1865, 273-4; leader of the House of Commons in Russell Government, 274; Disraeli versus Gladstone in House of Commons, 1866, 274-7; the Reform Bills of 1866-1867, 275; his versatile mind, 276; overawed by Disraeli, 276-7; disestablishment of Irish Church, 277; Prime Minister for first time, 1868, 277; his policy and his mind, 277-9; the Boer War, 1881, and Gordon in Sudan, 1885, 279, 318-20; his policy in Ireland, 280-1; his active and emotional mind, 281-3; unique in English history, 283-4.

MELBOURNE, WILLIAM LAMB, 2ND VISCOUNT, 103-52; history of Coke family, 103-4; history of Lamb family, 104-5; his father, 105-6; his mother, 106-7; Melbourne House, 107; Lady Melbourne's friends, 107-10; Egremont, George Wyndham, 3rd Earl of, 110-2; education at Eton and Cambridge, 112-3; attacked in *Anti-Jacobin*, 113; student of law, 114; at Glasgow University, 114-7; early letters to mother, 115-7; opinion of Napoleon, 116, 122; called to Bar, 1807, 117; life in fashionable political society, 117-8; death of elder brother, 118; enters House of Commons, 118; marriage with Lady Caroline Ponsonby, 118-9; opinion on reform of land laws, 120; speaks against autocratic action by Crown, 120-1; desire for political honesty, 121; attacks conduct of Duke of York, 122; difficulties of married life, 124-6; opinion of freedom, 124; letters from wife, 125; his love of books, 126-7; reënters House of Commons, 1816, 127; attitude toward "reform", 128; Secretary for Ireland under Canning, 1827, 129; his life and action in Dublin, 129-31; resigns office with Canningites when Wellington became Premier, 131; succeeds to peerage, 1828, 131; Home Secretary, 1830, in Grey Ministry, 132; his treatment of discontent and rioting, 132-38; attitude toward Reform Act, 1832, 138-40; becomes Prime Minister, 1834, 140; Municipal Reform Act, 1835, 141; Marriage Act, 1836, 141; reduction of Stamp Duties on newspapers, 141; attitude toward Chartists, 141-2; attitude toward trades-unions, 142-3; attitude toward free-trade in corn, 143; divorce proceedings, 144; trains Queen Victoria in constitutional duties, 144-50; Greville's account of life at Court, 145-48; his temporary resignation and difficult household posts 148-9; friendship with Queen, 149; resigns premiership, 1841, 150; continued correspondence with Queen, 150-1; returns to society life, 150-1; dies, 1848, 151; Greville's obituary notice,

Melbourne (*Continued*)
151; conversation with Benjamin Disraeli, 219.

PEEL, SIR ROBERT, 2ND BARONET, 155–202; contrasted with Melbourne, 155; the history of Peel family, 156–7; his father, 157–61; his mother, 158; birth, 1788, 158; father's plans for his son, 159–61; education, 161; at Harrow and Oxford, 161–2; enters House of Commons, 1809, 162; first speech, 163; Dean Cyril Jackson, 163; defends Wellington's action in Pensinsula 164; Chief Secretary for Ireland, 1812–1818, 164–70; disliked by Daniel O'Connell, 165; attitude toward political corruption, 165–6; attacked by O'Connell, 167; strengthens police; Royal Irish Constabulary, 168; manages political bribery, 168–70; resigns Chief Secretaryship, 1818, 170; chairman of Banking and Currency Committee, 171–73; supports severity against democratic discontent, 173; Home Secretary, 1822, 173; marries Miss Julia Floyd, 1820, 174; letters to wife, 174–5; criticises Mrs. Arbuthnot and Duke of Wellington, 175; his nervous nature, 176; reform of criminal law, 176–7; dread of rioting, 177; harsh treatment of the poor, 177–8; competes for Premiership, 1827, 178; resigns office with Wellington, 179; Home Secretary and leader of House of Commons, 1828, 179; Catholic emancipation, 179–82; loses seat for Oxford University, 181; his Bill for Metropolitan Police, 182–3; resigns with Wellington, 1830, 183; the Reform Bill struggle, 183; leads the new Middle Classes, 184; attitude toward Reform Bill, 184–7; refuses office, 187; policy behind the scenes, 187–8; Prime Minister, 1834, 188; Tamworth Manifesto, 189; the "Hundred Days" Government, 190; vote to reduce Prince Consort's allowance, 191; Prime Minister again, 1841, 191; economic crisis, 191; attempts to cheapen food, 192–4; his budgets, 193; the Factory Acts, 194–6; slave-grown sugar, 196; Maynooth grant, 196–7; the Corn Laws, 197–202; criticised by Benjamin Disraeli, 215, 232–3.

VICTORIA, QUEEN, 287–320; a ruler by profession and race, 287–8; her early education, 288–92; early experience, 292–5; appearance of Prince Albert, 295; preparing for the throne and succeeds, 296; Melbourne's guardianship, 297–9; Madame de Lieven's report, 298; Queen's handling of marriage arrangements, 298; the character of Prince Consort, 299; the "Victorian" Age, 299–301; her relations with husband, 300; the Prince creates Victorian propriety, 301–2; his power over the Queen, 302–3; her respect for him, 303; her intellectual powers, 304–5; her freedom from "class" prejudices, 305–6; rebukes Gladstone for undemocratic budget, 306; Gladstone's evidence of her ability and charm, 307–9; her struggle against Palmerston's diplomacy, 309–15; the Kossuth incident, 310–3; Napoleon's coup d'état, 313–5; the Danish